ISLAMISM AND REVOLUTION ACROSS THE MIDDLE EAST

Critical Studies on Islamism Series

The series Critical Studies on Islamism examines Islamism as a multifaceted, intricate, and evolving phenomenon. The aim of the series is to provide new and original interpretations of Islamism from a scholarly multidisciplinary, and interdisciplinary perspective. The series covers a wide range of topics that relate to Islamist movements, groups, networks, parties, and actors. The scope of the series is global and it covers the nature, dynamics, and evolution of Islamism at different contexts and regions from the Middle East and North Africa, South East Asia and Australia, to Europe and North America. To achieve disciplinary diversity, manuscripts from all related disciplines are welcomed including, but not limited to: political science, sociology, religious studies, history, political economy, sociolinguistics, media and cultural studies, and international relations. The emphasis is on producing books that provide original approaches theoretically and empirically.

Series Editor:

Dr. Khalil al-Anani
Associate Professor of Political Science, Doha Institute for Graduate Studies, Qatar

Advisory Board:

James Piscatori, Australian National University, Australia
Emad El-Din Shahin, Hamad Bin Khalifa University, Qatar
Nathan Brown, George Washington University, USA
Peter Mandaville, George Mason University, USA
Jillian Schwedler, City University of New York's Hunter College, USA
Heba Raouf Ezzat, Ibn Haldun University-Istanbul, Turkey
Nader Hashemi, University of Denver, USA
Francesco Cavatorta, Laval University, Canada
Omar Ashour, Doha Institute for Graduate Studies, Qatar

To contact the Series Editor:

csisibtauris@gmail.com

ISLAMISM AND REVOLUTION ACROSS THE MIDDLE EAST

Transformations of Ideology and Strategy After the Arab Spring

Edited by Khalil al-Anani

I.B.TAURIS

LONDON • NEW YORK • OXFORD • NEW DELHI • SYDNEY

I.B. TAURIS

Bloomsbury Publishing Plc

50 Bedford Square, London, WC1B 3DP, UK
1385 Broadway, New York, NY 10018, USA
29 Earlsfort Terrace, Dublin 2, Ireland

BLOOMSBURY, I.B. TAURIS and the I.B. Tauris logo are trademarks
of Bloomsbury Publishing Plc

First published in Great Britain 2022
This paperback edition published 2023

Copyright © Khalil al-Anani, 2022

Khalil al-Anani and contributors have asserted their right under the Copyright,
Designs and Patents Act, 1988, to be identified as Author of this work.

Copyright Individual Chapters © 2022 Khalil al-Anani, Tarek Chamkhi,
Mohammed Masbah, Hamzah Almustafa, Taha Yaseen, Mohammad Abu Rumman,
Mubarak Aljeri, Abdelwahab El-Affendi

For legal purposes the Acknowledgments on p. xii constitute an extension
of this copyright page.

Series design by Adriana Brioso
Cover image © Wolfgang Kaehler/LightRocket/Getty Images

All rights reserved. No part of this publication may be reproduced or transmitted in
any form or by any means, electronic or mechanical, including photocopying, recording,
or any information storage or retrieval system, without prior permission in writing
from the publishers.

Bloomsbury Publishing Plc does not have any control over, or responsibility for,
any third-party websites referred to or in this book. All internet addresses given in this
book were correct at the time of going to press. The author and publisher regret any
inconvenience caused if addresses have changed or sites have ceased to exist, but can
accept no responsibility for any such changes.

A catalogue record for this book is available from the British Library.

A catalog record for this book is available from the Library of Congress.

ISBN: HB: 978-1-8386-0630-5
PB: 978-1-8386-0628-2
ePDF: 978-1-8386-0632-9
eBook: 978-1-8386-0631-2

Series: Critical Studies on Islamism

Typeset by Deanta Global Publishing Services, Chennai, India

To find out more about our authors and books visit www.bloomsbury.com
and sign up for our newsletters.

To
Howaida, Mohamed, and Aly, again

CONTENTS

Preface		ix
Foreword		x
Acknowledgments		xii
Abbreviations		xiv

1   INTRODUCTION: ISLAMISTS AND REVOLUTIONS   1
    Khalil al-Anani

2   EGYPT'S MUSLIM BROTHERHOOD: AN ABORTED CHANGE?   7
    Khalil al-Anani

3   THE TUNISIAN ENNAHDA PARTY IN THE POST-ARAB SPRING:
    FROM ISLAMISM TO NEO-ISLAMISM   19
    Tarek Chamkhi

4   MOROCCO'S JUSTICE AND DEVELOPMENT PARTY:
    CONSTRAINTS ON PARTICIPATION AND POWER POST-2011   33
    Mohammed Masbah

5   TRANSFORMATION OF ISLAMIST GROUPS IN SYRIA: AHRAR AL-
    SHAM, JAYSH AL-ISLAM, AND THE SHAM LEGION   51
    Hamzah Almustafa

6   ISLAMISTS IN TRANSITION: THE YEMENI CONGREGATION OF
    REFORM—ISLAH PARTY   69
    Taha Yaseen

7   ISLAMISTS IN JORDAN: THE LONG JOURNEY OF THE MUSLIM
    BROTHERHOOD'S CHANGES   81
    Mohammad Abu Rumman

8   TRANSFORMATIONS OF THE ISLAMIC CONSTITUTIONAL
    MOVEMENT IN KUWAIT   101
    Mubarak Aljeri

9 ISLAMISM, AUTOCRACY, AND REVOLUTION: THE MORAL
   BANKRUPTCY OF ERADICATIONISM   117
   Abdelwahab El-Affendi

Notes   133
Select Bibliography   158
Contributors   161
Index   163

PREFACE

The theme of this book is both timely and significant for any individual seeking to understand the transformation of and changes in Islamism in the Middle East over the past decade. Since the outset of the so-called Arab Spring, Islamists have experienced significant changes ideologically, politically, and organizationally, which have shaped their political trajectories over the past years. The Islamist scene has drastically changed where some Islamists took power while others were subjected to severe and unprecedented repression. Furthermore, the civil wars in Syria, Libya, and Yemen, coupled with the regional counterrevolution led by the United Arab Emirates and Saudi Arabia, have significantly impacted the calculations of political activists, including Islamists, who face unprecedented repression and exclusion domestically, regionally, and globally.

Making sense of these new dynamics and understanding their impact on Islamist movements and groups prompts us to have a fresh and deep look into their actions, strategies, and behavior over the past decade. Therefore, this book provides an in-depth and detailed account of the changes in and transformation of Islamist movements over the past years from a critically comparative perspective. It thoroughly analyzes Islamists' ideological, political, and organizational changes in seven Arab countries: Egypt, Tunisia, Morocco, Syria, Yemen, Jordan, and Kuwait. Scholars who have contributed to this volume have deep knowledge of their respective countries. They provide a comprehensive, accurate, and original analysis of Islamist movements and groups in these countries. They apply different theoretical and methodological approaches in order to monitor, explore, and understand the changes and transformation that have occurred within Islamist movements over the past decade.

I have been following, monitoring, and writing about Islamists for almost two decades, and I can say, with no exaggeration, that Islamism, as a sociopolitical and religious phenomenon, remains one of the most complex, intricate, and evolving phenomena that requires more digging and research in order to understand and unravel its rationale and complexity. I hope this volume contributes to the existing and growing scholarship on Islamism and helps the reader to grasp its essence.

This book inaugurates the *Critical Studies on Islamism Series*, of which I am honored to serve as a series editor. The series critically examines Islamism as a multifaceted and intricate phenomenon and seeks to provide a rigorous and compelling understanding of its ideology, discourse, and behavior. The series is the first of its kind to focus specifically on Islamism and tackles it from multi- and interdisciplinary perspectives.

Khalil al-Anani
Fairfax, VA, Winter 2021

FOREWORD

Peter Mandaville
Professor of Government and Politics
George Mason University

The comparative political science literature dealing with the intersection of revolutions and Islamist movements has generally featured two tendencies. One entails the exploration of supposedly "Islamic revolutions," such as the 1979 Iranian Revolution and Omar al-Bashir's 1989 coup in Sudan. The other emphasizes the revolutionary nature of Islamist groups, treating these movements first and foremost as radical political actors seeking to fundamentally upend the status quo. *Islamists and Revolution Across the Middle East*, therefore, stands out as a uniquely valuable contribution precisely because it positions and examines Islamist groups as neither the ideological source nor the primary agents of revolution. It recognizes that, almost without exception, in the countries that experienced mass protests and political upheaval from late 2010 through 2011, Islamists were not at the forefront of those popular mobilizations. Caught largely unaware, Islamists—like most other political groups—were forced to improvise, adapt, and often make decisions on the fly in the face of rapidly evolving and highly fluid political environments.

The chapters that comprise *Islamists and Revolution Across the Middle East* explore the background and prevailing circumstances surrounding Islamist groups in the years preceding the dramatic events of 2010–11; analyze how these movements and political parties responded to upheaval and revolution; and explain how those different responses and actions yielded varying outcomes with respect to the current status and role of Islamists in countries across the Middle East. This volume allows us to understand how factors such as the level of presence and engagement with society in the period leading up to the revolutions help to explain the differential electoral performance of groups such as the Egyptian Muslim Brotherhood (robust social infrastructure and networks throughout the country) and the Libyan Muslim Brotherhood (virtually absent from social life) in early post-revolutionary ballots. Spanning multiple subregions, from North Africa to the Levant to the Arabian Peninsula, as well as varied regime types (republics and monarchies), the volume draws our attention to the ways different contextual factors—historical, economic, political—shaped the experiences, options, and, ultimately, political outcomes for Islamists during and in the aftermath of the Arab Spring. In this sense, *Islamists and Revolution Across the Middle East* makes a perfect companion volume (or perhaps an essential prequel?) to Shadi Hamid and William McCants' *Rethinking Political Islam* (2016), a text that explores how Islamist groups across the Middle East (as well as across South and Southeast Asia) responded to the 2013 military coup in Egypt.

In evidence across the case studies presented here—Egypt, Tunisia, Morocco, Jordan, Syria, Kuwait, and Yemen—are many of the key trends that seem to embody this period of political Islam in flux. From the Egyptian Muslim Brotherhood's initial hesitation to join the protests in Tahrir Square and their willingness to negotiate with the Mubarak regime to the careful tiptoeing of the Party of Justice and Development (PJD) in Morocco and the minimally oppositional stance of the Brotherhood in Jordan's parliament, we see a clear tendency toward Islamist self-limiting and accommodationism. The rethinking of the relationship between movement (*haraka*) and political party (*hizb*) is evident in both the Tunisian and Egyptian cases, with Ennahda redefining itself as a purely political entity and, from the summer of 2019, the Egyptian Muslim Brotherhood appearing to allow its followers to support political parties from across the political spectrum. Today, Islamists are also dealing with fundamentally existential questions about the nature and ongoing relevance of Islamism as a political project, a trend clearly evident in the rise of what Tarek Chamkhi labels "neo-Islamism" as well as in Ennahda's Rachid Ghannouchi's 2016 declaration to the effect that henceforth his group should refer to itself as "Muslim Democrats" rather than Islamists. And as Avi Spiegel suggests in his book *Young Islam*, for many younger activists drawn to groups such as Al Adl Wa Al Ihssane in Morocco, Islamism does not constitute a distinct ideological project with clearly defined goals. Rather, it often functions as something akin to a generic aspiration for a different kind of politics: something more ethical, affirming, and less corrupt than the status quo.

If Islamism is indeed at something of a crossroads today, then *Islamists and Revolution Across the Middle East* provides us with many resources we will need to discern the possible futures of political Islam from. Clearly, the next chapters in Tunisia's story will be key, as will the question of what happens to Muslim Brotherhood groups in those countries struggling with civil war (notably Libya, Syria, and Yemen): will they emerge as power brokers in the context of post-conflict political transitions? Finally, Islamism across the entire region has been inescapably shaped in recent years by a broader geopolitical rift between one bloc of powerful countries vociferously opposed to political Islam (the United Arab Emirates, Saudi Arabia, and Egypt) and another bloc that has tended to support Islamists (Turkey and Qatar). The waxing and waning of tensions within this rivalry constitutes a macro overlay that will continue to define the boundaries of the political possibility for Islamism.

In summary, by moving away from treating Islamism as an inherently revolutionary force and instead exploring revolution as something that happens *to* Islamists, the chapters in *Islamists and Revolution Across the Middle East* significantly advance our understanding of contemporary political Islam while adding valuable insight to the comparative study of revolutions.

ACKNOWLEDGMENTS

This book would have not been possible without the support of several individuals and institutions. It resulted from a research project that has been in the making for the past three years, where I benefited from the insights and views of several individuals. First and foremost, I would like to thank all interviewees from the leaders and members of Islamist movements and groups who agreed to participate and to be interviewed for this work. The contributors of this volume have spent hours talking to these individuals, and without sharing their personal tales, experiences, and views, this work would have lacked the thoroughness and the contribution it intends to make to the study of Islamism.

I presented some of ideas of this book at different workshops and conferences, including Middle East Studies Association (MESA), British Society for Middle Eastern Studies (BRISES), and the Project on Middle East Political Science (POMEPS) over the past few years. Also, the contributors of this volume have presented their respective papers at a workshop organized at the Doha Institute for Graduate Studies during the fall of 2018. I am grateful to the participants in that workshop from the faculty members and graduate students at the Doha Institute and scholars at the Arab Center for Research and Policy Studies (ACRPS) for their participation and for their useful comments. In particular, I would like to thank Dr. Azmi Bishara whom I had the pleasure to work with over the past six years and have several intellectual conversations that helped refine some ideas of this volume. Also, I would like to thank Professor Abdelwahab El-Affendi whom I had the privilege to work with and benefit from his insightful views on Islamism. I am also thankful to my colleagues and friends at the Doha Institute and the Arab Center for Research and Policy Studies (ACPRS). In particular, I would like to thank Professor Nabil Khattab, Dr. Ibrahim Fraihat, Dr. Mohamed El-Masry, Mr. Gamal Barout, Dr. Haider Said, Dr. Abdelfattah Mady, Dr. Morad Diani, Dr. Radwan Ziadeh, Dr. Ahmed Hussein, Dr. Saoud El-Mawla, Dr. Mustafa Menshawy, Mr. Abdou Moussa, Mr. Maen Albayari, Dr. Luai Ali, Dr. Adham Saouli, Dr. Omar Ashour, Professor Mouldi Lahmar, Professor Sari Hanafi, Dr. Azzam Amin, and Dr. Nawaf Altamimi.

Also, I would like to thank the contributors of this volume who worked tirelessly over the past few years to produce this insightful and rigorous piece of scholarship. In particular, I'm thankful to Abdelwahab El-Affendi, Mohammad Abu Rumman, Mohammed Masbah, Hamzah Almustafa, Mubarak Aljeri, Taha Yassen, and Tarek Chamkhi. I am also thankful to Professor Peter Mandaville for his continuous support and for writing the foreword for the book.

This project would not have been possible without the invaluable support I received from the Research Office at the Doha Institute for Graduate Studies.

Acknowledgments xiii

I owe a deep debt of gratitude to Raed Habayeb, Miriam Shaath, Maria Njeim, and Manar Arafeh for their dedication and support throughout this project. My research assistants Saif Alislam Eid, Rushdi Al Faouri, Omar Aziez, Mutaz Alnazer, and Mohamed Ahmed provided vital assistance throughout the journey of this book. I am indebted to Engy Farid, the Administrative Officer of the Politics and International Relations Program at the Doha Institute for Graduate Studies, who worked diligently to help organize the workshop and to handle the paperwork of this project. Special thanks go to the administrative assistants at the Doha Institute for Graduate Studies, Mrs. Takwa Zweiri and Mrs. Randa Al-Saadi, who provided vital support and assistance during the work on the book.

I am grateful to I. B. Tauris and Bloomsbury and their staff, particularly Sophie Rudland, the Senior Editor of Middle East Studies and Islamic Studies. I am indebted to Sophie's invaluable support, guidance, and encouragement throughout the journey of this project. Also, I am thankful to Yasmin Garcha, the Editorial Assistant for Middle East Studies, who provided vital help and assistance. I also thank the editorial team at the I. B. Tauris and Bloomsbury, particularly (the Senior Production Editor Giles Herman, Project Manager Mohammed Raffi and team at Deanta), who made this book possible. Special thanks go to the anonymous reviewers for their useful comments on the initial manuscript.

Last but not least, I am grateful to my family, particularly my spouse Howaida Soliman, whose love, sacrifice, and endless support made this work possible. Finally, I would like to thank my two sons, Mohamed and Aly, for their endless love and patience while I was working on this project.

Portions of Chapter 2 are reprinted with the kind permission of the *Democratization Journal* and *The Middle East Journal*. I acknowledge with thanks the permission of the publishers for the use of this material. This publication was made possible by a Doha Institute for Graduate Studies Major Research Fund grant (MRF0202). The findings achieved herein are solely the responsibility of the authors.

ABBREVIATIONS

AKP	Justice and Development Party (Turkey)
CPA	Civil Protection Authority (Syria)
FJP	Freedom and Justice Party (Egypt)
FSA	Free Syrian Army (Syria)
GCC	Gulf Cooperation Council
GPC	General People's Congress (Yemen)
Hadas	Islamic Constitutional Movement (Kuwait)
HTS	Hay'iat Tahrir al-Sham (Syria)
IAF	Islamist Action Front
IS	Islamic State
ISIS	Islamic State of Iraq and Syria
LIFG	Libyan Islamic Fighting Group
LIMC	Libyan Islamic Movement for Change
MB	Muslim Brotherhood
MTI	Islamic Tendency Movement (Tunisia)
NCA	National Constituent Assembly (Tunisia)
NSF	National Salvation Front (Tunisia)
PJD	Party of Justice and Development (Morocco)
PLO	Palestinian Liberation Organization
RCD	Democratic Constitutional Rally (Tunisia)
RPP	Rescue and Partnership Party (Jordan)
SIF	Syrian Islamic Front
SILF	Syrian Islamic Liberation Front
TMC	Tripoli Military Council
UGTT	General Labour Union (Tunisia)

Chapter 1

INTRODUCTION

ISLAMISTS AND REVOLUTIONS

Khalil al-Anani

A decade ago, the Arab Spring began with a glimpse of hope that democracy has finally reached the shores of the Arab world. The removal of Arab dictators in Egypt, Tunisia, Libya, and Yemen ushered in a new era of freedom, justice, and dignity. However, the Arab Spring has not produced the political change Arab people aspired for, and the hopes for democracy are fading away. Arab people ended up with civil wars in Syria, Libya, and Yemen, a brutal dictatorship in Egypt, and a shaky and fragile democracy in Tunisia. Despite the modest harvest of the Arab Spring, Islamist movements and groups have been significantly impacted by the Arab uprisings. After decades of repression and exclusion, Islamists became a key player in the new political scene after the Arab Spring. In Egypt, as well as in Tunisia, Morocco, Yemen, Syria, and Libya, Islamists' discourse, strategy, and behavior have shaped the outcome of the Arab uprisings. However, Islamists' role and performance varied from one case to another. For example, whereas Islamists succeeded in gaining and maintaining power in Tunisia and Morocco, they failed to do so in Egypt, Libya, Syria, and Yemen. Likewise, while the inclusion of Islamists led to their views and ideology becoming moderated in some cases, it created challenges and problems in others. Therefore, this book attempts to answer two key questions: first, how did the Arab Spring affect Islamists' ideology, strategy, and organizations? Second, how can we explain Islamists' different responses to the Arab Spring and what do these responses tell us about Islamists' diversity and heterogeneity?

This volume aims to provide compelling answers to these questions. It does so by examining the transformation of Islamists' ideology, behavior, and strategy since the beginning of the Arab Spring. The main argument of this book is that insofar Islamists were key players in the post-Arab Spring era, they have experienced different changes and transformations ideologically, politically, and organizationally. That is evident in the cases that are covered in this volume. Through an in-depth comparative analysis, the volume brings together a group of scholars who have profound knowledge and expertise on Islamism. The cases covered in the volume represent the countries that either witnessed revolts and uprisings in 2010 and 2011—regardless of the outcome of these uprisings, such as Egypt, Tunisia, Libya, Yemen, and Syria—or those that were affected by the ashes of the Arab Spring and had to accommodate Islamists, such as Morocco, Jordan, and Kuwait. These cases were deeply studied over the past four years as part of a research project that was funded by the Doha Institute for Graduate Studies between 2017 and 2019 (MRF0202).

Islamists and Revolution

With a few exceptions, mainstream Islamists tend to avoid revolutions and revolutionary change which can lead to unexpected consequences. Instead, they adopt a gradual reformist approach to realize their goals. They focus mainly on religious preaching (*da'wa*), education (*tarbiyya*), and religious commitment (*iltizam*) as key tools in advancing their agenda. Hassan al-Banna, the founder of modern political Islam, was once asked about staging a revolution against political regimes and his answer was that the Muslim Brotherhood does not believe in revolution because it can lead to chaos and instability. For him, change should happen through reforming individuals and society. Therefore, when the Arab Spring started, Islamists were reluctant, at least in the beginning, to join the uprisings that led to the downfall of autocratic regimes in Egypt and Tunisia. Furthermore, after taking power in the wake of the Arab uprisings, Islamists remained committed to their reformist and gradualist approach, which led, in turn, to the alienation of the revolutionary forces, particularly in these two countries.

However, Islamists were significantly influenced by the Arab Spring. Over the past decade, they have undergone significant changes ideologically, politically, and organizationally. They had to adapt to the new political environment that ensued after the removal of autocratic regimes, which forced them to make political and ideological concessions, develop a new strategy, and adopt different political tactics. As this book shows, Islamists' response to the Arab Spring was uneven. While some of them succeeded in adopting an open and flexible agenda, such as in Tunisia, Morocco, and Yemen, others failed to genuinely change their position and could not cope with the new changes, such as in Egypt and Jordan. Furthermore, moving from the opposition to power was a challenge for many Islamists who lacked the experience and skills of governance. Islamists who took power in Egypt, Tunisia, and Morocco were faced with the questions of poverty, corruption, and good governance. They had to practice politics from a power vantage point and show the ability to meet people's expectations. Some of them have succeeded, such as in Morocco and Tunisia, while others have failed miserably, as has happened in Egypt. Turning slogans into practical and viable policies constituted a challenge for Islamists. Raising slogans such as "Islam is the solution," imposing Sharia law, or establishing an "Islamic state" were tactics akin to a mirage. In some cases, the lack of political readiness and the almost nonexistent governing experience allowed the Old Regime to come back and end the democratic transition, such as in the case of Egypt. The Muslim Brotherhood's inability to govern and run the country resulted in a military coup in 2013, which removed the movement from power and reinstalled an unprecedented repressive regime. Furthermore, while some Islamists separated religious and political activities, such as in Tunisia and Morocco, others still mixed them, such as in Egypt and Jordan. Additionally, Islamists had to rethink and clarify their position on critical issues such as citizenship, individual and personal freedoms, national state, and democracy. Whereas some groups changed their views on these issues to become more progressive, others are still figuring out how to deal with them.

The Impact of the Arab Spring on Islamists

The French sociologist Olivier Roy argues that Islamists are shaped by politics rather than vice versa.[1] That was evident after the Arab Spring, which reshaped Islamist politics drastically. However, to understand how Islamists were affected by the experience of the Arab Spring, it is crucial to unpack the contexts in which they have been operating over the past few years. Here, we can talk about three key contexts. The first is the open and reformist context, in which Islamists enjoyed some degree of integration and acceptance within the political game, as in Morocco and Tunisia. In these cases, the inclusion of Islamists contributed to their ideological and political transformation, particularly with regard to thorny issues such as the relationship between religion and politics; issues of individual freedoms, human rights, and relations; and attitudes toward women and minorities. In this discussion, we should not forget that these contexts are not necessarily fully democratic nor ruled by Islamists in full. The second context is the authoritarian and repressive context in which interactions range from the partial exclusion of Islamists (as in Jordan) to total exclusion and eradication (as in Egypt and Syria). This context led to divisions and schisms within Islamist movements and parties and the rise of conservative voices and wings within these movements. This has led the Islamists to confront contradictory choices between acceptance, coexistence, rejection, and confrontation, both politically (Egypt and Jordan) and militarily (Syria). The only beneficiaries of this context were violent radical movements such as ISIS and Al-Qaeda, which dominated the Islamic landscape in these countries over the past years in a manner that served repressive authoritarian regimes and contributed to increasing regional and international support for them in their "war on terror."

The third context is characterized by armed conflict and civil wars that left Islamists with no choice but to engage in its interactions and dynamics so as not to be discarded or excluded by other players and conflicting parties, as is happening in Yemen, Libya, and Syria. This context has produced a mix of strategies and tactics among Islamists, depending on the circumstances of each country. In the Yemeni case, for example, the Yemeni Congregation for Reform party was forced to engage in a changing negotiation process, sometimes with the late president Ali Abdullah Saleh, sometimes with the Houthis, and sometimes with a third force against them, such as Saudi Arabia and the UAE. The party was forced to join the ranks of the popular resistance to confront the Houthis and stop their march toward the most important Yemeni cities, especially Aden and Taiz. In the Libyan case, the Islamists engaged in a military confrontation through militias and armed groups to counter the rebellion led by Khalifa Haftar in the eastern

4   *Islamism and Revolution Across the Middle East*

cities, especially Benghazi. Despite the openness of the Islamists to the option of an international solution, there is a determination from regional countries such as Egypt and the UAE to eradicate them completely from the Libyan political scene. In Syria, the situation is not very different. There is no single Islamic movement that has not taken up arms in the face of the war crimes and genocide waged by Bashar al-Assad against the Syrians. Past contexts certainly do not mean that they are the sole or main determinants of Islamists' movements and strategies, as if they were without their own self-will or independent visions. However, the point here is that the Islamists do not work in a vacuum, and that their decisions and movements remain governed by the nature of the context in which they are active. Notably, that the relationship between these contexts and the Islamists' behavior is not linear or mechanical, but an interactive dialectical relationship, in which many factors overlap and can lead to different outcomes. These contexts, however, do not mean that they are the sole or main determinant of Islamists' behavior and political calculations. Rather, it means that the Islamists do not operate in a vacuum and that their decisions are governed by the nature of the context in which they are active and function.

Theorizing Islamism

Islamism has been a subject of scholarly inquiry over the past decades. Scholars from various disciplines such as politics, sociology, and history have used different theoretical and methodological approaches to grasp the essence and complexity of Islamism. Some scholars have used social movement approaches—framing, collective actions, mobilization, etc.—to analyze Islamists' activism,[2] while others have employed political process and identity approaches to understand the transformation of Islamist movements.[3]

This volume builds on these efforts from critical and multidisciplinary perspectives where scholars draw their case studies using different theoretical and methodological tools. For example, some scholars in this volume question the very notion of Islamism and attempt to introduce new concepts that can help capture and explain the transformation of Islamists, particularly after the Arab Spring. For example, in his chapter, Tarek Chamkhi introduces the concept of neo-Islamism, which helps understand the transformation of the Ennahda Party in Tunisia after the Arab Spring. According to Chamkhi, the concept of neo-Islamism differs from the classical concept of Islamism in its scope, discourse, and tools. Neo-Islamism believes that Sharia is not an immediate priority for Islamists whose focus shifted from religious proselytization (*da'wa*) to political, social, and moral reform. It also differs from Bayat's concept of post-Islamism, which tends to focus on Islamist individuals and their apolitical activities. According to Chamkhi, the neo-Islamists, unlike the post-Islamists, remain active and involved in collective action through their parties and groups.

Furthermore, the volume makes the case for the intricacy and multifaceted nature of Islamism as a sociopolitical and religious phenomenon. It avoids the orientalist and existentialist approaches that treat Islamism as a rigid, static, and immutable phenomenon or mix it with Islam as a religion or system of faith. It rather treats Islamism and Islamist actors as dynamic, evolving, and mutable interlocutors who are affected by the social, political, and cultural environment in which they operate. A key contribution of this volume lies in its ability to show the wide spectrum of Islamists' strategies, tactics, behaviors, and discourses since the beginning of the Arab Spring. Moreover, it reveals how Islamists, like their ideological counterparts, were immensely affected by the events of the Arab Spring, which reshaped their discourse and strategy.

Methodologically, the volume critically engages with the traditional approaches in studying Islamism and provides new approaches that could help in analyzing and understanding the transformation of Islamists. For instance, it goes beyond the "inclusion-moderation" hypothesis that dominated the study of Islamism for the past two decades. It provides new ways to examine and explore the transformations of Islamism beyond the prism of moderation or radicalization to focus on the processes, dynamics, and settings that determine and shape these transformations. As Hamzah Almustafa points out in his chapter, the transformation of Islamists should not be attributed to their inclusion or exclusion but rather to the environment in which they operate, their structure and mobilization capabilities, and their framing processes and strategies.

Finally, it is worth noting that some terminologies in this book are used interchangeably. For example, "Islamism" and "political Islam" refer to the same entity of sociopolitical actors with a religious reference. While both terms are conceptually and theoretically contested, scholars use them interchangeably. Further, the "Muslim Brotherhood" is used interchangeably with the "Muslim Brothers" or the "Brotherhood." All these terms refer to a sociopolitical movement that emerged in Egypt in 1928 and became one of the most influential Islamist movements in the Muslim World.

Mapping the Book

This volume is divided into ten chapters. After the introduction, I examine in Chapter 2 the transformation of Egypt's Muslim Brotherhood since the uprising of January 2011. The chapter explores the response of the Brotherhood to the uprising and how they performed while it was in power in 2012–13. It reveals the ideological, political, and organizational changes the movement had undergone over the past decade, particularly after the coup of 2012. In Chapter 3, Tarek Chamkhi explores the transformation of the Tunisian's Ennahda movement since the uprising of 2010. He introduces the concept of "neo-Islamism" as a new analytical approach to understand the case of Ennahda. By analyzing Ennahda's statements and texts, the chapter reveals the ability of the movement to move from a traditional religious movement to a civic political party. In Chapter 4, Mohammed Masbah cogently explains the case of the Moroccan Party of Justice and Development (PJD). He unpacks the transformation of the PJD since 2011 ideologically, politically, and organizationally, in particular after taking power in 2011. He assesses the political performance of the PJD and how it was affected by the party's internal dynamics and leadership. Through several interviews with members and leaders of the PJD, Masbah draws a clear picture of the relationship between the party and the monarch over the past decade and how the latter shrewdly attempted to co-opt the former.

Chapter 5 discusses the Syrian case. Hamzah Almustafa provides a comprehensive and profound analysis of the transformation of Islamist groups in Syria, particularly Ahrar al-Sham, Jaysh al-Islam, and the Sham Legion. He examines the dynamics of Islamists' engagement during civil wars. Through several semi-structured interviews with members of these groups in Turkey, Al-Mustafa provides an original account of the internal dynamics, divisions, and transformations of Islamist groups in Syria. He also engages critically with the inclusion-moderation hypothesis and revisits its main assumptions, particularly with regard to the Syrian case. Chapter 6 examines the case of Islamists in Yemen with particular focus on the Yemeni Congregation of Reform (Islah Party). Taha Yaseen explores the changes in Yemeni Islamists since the uprising of 2011. He explains how Islah Party could become a key force in political changes after the removal of former Yemeni president Ali Abdullah Saleh. The chapter also highlights the impact of the war in Yemen on Islamists and how they respond to it. Through several interviews with Islamists and experts, Yaseen explains the changes that have happened within Islah Party and situate them within the larger context of the conflict in Yemen. In Chapter 7, Mohammad Abu Rumman explores the ideological, political, and organizational changes that have happened within the Islamist scene in Jordan with special focus on the Muslim Brotherhood. The chapter provides a comprehensive and cogent analysis to the ups and downs of the relationship between the Brotherhood and the monarch, and how this relationship shaped the former's political behavior and strategy. Chapter 8 discusses the Islamic Constitutional Movement (ICM) in Kuwait. Through several in-depth interviews with Kuwaiti Islamists, Mubarak Aljeri examines the changes in and transformation of the ICM over the past decade and how the Arab Spring experience affected the movement and shaped its strategy and political behavior.

Finally, in Chapter 9 Abdelwahab El-Affendi wraps up the book with an overview of the dilemma of Islamists under autocratic regimes. He explains how Islamists engaged with the Arab uprisings, particularly in Egypt and Tunisia. He draws parallels between the two cases to show how pragmatism can help not only Islamists but the democratic transition in general. The chapter shows how deep mistrust and a sense of insecurity among political actors can hamper transition, and highlights the importance of giving political and ideological concessions in order to avoid political failure in the future.

Chapter 2

EGYPT'S MUSLIM BROTHERHOOD

AN ABORTED CHANGE?

Khalil al-Anani

The abrupt rise and fall of Egypt's Muslim Brotherhood (al-Ikhwan al-Muslimun) has struck observers, commentators, and policymakers. Not only has the movement lost power dramatically after a military coup in July 2013, but it has also been significantly crushed by the post-coup regime led by General Abdel Fattah al-Sisi. With thousands of its members and sympathizers in prison for almost half a decade now, the movement has fallen into oblivion. While it is somehow difficult to gauge the impact of the current wave of repression on the Brotherhood, it is certain that this repression is the worst in the movement's history.

This chapter explores the transformations of the Brotherhood since the uprising of 2011. It seeks to understand the changes that have occurred in the Brotherhood's ideology, strategy, and organization since the uprising until now. The chapter argues that the Brotherhood was reluctant to make real changes in its ideology and organization in order to adapt with the post-uprising environment. It was mainly preoccupied with securing political gains and gaining power rather than opening up and modernizing its ideology and structure. This reluctance affected the Brotherhood's strategy and led to many miscalculations that contributed to its failure and fall from power in 2013. Moreover, I contend the Brotherhood experienced more changes and transformations after the coup than it did after the uprising of 2011. This argument goes against the inclusion-moderation hypothesis, which assumes that conservative and anti-regime movements tend to change their ideology and behavior in order to adapt with political openings and to widen their constituency.

The Brotherhood after the Uprising of 2011

In the pre-January 25 uprising era, the Brotherhood was preoccupied with two key objectives: maintaining its organization and enhancing its social and political clout. It achieved both goals despite the brutal repression of the long-standing regime of Hosni Mubarak. Over the past decades, the Brotherhood expanded its social network by creating several medical service clinics, educational centers, and Islamic schools throughout Egypt, in both urban areas and the countryside.

Deprived and disillusioned by Mubarak's economic policy in the late 1980s, many Egyptians found shelter in the Brotherhood's social and economic services. Unsurprisingly, the Brotherhood's social constituency grew exponentially during the 1980s and 1990s, which subsequently helped the movement enhance its political and electoral gains.

The Brotherhood has participated in formal politics since the beginning of the 1980s; it routinely took part in parliamentary elections, as well as elections within university unions and professional syndicates. Exhausted by fighting radical and violent Islamists, the Mubarak regime turned a blind eye to the expansion of the Brotherhood during the 1980s. However, by the turn of 1990s, the regime began to crack down on the Brotherhood and to undermine its growing political and social activism. Mubarak employed the surge of violence initiated by radical and violent Islamists as a pretext to suppress and crush the Brotherhood. The Brotherhood, in turn, sought to delegitimize the Mubarak regime and discredit its dominant and corrupt National Democratic Party (NDP). It thus boycotted the parliamentary elections in 1990 and attempted to reach out to other political forces, resulting in intensified repression against its leaders and members during the 1990s. As Carrie Wickham notes, "The Brotherhood's victories in the associations thus triggered a crackdown that reversed many of the gains it had made in the preceding decade."[1]

The change in the Brotherhood's leadership in 2004[2] and the US pressure on Mubarak to open up the political space represented a golden opportunity for the Brotherhood to enhance its political clout. Therefore, the movement reached out to other political forces such as the Kefaya movement, which emerged in 2004 as an anti-Mubarak movement and mobilized the people against his rule during the 2011 uprising. The Brotherhood also demonstrated against the regime for the first time since the 1960s, an act that previously resulted in the arrest of many senior officials.[3] Surprisingly, the Brotherhood won close to 20 percent of the seats in the parliament during the 2005 elections, which precipitated another clash with the Mubarak regime.[4] By 2010, the relationship between Mubarak and the Brotherhood reached a complete impasse.

After the downfall of Mubarak in February 2011, the Brotherhood emerged as a key player in Egypt's incipient political order. The movement persistently attempted to solidify its political gains after the uprising and was driven by a sense of hunger for power fueled by the immense vacuum left after the fall of Mubarak and the NDP. The movement's instinct for power was reinforced by the significant weakness of political parties and both the fragmentation and disorganization of youth movements. As Nathan Brown points out,

> The various forces that participated in the revolution spent little of the ten months since their stunning victory in Tahrir Square party-building, with many of them eschewing party politics on principle and others focusing, instead, on the politics of protest rather than of party organization.[5]

Expectedly, they were quickly outweighed by the more organized and well-prepared forces such as the Brotherhood and Salafis, the newcomers to Egyptian politics.

Building on their religious appeal and long-standing social networks, Islamists dominated Egyptian politics after the uprising. They established new parties, participated ardently in elections, and became heavily involved in negotiating the road map of the transition with the military.

The Brotherhood established its Freedom and Justice Party (FJP) in June 2011 and proceeded to win approximately 47 percent of parliamentary seats in the 2011–12 elections.[6] The FJP's platform was an amended version of the Brotherhood's political platform that was announced in 2007 and created internal discord over the position of the movement, particularly among women and non-Muslims. Perhaps the most prominent difference between the two platforms was the omission of a controversial provision granting clerics a formal role in politics and lawmaking. The Brotherhood's 2007 program called for the formation of a committee of senior religious scholars chosen in national elections to advise the parliament and the president, thereby creating a system that many found to be akin to the Iranian model. The FJP also removed an article regarding the importance of the state's religious functions, which implicitly prevented a Copt or non-Muslim female from becoming the head of state. The new platform did not rule out the election of women to government, although Brotherhood members have repeatedly stated they consider women "unsuitable" for the presidency.[7]

Overall, the Brotherhood chose to remain mum on controversial issues, hoping to dodge criticism from other political parties and segments of society. Even though the FJP labels itself as a civil party, religion had a heavy presence throughout its platform. The party declared as its primary objective to not gain power, as one would expect of any political party, but rather to "enhance Islamic morals, values, and concepts in individuals' lives and society," which are goals closer to that of a religious group than a political party. The FJP's platform was also ambiguous and inconsistent in the use of key terms. For instance, when discussing the nature of the state, the word "*shura*" (consultation) is used, as this is thought by Islamists to be a broader and more inclusive term than democracy. In other parts of the platform, "*shura*" and "democracy" are used interchangeably, an apparent reflection of the conflict between the party's religious ideals and its political ambitions. This usage also reflects the party's attempt to balance the discourse of the conservatives with that of the reformers within the Brotherhood, with "*shura*" being favored by the conservatives and "democracy" appealing to the reformers.[8]

The Brotherhood's Rise to Power

The Brotherhood's march to power was neither easy nor smooth. Not only did the movement have to try to resist the lure of power after more than eighty years in the shadows, but it also had to maneuver and adapted to new rules of the game. During the January uprising, the Brotherhood was keen not to provoke or alienate other political forces or the West. For instance, the Brotherhood announced that it would not impose Islamic law in Egypt.[9] Further, the Brotherhood adopted a self-restraint strategy to defuse fears after the fall of the Mubarak regime by repeatedly stressing that it did not seek full control of Egypt.[10] A few days before ousting Mubarak, the Brotherhood announced it would not field a presidential candidate and embraced the slogan of "participation, not domination" to emphasize its limited political ambitions.[11] In March 2011, the Brotherhood announced it would contest only 30 percent of the seats in the parliament. However, with time the Brotherhood became politically emboldened and could not rein in its political ambitions. Accordingly, it contested more than 50 percent of the parliamentary seats and fielded a presidential candidate. The Brotherhood justified its changed position on the basis of "the threats that face the revolution,"[12] a justification that raised many questions and concerns regarding its credibility and power-hunger inclinations.[13]

The Brotherhood's decision to contest presidential elections came amidst a standoff with the Supreme Council of Armed Forces (SCAF), which was running the country after Mubarak's fall. Following a short honeymoon period, a clash of interests surfaced between the Brotherhood and the SCAF. While the Brotherhood sought to secure more power after the removal of Mubarak, the SCAF was reluctant to relinquish its control over the state. Therefore, when Morsi eventually became president, he was significantly crippled and left with no real powers. The standoff between the two sides was not based on views over democracy, achieving the uprising's objectives, or meeting the demands of the people; rather, it was over each side's share of power and political privileges.[14] After reneging on its promise to hand over power within six months, the SCAF sought to secure as much power as possible from the emerging political order. For the military junta, their long-standing independence and privileges were a "red line" and therefore not a topic for negotiation with the new political regime, regardless of its political background. On the other hand, the Brotherhood became obsessed with the possibility of the Old Regime's return. For them, the only way to prevent this unacceptable condition was to step in and take power themselves. When the Brotherhood and the SCAF failed to identify a "consensual" candidate who could secure their interests, the clash between the two sides became inevitable.

The Downfall of the Brotherhood

After Mohamed Morsi became Egypt's first democratically and freely elected president in June 2012, it appeared that a new chapter in the Brotherhood's history was on the horizon. Following a short period serving as a government-in-waiting,[15] the Brotherhood became the new ruler of Egypt with all power aspirations and challenges included. The group's failure to make the needed transition from a vocal opposition movement to a ruling force became glaringly evident during Morsi's tenure, as the Brotherhood ironically embodied both identities. In addition, the Brotherhood encountered tremendous political, social, and economic challenges that required fundamental changes in the movement's discourse and strategy.

While many factors contributed to the downfall of the Brotherhood, including the resistance and plots of the "deep state" and the regional hostility against the

Brotherhood, its loss of power was accelerated and facilitated by three other factors pertinent to the Brotherhood itself: the burden of conservatism and lack of a revolutionary agenda, the organizational inertia and stagnation of the Brotherhood, and the lack of governance experience among the Brotherhood leaders, particularly President Morsi.

1 The Brotherhood's Conservatism

The Brotherhood is a conservative movement. Since its inception in 1928, it adopted an orthodox yet populist ideology and discourse that resonated with many ordinary Egyptians. Unsurprisingly, the Brotherhood has emerged as the most popular opposition movement in Egypt over the past century. The debate over whether the Brotherhood should espouse a "revolutionary" ideology and platform dates back to its early years. Hasan al-Banna, the founder and chief ideologue of the Brotherhood, was firm and clear in emphasizing the "reformist" character and approach of the Brotherhood. He explicitly stated that the Brotherhood "does not believe in revolution."[16] Over the past six decades, the Brotherhood avoided revolt or rebellion against Egypt's autocratic regimes despite their brutal repression and exclusion. The Brotherhood not only tolerated regime repression under Mubarak but also struck deals and bargains with it in some instances.[17]

By conservatism, in this context, I refer to the traditional and orthodox ideology of the Brotherhood that prefers reform over revolution, gradualism over radical change, and compromise over confrontation. While conservatism has helped the Brotherhood broaden its constituency by appealing to the low and lower-middle classes, particularly during the Mubarak era, it became a burden after the January uprising. The Brotherhood firmly believes in gradual reform based on a "bottom-up" approach that starts by reforming and purifying individuals at the bottom then begins capturing and Islamizing the state at the top. The Brotherhood's statements and texts eschew the very idea of "change," using the notion of "reform" instead. According to the movement's doctrine, this reform should come through a gradual and long-term process, not radical steps or moves.[18] Moreover, the Brotherhood always speaks proudly of its "gradualist" character and strategy, particularly when compared with extreme and radical movements that adopt violence as a political means. As one leader puts it, "gradualism and peaceful reform is our social capital."[19] More importantly, not only does this gradual and reformist strategy correspond with the broad and relatively ambiguous ideology of the Brotherhood, but it also resonates with the politically and socially conservative Egyptians who generally prefer gradual change as opposed to confrontation with the regime.

After the January 25 uprising, the Brotherhood's gradualist and reformist character became irrelevant. Not only has the movement struggled to adapt to the fast-changing environment, but it has also failed to uphold its objectives and aspirations. To be sure, the Brotherhood was torn between its embedded and long-lasting "conservativism" and the revolutionary momentum and spirit created after the uprising; it failed to rise up to the promises and objectives of the January uprising and to materialize them after taking power.

Furthermore, the conservative character of the Brotherhood was manifested in its "non-confrontational" and accommodative strategy, particularly in dealing with the state's antiquated institutions. It preferred to deal and bargain with the deep state; that is, it worked through traditional channels such as the military and the Ministry of Interior, rather than accommodating and allying with the young revolutionaries and activists who sparked the uprising. The Brotherhood also alienated liberals, leftists, and secularists by allying with the Salafis and former jihadis, a decision that further marginalized it from the revolutionary forces. Although Morsi made a bold decision to dismiss the minister of defense, Field Marshal Mohamed Hussein Tantawi and his chief of staff, Sami Anan, in August 2012, this decision was linked mainly to internal arrangements and a "time-for-change" mentality within the military rather than serving as a sign of his "revolutionary" policy. Moreover, some activists accused Morsi of striking a deal with the military in order to give a "safe exit" to Tantawi and Anan that shielded them from being prosecuted or held accountable for their actions.[20]

This "accommodative" approach is particularly evident in the 2012 constitution that was primarily drafted by the Brotherhood and Salafis, and granted more autonomy and powers to the military.[21] According to the constitution, the military's budget was not a subject of civilian oversight. It also preserved the trial of civilians by the military, originally included in the 1971 constitution, albeit narrowing its scope. Morsi was also hesitant to reform the Ministry of Interior despite the appeals of many activists and human rights organizations. On the contrary, Morsi surprisingly increased the salaries of police officers and praised their role in "the revolution."[22]

This conservativism, or lack of a revolutionary mindset and agenda, was a major impediment that precluded the Brotherhood from succeeding once in power. It also estranged activists who lost faith in Morsi's ability to build a democratic political system by the end of his first year in power, resulting in many turning against him, a movement that further legitimized calls for his removal.

2 The Organizational Stagnation

The Brotherhood has long been praised for its powerful and disciplined structure as a social movement. This organizational resilience, however, worked against the Brotherhood after the uprising and affected its political calculations. This tight-knit structure has also blocked attempts to restructure the group in order to become more participatory and transparent.

This organizational inertia has affected the Brotherhood in two different ways: first, the control and domination of the so-called conservative faction was enhanced at the expense of the so-called reformists; second, the rigidity and exclusiveness of the decision-making process within the movement increased. The domination of the conservative wing started during the middle of the 1990s, especially under the tenure of Mustafa Mashhur, the fifth General Guide of the Brotherhood. After a short time of balance between the conservatives and the reformists, the former became more powerful and dominant. This became clear when key reformist figures such as Abu Ela Madi and Essam Sultan broke away from the movement and sought to establish their own political party.[23] By the end of the 1990s, the conservatives were controlling the Brotherhood and solidifying their grip on power within the movement.[24]

Between 2001 and 2011, the conservatives dominated the Brotherhood's leadership entirely, restructuring its organization and controlling its decision-making process. Two key figures paved the way for these significant changes: Mahmoud Ezzat, the former secretary general of the Brotherhood,[25] and Khairat al-Shater, the Deputy General Guide, business tycoon, and strategist of the Brotherhood.[26] These two men became the most influential leaders within the movement. Not only have they created a narrow power center that has dominated and controlled the Brotherhood over the past decade, but they have also reshaped the structure of the movement and its chain of command to become reliant on them. This was evident when they reconfigured the top two institutions within the Brotherhood: the Shura Council and the Guidance Bureau.[27] The selection of these two institutions' members became based on their loyalty and allegiance to the movement's leadership more than their personal merits or qualifications. During the 2000s, many of the Brotherhood's senior- and mid-level leaders such as Mohamed Morsi, the former president; Sa'ad al-Katatni, the former spokesperson of the parliament; Sa'ad al-Hossini, the former governor of Kafr El-Shaikh during Morsi's tenure; and members of the Guidance Bureau were selected and promoted through the connections and blessings of al-Shater and Ezzat.

Tensions and bickering between the conservatives and the reformists simmered for almost two decades. However, it reached a tipping point after the January uprising when the Brotherhood expelled many of its reformist figures and youth. Abdel Moniem Aboul Fotouh, a prominent reformist figure, was banished and excluded from the Brotherhood after his bid for presidency. Ostensibly, he was dismissed for breaking the Brotherhood's vow not to contest presidential elections. Yet, this was a culmination of the long-lasting dispute between him and al-Shater. Other prominent figures such as Mohamed Habib (a former Deputy Supreme Guide), Ibrahim El-Za'farani, Khaled Da'ud, and Hitham Abu Khalil were excluded and had to leave the movement.[28] Similarly, many young members in the Brotherhood were unashamedly expelled despite their role in saving face for the Brotherhood during the uprising. Prominent young activists such as Islam Lotfi, Mohamed El-Qassas, and Mohamed Abbas, among others, were reproved as a result of their calls for internal change and restructuring in the Brotherhood to make it more open and progressive. Thus, they broke ranks with the movement and established a new political party called the Egyptian Current (Al-Tayyar al-Masry).[29]

The second piece of evidence of the Brotherhood's organizational inertia and stagnation is the rigidity and exclusiveness of its decision-making process, which was palpable in the Brotherhood's decision to field a presidential candidate. After its prior decision not to contest the presidential elections, the Brotherhood decided to nominate its powerful and leading strategist Khairat al-Shater for the presidency on March 31, 2012. Not only was selecting al-Shater a surprise, given his low public profile (at least compared with other Brotherhood figures such as Essam El-Arian and Sa'ad El-Katatni), but the process of selecting and nominating him was also highly controversial and divisive. Within the context of the Brotherhood's tense relationship with the SCAF, the Brotherhood's Shura Council was hastily summoned to discuss whether the Brotherhood should break its prior vow and field a presidential candidate. After three controversial rounds of voting, al-Shater was chosen to be the Brotherhood's presidential candidate. In the first two rounds, the majority of Shura Council members voted against fielding a presidential candidate. However, in the third round, the vote was fifty-six in favor versus fifty-two against nominating al-Shater as a presidential candidate.[30] The controversial voting process demonstrates more than the deep division within the Brotherhood over contesting the presidential elections—it also underscores the marginalization of the movement's grassroots elements from discussing such important and critical issues.[31] Therefore, in order to justify its new position and accommodate any internal opposition that might appear, the Brotherhood launched an internal campaign to legitimize its decision. As Ahmed Shehatah, the FJP's representative in Zagazig, explains:

The decision [of contesting presidential elections] was based on the movement's interest and the changing of political circumstances. The Brotherhood acts like a responsible collective entity whereby grassroots respect and follow the leadership's decisions.[32]

In addition, the Brotherhood's hasty decision to field a presidential candidate runs counter to its long-standing policy of caution and self-restraint. As Marc Lynch puts it, "The nomination of al-Shater seems to have been a response to threats and opportunities in a rapidly changing political arena, rather than the hatching of a long-term plan."[33] The absence of such a plan led Fahmy Howeidy, a well-known Islamist-leaning columnist and writer, to criticize the Brotherhood's presidential decision, describing it as a "trap they [the Brotherhood] have fallen into."[34]

Furthermore, the selection of al-Shater and then Morsi to run for presidency reflects the balance of power within the Brotherhood. While the former is a heavyweight leader within the Brotherhood due to his financial and organizational capabilities, the latter is a sheer example of how conservatives have created their loyal cadres and members within the Brotherhood. Morsi was selected as the Brotherhood's second choice for presidency. He was a loyal and committed member to the Brotherhood's leadership since he joined the movement in the late 1970s. In fact, his record of allegiance and submission to the Brotherhood's conservative wing paved the way for both his selection as the chairman of the FJP and the conferral of the old guards' blessings. After becoming president, Morsi was perceived by many Egyptians as the Brotherhood's man in the presidential palace instead of a president for all Egyptians. He also could not abandon the Brotherhood's ideology or change its ideas. Predictably, many of his assistants and advisers were either from the Brotherhood, particularly the group of al-Shater, or had Islamic leanings. Morsi also allied with Salafis and ex-jihadi parties such as

2. Egypt's Muslim Brotherhood

the al-Nour Party and the Building and Development Party (BDP), the political arm of al-Jama'a al-Islamiyya, at the expense of secular and liberal forces, as well as young revolutionaries.

3 The Incompetence of the Brotherhood

During Morsi's short tenure, the Brotherhood was in power but not in control. Not only did Mubarak's notorious bureaucracy and antiquated institutions (i.e., the Ministry of Interior, the judiciary, and most importantly, the military) vehemently reject the Brotherhood, the latter also lacked the experience and wisdom in dealing with them. During the past three decades, the Brotherhood had no access to public office; its leaders and members were systematically barred from holding ministerial and senior governmental positions. Individuals affiliated with the Brotherhood were always seen and treated by state institutions as "outsiders" who should not be trusted or tolerated. As a mid-level Brotherhood leader clearly states, "We were always treated as second class citizens under Mubarak. If you are a member in the Brotherhood, you will not join the army, become a minister or a governor."[35] This sense of deprivation and exclusion overshadowed the Brotherhood's policy and strategy while in power. Therefore, any attempt by the Brotherhood to reform or restructure the state's institutions was interpreted with mistrust and suspicion. In fact, the more the Brotherhood attempted to control these institutions, the more resistance they faced. Furthermore, the Brotherhood could not take over key state institutions such as the Ministry of Interior, the Ministry of Foreign Affairs, or the Ministry of Defence, and they barely controlled a few others such as the Ministry of Investment, the Ministry of Youth, the Ministry of Supplies, and the Ministry of Local Administration.[36]

Despite the fact that the Brotherhood is the largest social movement in Egypt with the highest number of professionals (e.g., doctors, lawyers, engineers, and teachers), it failed to govern Egypt effectively. While it is difficult to judge the Brotherhood's performance in power because of its short reign, it is safe to say that the Brotherhood's cadres and leaders lacked the basic governance skills and tactics that would have enabled them to deal with Egypt's daunting social and economic woes.

Additionally, examining the Brotherhood's indoctrination and socialization process is instructive to understand its unconvincing performance while in power. As a proselytization movement, the Brotherhood indoctrinates its members to become preachers (du'ah), not statesmen. The socialization process within the movement aims chiefly to reshape individuals' identity to become devout and pious members. As a result, the Brotherhood's members proved adept at protesting and opposing political regimes since its inception in 1928 but simply lacked the experience and opportunities to govern. Unlike their counterparts in Turkey's Justice and Development Party (AKP) who gained an opportunity to practice governance during the 1990s, the Brotherhood's leaders never had access to provincial or municipal administration in Egypt because it was entirely under the control of the former ruling NDP. Ultimately, the Brotherhood proved capable of operating mosques, syndicates, and welfare societies; however, they were never trained to be professional civil servants, a lack of experience that contributed significantly to their downfall.

The Brotherhood after the Coup of 2013

Since taking power, the post-coup regime has adopted a heavy-handed and repressive policy toward the Brotherhood; it brutally massacred hundreds of its members in July[37] and August 2013[38] and arrested thousands more.[39] The post-coup regime also implemented a comprehensive political, economic, social, and religious policy intended to eliminate the Brotherhood's activism.[40] In October 2013, for instance, the government confiscated and froze the financial assets of the Brotherhood leadership.[41] However, the turning point came when the government designated the Brotherhood as a terrorist organization on December 25, 2013.[42] Moreover, many of the Brotherhood's members have fled the country and are now taking refuge in various countries such as Qatar, Turkey, and the UK.[43] The post-coup regime capitalized on public anger and disappointment toward the Brotherhood in order to quash it, an effort that was wholeheartedly touted and amplified by the pro-military media.

More importantly, the significant and unequivocal regional support to the post-coup regime, chiefly from Saudi Arabia and the UAE, plays a crucial role in continuing the suppression of the Brotherhood. After the Arab Spring, Saudi Arabia and the UAE viewed the Brotherhood's rise as an existential threat that needed to be halted.[44] Therefore, after the coup, both countries have rewarded Abdel Fattah al-Sisi—the former minister of defense who ascended to power after overthrowing the late president Mohamed Morsi on July 3, 2013—by pouring billions of dollars into Egypt's ailing economy.[45] Since taking power in June 2014, al-Sisi has demonstrated significant reliance on financial inflows from the Gulf in order to make progress toward mitigating Egypt's social and economic woes, an arrangement whose conditions include ending the Brotherhood once and for all.[46]

The Brotherhood's response to state repression after the coup of 2013 has changed over time. In the beginning, the movement desperately attempted to undo the coup by mobilizing its constituency and supporters. Its leaders were in a state of shock and imbalance because of losing power after only one year in office. Al-Sisi adopted an unprecedented repressive policy against the Brotherhood. He threw thousands of its members into prison, seizing their financial and economic assets, and taking over their social, educational, and medical organizations.[47] Moreover, al-Sisi's regime killed several hundreds of the Brotherhood's members and supporters either by using excessive and brutal force against the protesters at sit-ins (e.g., the Rabaa massacre on August 14, 2013) or by torture and extrajudicial killing.[48]

The Brotherhood witnessed divisions on how to deal with regime repression. Some members called upon the leadership to legitimize retaliation against the regime, which created more problems and challenges for the movement. However,

2. Egypt's Muslim Brotherhood

the Brotherhood's leadership was aware of the consequences of any confrontational or violent reaction against the regime. These divisions were heightened after the Rabaa massacre when the security forces killed more than 800 members of the Brotherhood in one of the bloodiest massacres in Egypt's modern history according to the Human Rights Watch.[49]

Disoriented Adaptation

A few weeks after the 2013 coup, the Brotherhood had to make changes in its organizational strategy in order to mobilize its base. These changes enabled the movement to draw thousands of its members and supporters into the streets in urban and suburban areas, such as Cairo, Giza, Al-Fayoum, El-Mansoura, and Souhag. Protests and demonstrations unfolded with one goal: to "bring down the coup."[50] The Brotherhood attempted to create an anti-coup momentum that might change the status quo in its favor, and to maintain cohesion and solidarity among its rank and file. Therefore, it created and led a coalition of Islamist parties and groups that rejected Morsi's removal and called for reinstating him. It was called the "National Alliance to Support Legitimacy."[51] During the weeks between the coup and the Rabaa massacre, the Brotherhood succeeded in organizing daily protests across Egypt,[52] which provoked the post-coup regime and resulted in the use of brute force against the Brotherhood. As Ketchley notes, "The 14 August massacres would establish a precedent whereby soldiers and Interior Ministry-controlled security forces routinely used live ammunition, tear gas, and birdshot to disperse anti-coup protests."[53] After the Rabaa massacre, demonstrations became very tense and led to several confrontations between the Brotherhood and security forces. Therefore, to curb the Brotherhood's protests, an Egyptian court banned its activities on September 23, 2013, forcing the movement underground and its members to become more defiant.[54] The ban allowed the regime to intensify the campaign against the Brotherhood, and security forces continued the violent behavior against the movement's supporters. It also triggered a debate within the Brotherhood on whether to use self-defense tactics for maintaining protests and protecting the protesters from police attacks. The movement's leadership vehemently rejected any use of violence and directed its members to keep their protests peaceful.[55]

As a result of closing of the public space after the coup, the Brotherhood shifted its strategy toward schools and universities. The movement called upon its students to organize marches and protests against the regime and to maintain what it called "revolutionary activism" (*al-hirak al-thawry*).[56] Benefiting from its strong network and experience in students' activism, the Brotherhood used universities as a new venue to mobilize the public against the regime. Protests were organized and led by mid-level leaders and graduate students under an umbrella network called "Students Against the Coup," which was formed after the coup and was active at several Egyptian universities. However, the regime began to hamper the Brotherhood's activism at Egyptian universities by deploying security forces inside universities. Further, the pro-regime media launched a campaign against

18 *Islamism and Revolution Across the Middle East*

the Brotherhood's protests and described them as "thuggery."[57] The government attempted to counterbalance the Brotherhood's activism at universities by encouraging leftist and liberal students to protest and challenge Brotherhood supporters. While protests dwindled in cities and the streets because of police brutality, universities became the hotbeds of the Brotherhood's continued protests. It was not until the regime declared the Brotherhood a "terrorist organization"[58] that its supporters became more rebellious and the movement experienced significant divisions on how to respond to regime repression. By that time, the Brotherhood's leadership control of its youth was significantly weakened.

The Brotherhood's organizational adaptation led to the emergence of a new line of leadership among the youth who began to operate independently from the old leadership. With the absence of the movement's senior and old members, young members became responsible for maintaining the Brotherhood's existence and running its daily activities for the first time in the movement's history. Over the past few decades, the Brotherhood's young members were marginalized and excluded from the decision-making process. As a conservative movement, age, in addition to loyalty and devoutness, plays a key role in deciding members' seniority inside the Brotherhood. This has changed after the coup when young members became the de facto new leadership of the movement. More importantly, the new leadership became popular among the rank and file because of its confrontational discourse and uncompromising position toward regime repression. According to a young Brotherhood member named Mustafa Ahmed, "the new leadership is more revolutionary and knows how to deal with Sisi's oppressive regime and it will never surrender to it."[59]

Conclusion

The Brotherhood has undergone significant changes and transformations over the past decade. The movement witnessed several ups and downs that have affected its views, organization, and strategy. Ironically, the pace of changes within the movement after the coup of 2013 overshadowed those after the uprising of 2011. The coup of 2013 left the movement in a state of confusion and dismay that it is still struggling to deal with. It is no exaggeration to say that the movement is witnessing one of the darkest episodes in its long history. Not only has the Brotherhood lost many of its supporters, but it is also suffering regionally and globally. At this stage, the movement finds itself fighting two battles simultaneously: the battle merely to survive and the more desperate battle to change the post-coup regime. Yet, it lacks both a clear vision and a coherent strategy to win on either of these fronts. As this chapter demonstrates, the anachronistic and conservative ideology of the Brotherhood and its stagnant structure played crucial roles in contributing to its political miscalculations and eventual downfall. In this sense, admitting its political blunders and reinventing its ideology and structure seems a sine qua non in order to regain its status as a key political actor in Egyptian politics.

Chapter 3

THE TUNISIAN ENNAHDA PARTY IN THE POST-ARAB SPRING

FROM ISLAMISM TO NEO-ISLAMISM

Tarek Chamkhi

The rise of Islamists in Turkey, Morocco, and Tunisia, and other attempts to grab power briefly in Egypt (2012–13) trigger questions regarding the neo-Islamists' doctrine, motivation, and "true colors" in terms of their democratic commitments, liberalism, Islamist ideology, and constant evolution.[1] The obvious differentiation between Islamists who accept and are willing to participate in the liberal democratic system and those who do not has brought "a new focus to the study on Islamism. Have the beliefs and practices of Islamist groups changed over time? What processes, mechanisms, and institutions promote moderation?"[2]

This chapter explains the transformation of Islamists in Tunisia after the Arab Spring. It focuses on the case of the Ennahda Party and how it became the most influential political party in Tunisia. Like other chapters in this volume, this one argues that the experience of the Arab Spring has affected Ennahda and led to several changes in its discourse and strategy. It argues that the political inclusion of Ennahda after the removal of Ben Ali's regime led to significant transformation in its ideology, strategy, and tactics. The chapter introduces the concept of neo-Islamism as a frame of analysis to better understand the case of Ennahda.

The neo-Islamists are an undeniable political force in the mainstream political arena in the Middle East. They are Islamists for a reason, despite their tremendous ideological shift toward liberal ends such as participating in democracy and condoning violence and extremism—they are not (yet) post-Islamists. Such a short chapter might not be able to give detailed answers to the ambitious set of questions it brings to attention; however, it can be worthy in provoking a discussion on the old-fashioned conception about Islamism in the Muslim world. Questions such as these: What processes, mechanisms, and institutions essentially contributed to the major refurbishment of Ennahda after the 2011 revolution? Does repression force moderation while democracy and inclusion enable Islamization? Is neo-Islamist moderation a conscious (ideological) choice, a tactical measure, or just a natural evolutionary endpoint?

The Arab revolutions' liberal language affected Islamists and drew their attention to new realities. During the election campaigns in Egypt, Tunisia, and

Morocco in 2011–12, Islamist parties abandoned their traditional motto ("Islam Is the Solution") their utopian discourse, and their dogmatic propaganda. Al-Anani observed:

> They did not promise paradise as a reward for those who would vote for them but rather pledged to improve the economy, fight corruption and attract foreign direct investment (FDI). Islamists increasingly realize that their legitimacy does not stem from the "mosque" but rather from their performance in public office.[3]

The 2011 uprisings marked a milestone in the relationship between the state and Islamism. The process of Arab weakening, which arguably began nearly ten years earlier with the widespread shock of the US invasion of Iraq and the toppling of Saddam Hussein in 2003, continued with regime changes in Libya and Yemen, as well as the civil war in Syria. The weakening of state power in all these cases vastly increased the salience of non-statist Salafi and jihadi movements. In Egypt and Tunisia, the Arab uprisings fundamentally challenged the "cronyistic" development strategies pursued by the Mubarak and Ben Ali regimes. In neither case, however, did the Islamist beneficiaries of these uprisings offer compelling alternatives to this economic model. Ennahda in Tunisia—and the political opposition as a whole—remained vulnerable to bottom-up pressure from the marginalized (*muhammishin*), who looked to Salafism as a more promising vehicle for social inclusion.[4]

This chapter focuses on the ideological and political shifts within the Tunisian Ennahda Party after the 2011 revolution, which showcased the Tunisian neo-Islamists as the spearhead of a new trend of politicians with the opportunity to initiate an unprecedented Muslim democratic movement. Further, it focuses on Ennahda's use of democracy, power sharing, and adaptation to moderate liberal concepts of conservatism and religiosity, as well as on their actions toward Sharia law, shariatization, and the Islamic state. To this day, some believe these aspects are the most challenging and evolutionary steps ever taken by mainstream Islamists.

The Phenomenon of Neo-Islamism

Neo-Islamism is distinguished by an ethical and theological emphasis on Islam that combines social conservatism with political moderation. Neo-Islamists are united in the view that Sharia is not an immediate reform priority; however, there are divisions over whether this is a tactical pause toward the ultimate pursuit of shariatization, whether it should be diluted if introduced at some future point, or whether it should never be introduced at all.[5] Neo-Islamism differs from classical mainstream Islamism (mainly that of the traditional Muslim Brotherhood [MB] movement) in several key ways, such as being a new form of religiosity, demonstrating a tendency toward gradualism, highlighting the grassroots' role in change, modernizing Islam into a contemporary ideology and political worldview, and emphasizing moderation in either personal religiosity or political behavior, nationalism, and friendly relations with the West.[6]

3. The Tunisian Ennahda Party in the Post-Arab Spring

Definitions of Islamism differ widely among its adherents, who sometimes contradict each other on a wide range of matters, including ideology, policy, and goals. In some cases, the *Salafi Jihadis* declare each other to be heretics, resulting in bloodshed as seen in Iraq, Afghanistan, Algeria, and Syria.

Historically, the term "Islamist" did not have currency amongst Muslim scholars, theologians, and historians. However, one of the rare exceptions was that of a famous Muslim theologian during the tenth century, Abu al-Hasan al-Ash'ari (874–936) whose influential book *The Essays of the Islamists* featured a compilation of various narratives by Muslim scholars and theologians. Modern Islamism, however, has very little to do with theology or even Islamic laws or Sharia. It is an ideological phenomenon that aspires excellence, viewing Sharia as a part of the utopian political system. Islamism has social and political aspirations, aiming to integrate Islam as such into politics, state affairs, economics, and civil and constitutional laws. The most accurate definition is probably that of Mohammad Ayoob, who described Islamism as "a form of instrumentalization of Islam by individuals, groups and organizations that pursue political objectives."[7] Ultimately, political Islam is a contemporary political ideology rather than a religion, religious cult, or theology.

On the other hand, while the term "neo-Islamism" is rarely used within the academic context, it remains vague and ambiguous in journalistic settings. Robin Wright, however, insightfully describes neo-Islamism as

> more flexible [than other traditional forms of Islamism], informed, and mature in their political outlook. For them sharia is about values, civilization, and political context. Neo-Islamists are seeking the ultimate objectives of sharia but without bonding each situation to a certain religious text. They believe that Islam is dynamic and not a set of fixed rules and tenets, but rather an organic belief system that can adapt to or live with the times. Neo-Islamists can be progressive and, on some issues, even liberal. [The] Neo-Islamists trust the reform scholars.[8]

Wright's characterization provides a description of neo-Islamist values and some of their activities, rather than delivering a precise definition or method of distinguishing it from other types of Islamism. Modern mainstream Islamism had several major turning points prior to the Arab Spring. This includes Gamal Abdel Nasser's persecution of the Brotherhood in Egypt during the 1960s, the Iranian Revolution in 1979, the First and Second Iraq Wars in 1991 and 2003, civil wars such as the Afghan jihad during the 1980s, and the Algerian, Bosnian, and Chechen Wars during the 1990s. However, neo-Islamism can be traced back to the Sudanese Islamist leader Hassan al-Turabi (1932–2017), who influenced other Brotherhood leaders and activists in the region during the 1990s, including Rached Ghannouchi himself.[9]

Within the literature on Islamism, Olivier Roy mentions the emerging new Islamists post-Arab Spring[10] but fails to distinguish them from the post-Islamists and activists. Asef Bayat overlooks this matter despite being the pioneer who coined the term "post-Islamists."[11] Neo-Islamism is different from what Bayat and Roy call post-Islamism for four main reasons: first, neo-Islamists, unlike the post-Islamists, remain active within traditional Islamic parties and prefer organizing by political/religious parties rather than through individual efforts or other means. Second, neo-Islamists, unlike the post-Islamists, have not given up on the idea of Sharia or shariatization of the state and society; rather, neo-Islamists use gradualist tactics to further their agendas. However, some neo-Islamists also exhibit their abundance of traditional Islamic movement agendas, as is the case with some Ennahda Party leaders during their tenth General Congress in 2016.[12] Third, the neo-Islamists, unlike the post-Islamists, do not explicitly give up the ideal of the Islamic state, though they might do so in the foreseeable future. Fourth, the neo-Islamists, unlike the post-Islamists, continue to be deeply concerned about *da'wah* (religious preaching and spreading the call of Islam) as much as they are concerned about gaining power, democratization, human rights, and fair treatment by governments. Post-Islamists tend to keep their religiosity private and focus mainly on social changes, democratization, and economic prosperity, normally within liberal setups.[13] Shadi Hamid[14] may be the only one who questions the neo-Islamists' moves toward democracy and existing liberal setups, temptation of power, and moderation through exclusion, despite his reluctance to describe the neo-Islamists as new or theoretically different from the traditional MB and its affiliates across the Muslim world. Others discuss in depth the shariatization of Islamist parties post-Arab Spring, with a focus on parties like Ennahda, but fail to distinguish them as sophisticated projects with common factors, empowering themselves by their members' achievements in the region and forming a potential game-changer for the Middle East and North Africa in the foreseeable future. Some believe the most important development in the evolution of Islamism occurred during and after the Arab Spring. This is not

> only because it allowed Islamists to take power through the ballot box but most importantly because of the consequences of such development on Islamists' ideology and tactics. Moving from opposition to government, Islamists will face enormous risks and challenges. . . . Islamists will have to compromise, bargain and negotiate, which will make them more prone to change and transformation.[15]

Potential of Neo-Islamist Parties in the MENA Region

In the four states where there is a potential for neo-Islamists to acquire power (such as the Brotherhood in Egypt), or are currently in power (such as the Justice and Development Party [AKP] of Turkey, Ennahda of Tunisia, and Justice and Development Party [JDP] of Morocco), we examine those parties that are gaining tremendous experience and controlling populations exceeding 214 million in total (Egypt, 90 million; Turkey, 78 million; Morocco, 35 million; and Tunisia, 11 million). For the neo-Islamists who are currently in power, this equates to 124 million inhabitants, which is roughly one quarter of the population of the European Union.

In addition, the GDP of these four countries exceeded 1.3 trillion USD in 2015 (Egypt, 330 billion; Tunisia, 48 billion; Morocco, 110 billion; and Turkey, 859 billion). Not including Egypt, which has no neo-Islamist influence at the moment, the GDP of Tunisia, Morocco, and Turkey is still approximately 1 trillion USD.[16] After the Arab Spring, for the first time since 1928 (just after the fall of the Ottoman Empire), the Islamist parties in Tunisia, Morocco, and Egypt had to contend with the fundamental yet complicated and unfamiliar

> matters of state and government. They had survived. They had gained power. Now the question dogging them for years remained: what did they hope to do with that power? Islamists were Islamists for a reason. They weren't liberals in disguise. If there was a demand for Islamism—and, in countries as varied as Egypt and Tunisia, there most certainly was—then someone would need to supply it.[17]

In addition, the powerful growth of the Turkish economy under the rule of the neo-Islamist AKP since 2002 empowered the Middle Eastern and North African neo-Islamists enormously. They grabbed the democratic momentum and contested in elections after the 2011 revolutions, emulating the Turkish model, even if they publicly denied doing so for political reasons or national pride.

The neo-Islamist discourse has many layers, starting with a focus on the neo-Islamists' goal of power, use of liberal democracy, power sharing, de-secularization or adaptation to liberal concepts, and their latest actions toward Sharia law, shariatization, and the Islamic state. Such a discourse leads us to several urgent questions, such as what processes, mechanisms, and institutions essentially contribute to moderating the neo-Islamists?

In fact, the mainstream Islamists, especially those who transformed into neo-Islamists, are no longer a marginalized and repressed underground movement. They are an undeniable political force of the mainstream political arena in their countries. They are Islamists for a distinguishable outlook, and despite their tremendous ideological shift toward liberal ends and participating in democracy and condemning violence and extremism, they are not (yet) post-Islamists.

Ennahda: Toughest Power Challenges

The Tunisian Ennahda Party has been in power continuously since 2011, first winning the plurality in the popular vote and later as part of the ruling coalition in the 2014 general elections. Observing Ennahda's political behavior provides this chapter with insights (or affirmations) in terms of the neo-Islamist temptations with power, Islamist gradualism, priorities, pragmatism, and level of political flexibility. Following its electoral victory in the November 2011 election, Ennahda began leading the coalition government comprising mostly of Ennahda, the Congress for the Republic (CPR), and the Democratic Front of Work and Liberties (Ettakatol)[18] in December 2011, which later became famous by the name of the

"Troika government."[19] At that time, law and order was nearly absent in the country owing to the vacuum left by the fall of Ben Ali. Tunisians awoke every morning to concerning security reports. According to the International Crisis Group,[20] the Interior Ministry stated that between February 2011 and February 2012, more than 400 police stations were attacked and 12,000 individuals were arrested for looting, assault, or attempted murder. Subsequently, Ennahda was obliged to conduct a deep review of its preconceptions, ideology, and political day-to-day tactics. The results were quite apparent and sometimes surprising. Ennahda can be evaluated on the basis of three tests in order to determine whether it is capable of participating in and furthering the democratic transition in Tunisia. The first test, involving moderation, examines Ennahda's attitudes toward democracy, an open society, and the free market economy; Tunisia's non-Islamic political parties; and tolerance toward differing religious and political points of view in general terms.

The second test examines Ennahda's contribution toward remedying the post-revolution economic crisis. Has Ennahda gained any success in resolving any of the country's economic problems during its relatively short time in power, and within the transitional and counterrevolution setbacks? Does Ennahda have a viable economic policy to bring Tunisia out of its economic struggles in the long term? Or broadly, does Ennahda produce any Islamic or neo-Islamic economic blueprint? The third test examines whether Ennahda's actions toward and reactions to Salafist influence have been successful.[21] Salafist influence includes terrorist threats, which Ennahda has experienced since its first day in power. More challenging from a political standpoint have been union strikes, coup attempts, and hostility from former RCD (Democratic Constitutional Rally, ruling party of Ben Ali) activists and security forces. The Salafist question is particularly important because Ennahda's enemies and competitors within the secularist camp have used Salafists (mainly Ansar a-Sharia) or the fear of Salafists to attempt to oust Ennahda from power. Once in power, Ennahda declared its most important tasks were to finalize the new constitution and move the country toward new, permanent institutions.

During the Troika alliance's two-year rule (2012–13), Ennahda suffered from both counterrevolutionary forces, which had some success in regrouping, and their long-standing hostile relations with the leftists of the Tunisian General Labour Union (UGTT). These forces were comprised of various groups sharing the common cause of anti-Islamist rhetoric.[22] Among these were supporters of the Ben Ali regime who were under the umbrella of the RCD. After the 2011 revolution and the dissolution of the RCD, they formed many new parties. One of the major parties is Nidaa Tounes, which is comprised of old-regime supporters and allies. Nidaa Tounes was established in early 2012 during the rule of Ennahda and is headed by the charismatic leader Beji Caid el-Sebsi (a veteran member of the Destour Party and the RCD, and a speaker of parliament in the Ben Ali era). The Popular Front, which is a coalition of various leftist parties, entered an alliance with Nidaa Tounes after the assassination of Chokri Belaid, general secretary of the Democratic Patriots' Movement (PPD), in February 2012. The National Salvation Front (NSF), established later, has more components than Nidaa Tounes and the Popular Front, including various civil nonprofit organizations and UGTT and security syndicates, which played critical roles in suppressing Ennahda during the autocratic era.

This alliance continually attacked Ennahda when it was in power. The secular groups placed blame on Ennahda for its soft stance against Salafist political violence. According to the ICG,[23] there is "not much doubt that the non-Islamist opposition has displayed excessive and premature alarm and that it sometimes levels unsubstantiated accusations. Nor is there much question that it is finding it hard to accept the reality of Islamists governing their country." Leftist parties and UGTT activists decided to depose Ennahda at any cost and organized union strikes across dozens of work sectors. These strikes occurred almost daily, culminating in thousands of strikes in 2012 and 2013. This union-led chaos contributed to Tunisia's economic crisis and general discontent across the population.

Between August and September 2013, the situation in Tunisia deteriorated nearly to the same levels seen in Egypt following the military coup that ousted President Mohamed Morsi. One of the dramatic consequences was Ennahda's prime minister Hamadi Jebali's resignation in early March 2013, immediately after the assassination of Belaid. Prime Minister Ali Larayedh (interior minister in the first cabinet), also a member of Ennahda, took over. From that position, Ennahda ceded control of the interior, defense, and foreign ministries to independent technocrats; this was a concession secularists had been demanding for some time.[24]

After the assassination of National Constituent Assembly (NCA) member Mohamed Brahmi in August 2013, the situation worsened and roughly sixty members of the parliament (MPs) resigned from the NCA. Many of these MPs joined the sit-in at Kasbah, where the opposition launched a youth movement called *tamarod* (Rebellion) movement, similar to those in Egypt when Morsi was ousted on July 3, 2013. Tunisia's *tamarod* claimed to have gathered over 870,000 signatures in support of a petition to dissolve the country's parliament and replace it with a government of "national salvation." In early August, Ettakatol's Mustafa Ben Jaafar, the speaker of the NCA, suspended the assembly's work.[25]

Moderation through Inclusion or Exclusion?

Ennahda went through a repressive era during both the Bourguiba and Ben Ali regimes, and subsequently shifted its ideological discourse up to the 2011 revolution and Tunisia's new era of democratization. On March 1, 2011, the party legalized democratic free elections and then proceeded to win the first such election on October 23, 2011, taking an impressive 89 seats out of 217 in the constituent assembly. Ennahda tried to go mainstream once before, during the early two years of the Ben Ali rule, and before the major regime oppression during the 1990s. Straight after Ben Ali seized power in November 1987, the 1987–1989 period represented a short break in Ennahda's very long journey of confrontation with the regime. During this period, Ben Ali offered opportunities for the Islamists through three avenues. First, the movement was permitted to take part in the High Council of the National Pact by the end of 1988. Second, the movement was allowed representation in the Islamic High Council, through its second-in-charge Abdelfattah Mourou, in early 1989. Finally, Ennahda was permitted to take part in the parliamentary elections of 1989, despite its fabrication throughout. Further, the movement was allowed an Islamic student union (the Union Générale des Étudiants Tunisiens, UGET), established on December 17, 1988; during this period, the party changed its name from "MTI" (Mouvement de la Tendance Islamique or Movement of Islamic Tendency) to Ḥarakat Ennahḍha in order to show the regime a goodwill and thereafter its eagerness to participate in the political sphere. In fact, Cavatorta and Merone observe that Ennahda's ideological moderation was in action since the 1989 elections.[26] The

> principal variable to explain this shift can be resumed in "moderation through inclusion," whereby the progressive inclusion of radical and anti-systemic parties into the political system forces them to compromise with their original extreme views in order to be able to compete in a pluralistic environment where shared rules have to be designed and where the constraints of participation inevitably force a review of strict ideological positions to attain at least some of the political goals the party has.

Moderation through inclusion might explain why Ennahda relinquished power in early 2014, following the overwhelming vote for the new constitution in January 2014, as well as Ennahda's controversial decision to separate da'wah (religious preaching) from politics in its tenth general assembly in 2016.

Ennahda did not moderate through inclusion from the 1970s up to March 2011. It went through countless repressive cycles, including losing its legal status; being subjected to kangaroo court trials, torture, exile, etc.; and being forced to campaign for freedom and existence while being underground for most of this period. Ennahda's moderation during the 1980s and 1990s might be explained through another variable—moderation through exclusion despite the dominant belief that exclusion from public space contributes to radicalization, underground violence, and terrorism. Ennahda developed and promoted itself as a moderate, tolerant movement from the start. When Ennahda took power after the October 2011 election, the official tune of moderation grew louder. The party at times seemed obsessed with its image of moderation. However, some scholars observed that the theory of moderation through inclusion does not apply to Ennahda. Cavatorta and Merone[27] argued that Ennahda gained its prominence and success as a political party through a policy of "moderation through exclusion." This runs contrary to most works on extreme-parties-turned-moderate, as moderation—namely, the acceptance of democratic procedures, human rights, and a market economy—comes about through inclusion. The inclusion theory appears sound when one analyses a number of Islamist parties having contributed to the progressive democratization of their respective countries. The Tunisian case, however, offers a different perspective on moderation. Cavatorta and Merone argue that Ennahda, through a painstaking process of exclusion—namely, through repression and social marginalization—shifted from its extreme anti-systemic position of the

3. *The Tunisian Ennahda Party in the Post-Arab Spring*

1970s to its mainstream position today.[28] The state of repression is critical in the development of the neo-Islamist ideology following the First Iraq War (1991) and shaped the destinies of neo-Islamists throughout Turkey, Egypt, Tunisia, Morocco, and Algeria. Shadi Hamid observes that Islamists under autocracy were obsessed with a commitment to gradualism.[29]

In this regard, Ennahda's path runs contrary to Turkey's AKP or the Moroccan PJD, which have come to embody the very notion of political moderation, accepting democracy and human rights, taking a market-oriented position on economic matters, and adopting a pragmatic stance on sensitive, strategic issues of importance for the West. In a strict institutional sense, Ennahda was not afforded the opportunity of participating in the political system before January 14, 2011, and cross-ideological cooperation with other ideological groups never occurred prior to the mid- to late 2000s.[30] Ennahda already advocated for the parliamentary system to eliminate the possibility of presidential autocracy reoccurring as it existed under Ben Ali. During its two years in power, Ennahda made concessions on several issues affecting the non-Ennahda populace. In March 2012, the party announced it would not insist that the constitution list Sharia as one or the only source of legislation. By October 2012, it appeared Ennahda preferred to give further concessions and would not insist that insulting religious values would be made a crime (apostasy). Angrist states, furthermore, that by May 2013 "a compromise had been reached wherein neither the president nor the prime minister would exercise sole control over the executive branch."[31]

On January 9, 2014, the Troika government effectively stepped down after the new constitution was signed by coalition leaders President Moncef Marzouki, NCA speaker Mustafa Ben Jaafar, and the officially resigned Prime Minister Ali Larayedh. Mehdi Jomaa one of Ali Larayedh's ministers, took over as prime minister and formed an independent caretaker cabinet. The new prime minister, with this purported independent cabinet, was charged with leading the country toward post-constitution parliamentary and presidential elections, which indeed took place before the end of 2014. This highlights the extent of Ennahda's visible moderation and political savvy which had been demonstrated during its years in power. Since the October 2011 elections, Ennahda has shown a strong inclination "into the mechanisms of compromise and bargaining, the very foundation of the liberal democratic game."[32]

However, the Egyptian military coup in July 2013 shook up Ennahda's coalition and undoubtedly forced Ennahda to play as safe as it could. Ennahda's enemies called upon the Tunisian army and other security forces to take over, to "copy and paste" the Egyptian counterrevolution experience in a coup d'état that would supposedly protect the country from Ennahda's wrongdoings.[33] The Tunisian army, as discussed earlier, was not brought up to be involved in politics—unlike the Egyptian Army, which is a state within a state, with a wide range of income sources, such as industrial investments, shopping centers, and political connections within Egypt and abroad. In fact, when President Marzouki eliminated high-ranking officers in the Tunisian army, he strengthened the possibility of Ennahda's future survival and confirmed that despite the professionalism of the army, some high-ranking generals were seduced into buying into the coup conspiracy.

Neo-Islamists' Ruling Failures

Ennahda was blamed for several failures of the administration. Critical emphasis can be made on the following:

1. Ennahda emphasized divisive political and social issues during negotiations about what should and should not be included in the new constitution. Issues such as the national identity, the status of women, punishment of blasphemy, the nature of the political system, and the state in general had become propaganda tools rather than the standard issues of the election period.
2. Ennahda has been accused by its secularist and leftist opponents of coddling the Salafis.[34] Such critique varies between accusing Ennahda of doublespeak, of condemning acts of terrorism and violent jihadi Salafis but taking little concrete action, and accusing Ennahda leaders of openly encouraging extremism, either because Ennahda leaders actually support a more extreme agenda, or because a strong and visible Salafi militancy strengthens Ennahda's support from secular voters and parties.
3. Some intellectuals, journalists, and even Ennahda supporters have accused Ennahda of obstruction, foot dragging, and making partisan decisions.
4. Ennahda has been accused of delaying work on the new constitution and new elections in order to have the opportunity to shape a text that would impose its values and populate the state apparatus with loyalists.
5. Critics furthermore accused Ennahda of stalling while it loaded the Interior Ministry and other offices with party loyalists rather than competent managers.[35]
6. Ennahda has been blamed for neglecting the economy in favor of focusing on ideological clashes with the opposition and on enhancing its power. It has neglected to address the social and economic grievances that fueled the rebellion against Ben Ali.

In the process, the achievement of a safe and smooth democratic transition has been somewhat diminished despite Tunisia's success in retaining its fledgling democratic institutions. Furthermore, goals such as tolerance and mutual acceptance that should have dominated the rules of engagement in this transitional democratic scene have been overshadowed by murder, fear, and divisiveness. Despite this, the constitution was ultimately enacted by early January 2014.

In late May 2012, Ghannouchi declared from Washington:

> Islamists' arrival to power does not mean that they will dominate the state, the society, and the revolution because they are the most popular party, as practiced by tyrannical systems. The state's role is not to impose a certain way of life on the people. . . . However, when we faced serious differences around issues like sharia, choosing a presidential or parliamentary political system, freedom of conscious, the universality of human rights, we had to organize a national

3. The Tunisian Ennahda Party in the Post-Arab Spring 29

dialogue between the main parties to reach consensus. This lasted for nearly five weeks and we ended up reaching compromises around these different issues, hence we accepted to leave out any mention of sharia in the constitution because this notion wasn't clear to the Tunisian people.[36]

Observers like Cavatorta and Merone[37] note that harsh security measures, torture, and oppression were imposed on Tunisians for decades, requiring many political players, including the Islamists, to find alternatives and make concessions on the go. Additionally, the rejection the party faced by a large section of the Tunisian society made it possible and necessary for Ennahda to entirely re-elaborate how political Islam could contribute to the developmental trajectory of the country. From this elaboration flows the acceptance of the dominant discourse of democracy, liberalism, and market economics without which the party would not have been able to find much space in Tunisia.

Ennahda as a neo-Islamist party has performed well in recent years to convince the outside world of its moderation and democratic attitudes. For instance, there is a significantly wide acceptance that the party has come a long way since its foundation in terms of its attitudes toward the fundamental principles of electoral democracy and basic human rights. As a matter of fact, since the October 18, 2005, "collective" (better known as "Call for Tunis"), Ennahda no longer faces widespread rejection from the political and social representatives of many sectors of the Tunisian society; "moderation is recognized as having been attained."[38]

Separation between *Da'wah* and Politics (Mosque and State)

In an internal paper distributed among Ennahda members in exile only a few months before the 2011 revolution, the organization acknowledged its long journey from political stagnation and revolutionary naivety toward pragmatism and political moderation. According to the document, Ennahda started as a group dominated by rejection of most choices made by the postcolonial state in dealing with development and nation-state building. It was acting from a revolutionary position. It was clear about what it did not want but unclear of what it wanted as goals and objectives of change. As the years passed, the list of rejections shrank, and were replaced with a mentality of proactivism, realism, and positivity; thereafter, a reasonable method of change was arrived at, which was characterized by flexibility and gradualism. However, almost everyone would agree that the party is very much influenced by the development of Ghannouchi's political thinking during the last twenty to thirty years.[39] Ennahda's historic leader continued its evolution after 2011, coming up with more controversial concepts within the wider Islamist community. It is worth stating here that Ghannouchi's *Public Liberties within the Islamic State* (1993), which he penned in jail after the declaration of the Islamic Tendency Movement (MTI) on June 1981, contains his major theoretical work that has only been available in Tunisia after Ben Ali's ouster in 2011. Cavatorta and Morene[40] describe it as the pillar of the attitudes and policy positions to public freedoms in the direction of cementing democracy as the only viable political system. Ghannouchi's intellectual work continues to constitute significant development for Tunisia because it informs and seeks to constrain the actions of militants from this point onward, as self-reflection would be increasingly discussed and eventually accepted from within.

Cavatorta and Morene[41] also observe that Ennahda reached the internal conclusion to support the creation of a "civil state" (*dawla madaniyya*), "openly subscribing to the idea that references to religion are purely identity-based and not sources for public policy-making." Ghannouchi himself declared in 2013, "We believe in Shari'ah and believe that is all justice and compassion. But the implementation of Shari'ah was marred by some vices like restrictions on the freedom of women, thought, and fine arts, as regrettably happened in more than one Islamic country."[42]

On October 31, 2011, Ghannouchi concluded on Al Jazeera TV that Sharia never left Tunisia, adding that there were many breaches of Islamic laws, but that these should be addressed gradually through awareness and "within the laws of time, place, and reality."[43] These statements were made in order to elucidate the party's decision not to insist on including Sharia in the draft constitution. Such pragmatic and diplomatic answers in public statements have become typical of Ghannouchi's post-Arab Spring thinking. When John Voll asked whether Islam is compatible with democracy, Ghannouchi stated, "I don't answer that question, because I think democracy is a part of Islam; if a system is not democratic, it can't be identified as being Islamic."[44] Ghannouchi's statements suggest Ennahda is driven by the exigencies of politics, which allow for a wide interpretation of its doctrine. The constant policy repositioning depends on need and a formulaic calculation within the objectives of Sharia (*maqasid al-sharia*), which is a very trendy scholarly field within contemporary Islamism, dealing with the rethinking of the aims or objectives of Sharia laws, in order to comprehend the reasoning behind the god giving laws itself. This elasticity is a core characteristic of neo-Islamism, especially post-Arab Spring.

Comparing Ennahda to Egypt's Brotherhood reveals Ennahda's political savvy, particularly with regards to adopting neo-Islamism. President Morsi was in office for roughly one year before the army ousted him. While in office, he issued a controversial sort of constitutional coup, which demonstrated Morsi's tendency toward autocracy and a refusal to cooperate with the opposition, let alone share the administration with the opposition and politicians from outside the Brotherhood. Ennahda, on the other hand, was eager to share power, make concessions, and stick to the civil secular state, despite occasional controversial statements from some Ennahda leaders. Ennahda's awareness that its victory in October 2011 did not deliver an absolute majority that would have allowed it to monopolize power is worth noting; in contrast, the impressive results in the Egyptian elections were viewed by the Brotherhood as a mandate to act strictly according to its own agenda. In mid-2016, Ennahda organized its tenth general conference around a major controversial topic—the separation between Ennahda as a national political party and a religious preaching movement—to secure several goals such as efficiency, transparency, expertise in politics, and specialization.

In an internal paper distributed in February 2016 among Ennahda members to generate discussion and dialogue ahead of the May 2016 general congress, the authors criticized the movement's totalitarianism—namely, the tendency to control and change everything by themselves—and called for separation between *da'wah* and politics in favor of specializing in the political arena.

While the domestic media, TV shows, and social media discussions acknowledged to various extents that this conference was necessary for the country's emerging democracy, many of party followers were unhappy with the intense dose of dramatic changes. The unhappy members and sympathizers criticized top leaders of hijacking the Islamic movement legacy, principles, and continuity in favor of secular gains. This undoubtedly adds to the mounting degrees of rebellion against the coalition between Ennahda and Nidaa Tounes after the 2014 elections, where Ennahda chose to enter a coalition with the remnants of Ben Ali's ruling party RCD. Rached Ghannouchi, the party's historic leader, was on top of the critics' list. Eventually, the conference decided to go ahead with transforming the party into a purely political party and encouraged its members to practice their *da'wah* and other nonpolitical affairs in an independent nongovernmental and nonprofit associations.

However, up to this day, little of the tenth general conference decisions have been realized. Despite Ennahda's win in the May 2018 municipal elections, many of its members continue to express their resentment of the coalition with Nidaa Tounes and abandonment of the historic Islamic movement's literature and legacies, while others praise Ghannouchi's wisdom and stand in appreciation of the latest evolution, which took place within a troubled local and regional atmosphere.

Conclusion

In conclusion, Ennahda's journey toward moderation, which started in the 1970s and culminated in its rise to power in late 2011, has been quite a long one. It is a "journey towards moderation in so far as it accepts the dominant values and discourses that the majority of the international community subscribes to."[45] During its two years in power, Ennahda did not show visible signs of reversing its practice of moderation, although the party has suffered from challenges and power struggles within a mostly hostile environment. Such practical developments shed light on whether the attempt to reconcile Islam with democratic politics is inherently problematic or contingent on the factors addressed in this study. Ultimately, although there has been plenty of opportunity to watch Ennahda in power over two years, this transitional period is not sufficient to determine with certainty whether Ennahda's future will be a deep, strategic Islamization, or inclusion in a secular political system.

Can the neo-Islamists become real democrats? The answer to this question partly depends on whether neo-Islamism will continue to be a major factor in the region after the Arab revolutions and whether Tunisian-style neo-Islamism will continue to be influential in Tunisia and the broader Arab and Muslim world. However, the three short years of Ennahda's participation in the Tunisian democratic transition showed that the version of political Islam it represents can be a genuine democratic player. Neo-Islamists may be politically illiberal while being democratic nevertheless.[46] Despite remarkable ideological reforms, neo-Islamists continue to carry out painful soul searching related to the preservation of their basic existence. This contemplation has been made more difficult within the chaos, civil wars, and changes of power in countries affected by the Arab Spring. The need to evolve amidst the chaos might lead over time to adoption of new agendas that swing to the liberal or illiberal ends of the spectrum, including varying levels of commitment to democracy and civic participation. In various scenarios, neo-Islamism may morph into post-Islamism, where shariatization is not on the agenda and Islam serves as only a moral guide. It is crucial to keep in mind that neo-Islamists remain the legitimate children of their religious communities and wider societies. There is no particular reason to suggest that Islamic "reform" would lead inevitably, for example, to liberalism in the way that the Protestant Reformation led, eventually, to modern liberalism.

Ennahda's participation in Tunisia's newly free political arena has been observable for only about seven years, which is insufficient time to make definitive statements about its democratic behavior. The party has repeatedly stressed that it remains committed to a democratic regime based on Islamic principles and that such a position is compatible with liberal democracy and the protection of basic individual liberties.

Despite setbacks, neo-Islamism remains a source of hope for the region. With the rise of emerging jihadist militias such as the Islamic State of Iraq and the Levant (ISIL), there is in fact an urgent worldwide call to cooperate with, strengthen, and support neo-Islamist bids to convert their societies' economic and political crises into smooth transitions to democratization.

Chapter 4

MOROCCO'S JUSTICE AND DEVELOPMENT PARTY

CONSTRAINTS ON PARTICIPATION AND POWER POST-2011

Mohammed Masbah

The Arab Spring paved the way for Islamist parties to participate in the electoral process and attempt to govern. In Egypt, the Freedom and Justice Party won a third of parliamentary seats in the 2011 election, and Muslim Brotherhood candidate Mohamed Morsi assumed the presidency in June 2012. Likewise, in Tunisia, the Ennahda Party succeeded in achieving impressive electoral results in 2011, bringing the party to power until the end of 2014. Islamists in Morocco were no exception to this trend; the Moroccan Party of Justice and Development (PJD) managed to take the lead in the 2011 parliamentary election, which led to the appointment of the party's leader as prime minister. However, after a brief period of rule, the majority of Islamist parties lost their footing because of either a military coup such as the case in Egypt or electoral defeat such as with Ennahda in Tunisia after the 2014 elections.

This chapter examines the case of Islamists in Morocco. It highlights the impact of the Arab Spring on the PJD's discourse and strategy, and how it could maintain power over the past decade. It argues that contrary to the short-lived reign of Islamists in Tunisia and Egypt, Morocco's PJD emerged as the only Islamist party in the Arab world to maintain power for two successive government mandates and win back-to-back electoral victories in the post-2011 period.[1] The party won 107 of 395 parliamentary seats in the 2011 election, followed by 125 seats in 2016 with a voting bloc that grew by approximately one-third relative to 2011. In addition to retaining control of the government, the PJD achieved remarkable electoral gains as well. Though it faced both internal and external challenges—particularly after the king's dismissal of Abdelilah Benkirane from the premiership in March 2017—the PJD was the only political party in Morocco and the Arab world that managed to achieve long-term government participation in the period that followed the Arab Spring.[2]

Moreover, the PJD represents the only case in the Arab world in which Islamists rose to power by way of political consensus without leading to political turmoil,[3] unlike other countries (e.g., Egypt, Tunisia, and Libya) where Islamists came to power through revolution. Thus, the important question is: How can we explain the JDP's ability to maintain the government for two consecutive terms and the subsequent impact on the party's ideological and organizational structure? Prior to answering this question, it would be helpful to draw attention to the analytical frameworks used to interpret Islamist political movements as the key to understanding this phenomenon. The subject of Islamists' political participation has been a long-standing topic of interest among academics. The majority of the literature prior to 2011 focused primarily on the role of political participation in the moderation of Islamist movements by examining the circumstances under which Islamist parties undergo moderation. During that period, a broad range of interpretations was presented, some of which focused on political participation as a key factor in the process of moderation,[4] while others focused on the role of political exclusion[5] or the presumed role of building alliances across ideologies on the moderation of Islamists.[6] Interest in the issue of moderation is primarily the result of the tendency of many Western countries in the post-September 11 period to question the compatibility of Islam and Islamists with the principles of democracy. During that same period, many Islamists were in opposition or exile and therefore did not yet have the chance to rule or else had abandoned their mission before taking power, as was the case in Algeria in the early 1990s.

The pre-2011 paradigm is not as effective in understanding current developments that evolved from a number of Islamist parties' rise to power. Despite the importance of the integration and moderation approach, it fails to give sufficient consideration to the content of participation and its impact on the ideological and organizational structure of the parties. In exchange, interest in recent years has shifted to the issue of Islamists' ability to adapt after assuming power.[7] A study by the Project on Middle East Political Science (POMEPS) proposes a framework for analyzing Islamist political movements through the application of "adaptation strategies."[8] Scholar Khalil al-Anani emphasizes the importance of analyzing the outcomes of political participation over confirming or negating the premise of integration and moderation in an effort to understand the reasons behind Islamists' adoption of a method of adaptation under a particular type of pressure or motivation.[9] Thus, the time period between Islamists' rise to power in 2011 and 2018 lends itself to the construction of analyses and evaluations of the content of their participation and its effects on these parties, both ideologically and organizationally.

From an analytical standpoint, this chapter proposes an interactive framework to examine the complex processes that contributed to Moroccan Islamists' ability to adapt in the post-Arab Spring period. This framework consists of observation and analysis of overlapping factors in the adaptation process and the effects of government participation on the organizational and intellectual foundations of the PJD. This includes the party's relationship with the ruling elite, especially the royal family and the Ministry of the Interior. The framework also examines the effects of participation on the party and its organizational cohesion after Abdelilah Benkirane's dismissal in March 2017. The chapter will describe the results of participation on the party's ideology and the relationship between Islamic preaching (da'wah) and politics, as well as the way in which the party has

4. Morocco's Justice and Development Party

established a relationship with its strategic partner, the Unification and Reform Movement, and the consequences of this partnership.

This chapter argues that the PJD party's governance over two successive mandates and its consecutive electoral victories cannot be explained by party moderation or the state's desire to placate an angry polity. Rather, it must be interpreted through a number of dynamic, overlapping factors. Simply reducing complex political phenomena to an interpretation based on one or two factors precludes a deep and accurate understanding of the complex processes that govern these phenomena. Thus, this chapter argues that revealing these complex processes is best achieved through a consideration of both the actors and the infrastructure, as well as the interaction between them through a thorough description and comprehensive detailed analysis of the situation. The individual and psychological dimension can be important elements in the analysis and understanding and no less important than structural factors.[10]

Considering these elements in its analysis, this chapter proposes a tripartite interpretation of the JDP's post-Arab Spring adaptation process. First, the Arab Spring protests aided in the Islamists' arrival to power. Fear of the Arab protests, which spread rapidly across the region, motivated the monarchy to open the political field to competition. This move made it possible for the PJD to benefit from an atmosphere of political openness after the surge of political protests in 2011. Thus, the political climate, the constitutional framework, and the monarchy's opening of the political field to Islamist participation within predetermined boundaries all contributed to their continued participation in governance. But, at the same time, these factors limited their power and ideological ambitions.[11]

The second element of the interpretation is the interdependence between the monarchy and the PJD. The party's sustained governance and its achievements would not have been possible without the direct and indirect support it received from the monarchy. Royal authorities in Morocco saw the party as a safety valve[12] in the post-Arab Spring period, betting on its popularity to quell public outrage, which led to their strategic cooperation. The relationship between the palace and the PJD fluctuated, but on the whole, it trended toward stability and coexistence. The party quickly understood that if it wanted to stay in power, it would need to earn the confidence of the palace. To this end, it had to be flexible and pragmatic. By the same token, it was not in the palace's interest to thwart the Islamists' governmental experiment for two reasons: first, because the PJD, as a pro-monarchy party, did not pose a vital threat. The second, more important, reason is that Benkirane and his party enjoyed the growing popularity.[13]

On the other hand, we see that the limits of this pragmatism are put to the test when the concerns of the two sides contradict one another. A complex view of this scenario suggests that the PJD was a victim of its own electoral success.[14] The palace considered that the party's continual and growing success could pose a threat to the monarchy's power in the event that the party continued to make electoral gains, positioning itself as a political force that could alter the balance of power, which currently leaned in favor of the monarchy. This is one possible interpretation of the palace's refusal to cooperate with Benkirane in his second

36   *Islamism and Revolution Across the Middle East*

mandate, which led to his inability to form a political majority in the wake of the 2016 election.

The third element in interpreting the PJD's maintenance of power is its pragmatism and the efficacy of its political mechanism. Owing to its flexibility and pragmatism, the party was able to navigate the constraints imposed by anti-Islamist sentiments in the local and regional environment and to overcome the obstacles that stood in its path. The nature of the electoral system in Morocco (electoral partitioning, a voting system based on proportional representation) does not allow for any political party to win the absolute majority, and therefore, the winning party must always build coalitions in order to form a government. For this reason, the PJD was continually forced to negotiate with its political competitors and make concessions in and outside of the government. Moreover, during the period of Benkirane's leadership, the party successfully implemented an effective communication policy that worked to strengthen its political mechanism. This allowed the party to maintain its voting bloc, even with voters who were angry about rampant corruption during the party's leadership in government.[15] The party presented itself as an opposition party that would drive the government. Thus, the primary factor that explains continued popular support for Benkirane's government ultimately goes back to the communication strategy that the party relied on at the time. The strategy centered on his rhetorical skills, his argumentation abilities, and his public speaking in front of an audience more than it did on economic achievements. It may even be the case that the party's communication policy compensated for the lack of economic achievements of Bekirane's government. This disparity becomes clear after Benkirane's removal and his replacement by Saadeddine Othmani, as will be detailed in the forthcoming analysis.

The chapter's methodology is based on the researcher's close following of the PJD's trajectory since 2011, utilizing reliable sources of information and primary data from the researcher's network. This includes official positions expressed by the party through official documents, statements, and the positions of its leaders, in addition to interviews with party leaders and other members that took place between 2011 and 2018. Lastly, this chapter relies on other academic studies and analyses of press coverage of the party during the period of the study.

The PJD's Rise to Power

Before analyzing how the PJD adapted during its governmental tenure, it would be beneficial to shed light on the factors that contributed to the party's rise to power. The way in which the party was managed during the 2011 period can be considered a key to understanding the JDP's political participation, as it reflects the party's operational methodology, which will later help in tracing the way it managed the government and its implications for the party.

As was mentioned previously, the PJD benefited from the limited openness of the political environment that Morocco experienced in 2011 in order to achieve electoral progress and subsequently arrive in government. At the outbreak of

4. Morocco's Justice and Development Party

protests on February 20, 2011, the monarchy dealt with them lightly. Instead of resorting to oppression, the monarchy responded, at least in part, to the demands of the protester through two processes: a constitutional one and a political one. The constitutional process included a broad revision of the 1996 constitution, announced in a speech by King Mohammed VI on March 9, 2011. The amendment was comprised of seven basic principles, including the constitutional enshrinement of the pluralistic nature of Moroccan identity (in particular, the constitutionalizing of the Amazigh language), the consolidation of the rule of law and the incorporation of the expanded regional project, the independence of the judiciary, the expansion of powers of the government and the parliamentary opposition, the strengthening of mechanisms of public life, the linking of the exercise of power and public responsibility to oversight and accountability, and finally the enshrinement of institutions of good governance, human rights, and the protection of freedoms in the constitution.[16] On the other hand, the constitution retained the broad powers for the king in the realms of religion and security. The king would continue to oversee the work of the government through the council of ministers, over which he presided, joined by his personal advisers. The king also retained powers to dissolve parliament and declare a state of emergency.[17] Among eligible voters, 98 percent voted in favor of the new constitution, with a participation rate of about 72 percent. Chapter 47, considered among the more progressive chapters of the constitution, confirms that the king should appoint "the prime minister from the political party that takes the lead in parliamentary elections, and on the basis of these results." The prime minister also proposes members of government to the king.[18]

The process of political openness arose through a number of indicators. First, through the increased use of consultation in the writing of the constitution. For the first time in Morocco's history, civil society and political parties contributed to the drafting of the constitutional text. Although the constitution drafting committee was not democratically elected, as was the case in Tunisia, the consultation process was largely integrated. With the exception of Al Adl Wa Al Ihssane, which was excluded from the consultation, influential elites, political parties, and civil society were all invited to participate, including the activists of the February 20 Movement (although they refused to participate) and the Democratic Way party. The PJD had an influence in the drafting of the constitution through its political mechanism, which included leaders of political parties and the body responsible for drafting the constitution. The party was particularly influential in expanding the powers of the government, parliament, and general freedoms on the one hand, and in establishing the Islamic nature of the state on the other hand.

The second indicator of political openness was represented by the king's call for early elections in November 2011. The elections would take place under the same electoral laws, but the Ministry of the Interior, which oversees the organization of the elections, would take a more neutral role. This led to elections that were more competitive and transparent than previously.

The PJD harnessed the open political climate for its own interests by launching a political initiative called the "Democratic Reform Initiative,"[19] which sought a "third way"—the party explained it as an effort to "seek reform under stability."[20] This rhetoric—reform within the framework of stability—was attractive to the middle class, who wanted greater transparency and to fight corruption while maintaining the country's stability. This has led some researchers to explain the electoral success of the PJD in the 2011 elections as being mainly based on the absence of political alternatives and the slow pace of reform projects.[21]

After the PJD's electoral victory in 2011, the palace demonstrated a willingness to cooperate with the party. This formed the foundation to facilitate the process of forming a government and its subsequent overhaul after the departure of the Independence Party in May 2013. This behavior reflects a pattern for the Moroccan monarchy, which is distinguished by its tendency to resort to gathering popular support in moments of political crisis.[22] The monarchy has demonstrated its ability to adapt to various political conditions, providing the foundation for the PJD to rise to power, but their relationship has always ebbed and flowed.

The PJD and the Monarch: A Complex Relationship

The relationship with the royal institution is the second key to understanding the PJD's continued participation in government. It is also key to understanding the party's decline after the 2016 elections. The period of Abdelilah Benkirane's premiership was characterized by uneasy coexistence and interdependence between the monarchy and the PJD. The relationship was marked by fluctuations based on context, local and regional circumstances, and the ups and downs of various levels of cooperation and noncooperation.

Upon close observation, the nature and quality of this relationship seem to have greatly influenced the party's course and its effectiveness during the post-2011 period. In moments when the palace shows cooperation with the PJD, the party demonstrates its capacity for resilience and realizes some achievements. On the other hand, when the monarchy does not cooperate with the party, it often fails to achieve its objectives. This is evident in two cases: first, in the formation of the government and maintenance of the coalition government, and second, in the implementation of government reform projects. But before delving into the details of the relationship between the palace and the party after 2011, it is beneficial to take a moment to describe the way in which each side views the other, which will help in understanding the calculations and behavior of each side.

Impressions of the Monarchy

The PJD recognizes that it works within a political system in which the monarchy is the cornerstone and that any attempt at political change would be unsuccessful without the blessing of the royal institution. In the early day of its electoral participation, the party firmly believed that the relationship with the monarchy should be governed by cooperation rather than competition. This was the party's sentiment as expressed in its official documents since its foundation and until today. This perspective is likely governed by two factors. The first is the fact that Islamist movements that entered into a confrontation with their regimes in other contexts failed, such as in Algeria in the early 1990s after a military coup that led to a civil war that lasted 10 years, which ultimately led to a failed political process and more severe authoritarian rule. This is why the leaders of the PJD were able to accept limited participation in elections in the late 1990s, owing to the fear of harsh reactions from the regime, similar to what happened in neighboring Algeria when Islamists swept the elections.[23] This prompted leading Islamists to adopt a strategy of scaling back in order to avoid confrontation with the state. The second factor is linked to the PJD's reading of Moroccan political history. The party believes that the cause of the failure of the democratic experiment after independence was mainly a power struggle between the left and the monarchy. Following a tug-of-war in the post-independence period, the monarchy managed to gain power and marginalize nationalist parties. Leaders of the PJD believe that the monarchy cooperated with a corrupt political elite owing to its fear of nationalist parties and therefore gave broad powers to the then-interior minister Mohamed Oufkir. In order to justify cooperation with the monarchy, Benkirane expressed in a 2016 conversation that his party was more loyal than the Oufkiri Movement, which in his view was the most corrupt party in power[24] because it posed a risk to the monarchy itself based on its greed and unbridled political ambition. Mohamed Yatim confirmed this, saying, "the PJD does not want to repeat the mistakes of the left that have entered into a confrontation with the monarchy."[25]

On the basis of these two factors, leaders of the PJD recognize that coexistence with the monarchy remains the best option to avoid repression. At the same time, the party realizes that the palace needs a political party that is loyal to the monarchy and has a popular base, as this will provide legitimacy for the regime and create a political balance. Hence, the PJD believes, despite external pressures, that its own interests require that it remain a political actor under an authoritarian regime but without aligning itself with the *makhzen* (the palace, the Ministry of the Interior, and their related network of interests). In an interview with the researcher, Abdellah Baha, former deputy secretary of the PJD, referred to the nature of the relationship that binds them to the state with the following example: "The Makhzen is like a fire; you need its warmth, but if you get too close, it might burn you." Thus, he suggests that regulating the distance between the party and the regime is important. In his view, "You need to be far enough away that you don't get burned, yet close enough that you don't freeze to death."[26] This explains, for example, why the party did not orient itself toward the opposition after Bekirane's dismissal in March 2017,[27] which was most likely due to fear of retaliation from the palace. According to the party's leadership, joining with the opposition at that time would constitute a challenge to the royal decision to dismiss Benkirane and would launch an open confrontation with the state and its authorities.[28] The Egyptian experience—especially after the coup of June 30, 2013 and the Rabaa al-Adawiya massacre—cast its shadow over the unconsciousness of PJD leaders, which was sometimes hinted at[29] and other times overtly mentioned in interviews.

The Ups and Downs of the Relationship

The PJD's relationship with the monarchy is characterized by ebbs and flows. Sometimes, the monarchy supported Benkirane during his first government mandate, and at other times, there was obvious tension between the two sides. In fact, the monarchy showed support for the PJD on a number of occasions. In the beginning, it supported the PJD in facilitating the process of forming its first government. It also facilitated Benkirane's 2013 mission to restore the coalition government after the Independence Party's withdrawal, not to mention the royal support of many of the political and economic reform initiatives initiated by the government, most notably the reformation of the justice system, the reformation of the fuel subsidy system (the compensation fund), and that of the pension system and the support for widows.

It is worth noting that the palace had a prime opportunity to rid itself of the PJD during the summer of 2013. At the time, the party did not have a majority in parliament after the Independence Party withdrew from the government coalition, and the regional climate was hostile toward Islamists after the military coup in Egypt on June 30, 2013. But the palace instead chose to keep the PJD in power, though it put pressure on the party to accept painful adjustments, such as abandoning the most important ministries, including the Ministry of Education and the Ministry of the Interior, to the benefit of technocrats.[30] Indications of rising tension in the relationship between the palace and the PJD emerged in the wake of the 2015 and 2016 elections. During this time, the palace worked to put in place a number of obstacles and legal measures to stop the JDP's electoral progress, in addition to its routine attempts to tame political parties through encouraging internal divisions and controlling the political landscape.

As a result of this tension, the Ministry of the Interior reverted to its previous practices of curtailing the PJD's electoral trajectory and controlling the pace of its electoral progress. The state used a number of classic tools, namely, blocking party leaders and Benkirane through attempts to prevent them from shaping the political views of citizens by forbidding Benkirane from convening organizing activities with citizens for security reasons. Likewise, anti-Benkirane actors were allowed to disrupt a number of these activities. Similarly, the monthly session in which Benkirane met with the parliamentary opposition was suspended. These parliamentary sessions constituted one of the means through which Benkirane could connect with broad segments of society that followed the political discussion. The palace's apprehension toward the PJD was demonstrated through its retention of parties close to the palace, which were used as tools to control the political balance in the country. Despite the bitter criticism received by the Authenticity and Modernity Party during the February 20, 2011 protests, the palace continued to offer its support, especially in the 2015 local elections, in which it took the lead in terms of the number of seats, and also in the 2016 election, in which the party came in second behind the PJD.

Despite leading the government and supervising the organization of elections, the PJD frequently complained of electoral bias on the part of the Ministry of the

4. Morocco's Justice and Development Party

Interior.[31] In the 2016 election, the Ministry of the Interior worked to reduce the party's electoral threshold to 3 percent using electoral partitioning inconsistent with population development. The majority of seats were allotted to rural districts, which usually vote for administrative parties with the aim of Balkanizing the political scene. Voter registration was also controlled by reducing the role of parties in registering citizens to vote. This decision was directed mainly toward the JDP, as it was the most active party this regard, having organized a coordinated campaign specifically to encourage voter registration. In addition, the pressure was placed on some businessmen to run as representatives of the JDP, at least in the case of Boussouf and Mohamed Awad. Although Benkirane reduced these measures, he admitted that there had been some abuses.[32]

Since the summer of 2015, the relationship between the palace and the PJD experienced growing tension. This was mainly due to the fact that it was an election period. Indications of tension began to appear after Abdelilah Benkirane's speech in April 2016 before members of his party in which he offered a thinly veiled criticism of those surrounding the monarchy.[33] The tension escalated after Benkirane appeared in a conversation on Al-Aoual's website in the summer of 2016 in which he directly criticized the private adviser to the king, Fouad Ali El Himma, and accused him of being a symbol of "control." He also hinted at the fact that the royal milieu contained corrupt actors, likening them to Mohamed Oufkir, who appeared to be loyal to the monarchy, but was actually concealing intentions to organize a coup.[34] This conversation, which led to considerable tension in the relationship between the palace and Benkirane,[35] was leaked to *Jeune Afrique*, a magazine with close ties to the palace. The magazine indicated that the monarchy was outraged by Benkirane.[36] The same source from the palace that leaked the news said that Benkirane "is working as prime minister during the week, and as a political opponent on the weekends"[37] in reference to the planning meetings that Benkirane regularly held with his party's base in which he criticized the difficulties that he faced in his work in the government. In September 2016, the royal court issued a strongly worded statement[38] against a statement by Nabil Benabdallah, secretary general of the Party of Progress and Socialism, in one of the national newspapers, which said that the problem was not the Authenticity and Modernity Party, but rather the person who supported and founded the party (El Himma). This resulted in a crisis within the Party of Progress and Socialism that nearly led to the resignation of Nabil Benabdallah from its leadership.[39] The Royal Court's statement was most likely aimed at hitting two birds with one stone. For one, it targeted Nabil Benabdallah because he led a small party that was also one of the biggest supporters of Benkirane. But the second goal was to send a message to Benkirane to avoid using the term "control" in combination with "the palace," as he had done in his speeches. Indeed, the statement succeeded in restraining Benkirane from using the term during his 2016 electoral campaign.[40] This tension also manifested symbolically when the 2016 parliamentary election results were announced unilaterally by former minister of the interior, Mohamed Hassad. The absence of the minister of justice and liberties, Mustafa Ramid, at the announcement was unexpected, given that he was the second in command of the "National Committee for the Oversight of Elections."[41] Despite the fact that Abdelilah Benkirane was granted a second royal appointment after the 2016 elections, demonstrating the king's respect for the constitution, the palace's lack of cooperation was one of the main reasons behind Benkirane's failure to form a government after a six-month deadlock. After attempting to negotiate with the parties involved in the formation of the majority government, Benkirane understood that the palace was not going to make his task easy. This led him to issue his well-known statement, "the conversation is over,"[42] in which he expressed that Aziz Akhannouch was not in charge and that the discussion would take place between the parties concerned, in reference to the palace. This was an indication that Benkirane felt that he would not be able to form a government without agreeing to the conditions set out by Aziz Akhannouch, who represented the party closest to the palace. Days before his dismissal, Benkirane expressed his intention to submit his resignation with the king upon his return from Africa. He had even written the letter of resignation and contacted the court to inform the king.[43] However, the king did not meet Benkirane personally but sent four of his advisers to inform him of the decision to dismiss him. Benkirane was carrying his letter of resignation that he intended to present to the king but refrained upon receiving the decision of his removal.[44]

From Identity to Administration

The PJD's course is fertile ground for the study of transformations experienced by Islamist political parties upon their arrival to power. Experience in government puts many of their basic assertions and assumptions to the test. During its government tenure, the PJD displayed remarkable flexibility and pragmatism, demonstrating the party's capacity to learn and adapt,[45] both from its own experience and from that of other Islamist parties, especially those that failed. The impact of political participation on the party's ideology is reflected on three levels: first, with regard to the relationship of the religious and the political; second, regarding identity issues; and finally, concerning the party's method of managing political conflict.

1. Islamic Preaching (da'wah) versus Politics

The relationship between Islamic preaching (da'wah) and politics represents one of the keys to understanding the flexibility and adaptability of the PJD. The Moroccan experience is an interesting case in this respect. Some scholars consider the nature of the relationship between the PJD and its parent movement (the Unification and Reform Movement) to be one of the factors in understanding the moderation of Islamists in Morocco.[46] In their view, this goes back to the fact that the independence between the party and the movement forced the PJD to be more self-reliant, both in terms of building up its own resources and establishing the party independent of the movement.[47] The reality is that the separation between da'wah and the politics is not static, but develops dynamically alongside the ideological

4. Morocco's Justice and Development Party

and organizational maturation of the experience as well as the constraints of the political environment. Ideological adaptation is, therefore, a process that preceded the party's government experience that began in 2012.

The period prior to 2011 can be separated into two stages. The first stage included the 1990s, which was characterized by tactical moderation—that is, the acceptance of political participation without adjusting political convictions. The relationship between *da'wah* and politics was the subject of internal discussions since the mid-1990s, culminating in the formulation of the "specialization policy" adopted by the Unification and Reform Movement, which required a gradual policy of differentiation between the movement and the party with regard to functions, figures, and rhetoric,[48] despite the strong presence of religious rhetoric in the party's discourse.

The post-2000 stage is considered the most important stage in the process of differentiation between *da'wah* and politics in parallel with the party's ideological maturity. The need for greater electoral support and to formulate a response to broad transformations that the society experienced led the party to break from its strict religious codes and move toward greater ideological openness.[49] Hence, the movement and the party worked to expand the "specialization policy" to include a greater distinction between the movement and the party such that the movement would focus its activity on *da'wah*, education, and training, while the party would focus on elections and public policy.[50]

This process of differentiation between the movement and the party required a separation, not only on the level of domains of activity but also an organizational distinction between the two institutions. Thus, membership in the movement was not considered a condition for obtaining a leadership position in the party. Accordingly, most members of the party today do not belong to the movement. Therefore, the movement's consultative council adopted a document called "Directions of the Movement," which included the principle of differentiation between political work and *da'wah*. According to the movement's chairman, Abdelrahim Chiki, this meant that "the movement and the party are independent institutions, each with its own choices, decision-making, and funding; the two are distinct on the levels of their functions, discourse, and leadership."[51] At the same time, he recognized the existence of members of the movement who belonged to the party and vice versa. In theory, party-specific decisions are not to be discussed within the movement. The former head of the Unification and Reform Movement, Mohamed Hamdawi, said, "I read about the formation of the government in the newspaper."[52]

However, the movement maintained institutional channels with the party primarily through the leaders who headed both groups, such as Mustafa Al-Khalfi, Mohamed Yatim, and Abdellah Baha, all of whom were members of the executive offices of both institutions. Likewise, the parliament members and ministers of the party maintained financial commitments to the party, given their status as party members. The movement does not officially advocate for party candidates nor does it allow leaders of Friday prayer to run for office. This rule was violated, however, with the nomination of the former head of the movement, Mohamed

Hamdawi, in the 2016 parliamentary election, not to mention that the movement implicitly mobilizes its members to vote for and support candidates of the party.

The truth is that the decision to separate propaganda from politics was not exclusively internally motivated. It was also brought about by pressure from the state after the bombings of May 16, 2003, which prompted some left-wing parties to call for the dissolution of the PJD. Likewise, the constitutional framework also prohibits the establishment of parties on a religious basis.[53] Thus, in an official speech after the 2003 bombings, King Mohammed VI stressed that as emir of the believers, he is considered the "sole religious authority for the Moroccan nation, so there would be no room for parties or associations that aim to speak on behalf of Islam as a whole or its guardianship."[54] The pressure that accompanied the May 16 bombings was another opportunity to advance the separation between religion and politics. Thus, the PJD had no choice but to formally declare the dismantling of all organizational and ideological links to the Unification and Reform Movement.

The PJD has solidified its intellectual position on the issue of the relationship between *da'wah* and politics through two processes. First, through the writings of its intellectual leaders, and second, through the adoption of official party documents that outlined the separation between *da'wah* and politics. Saadeddine Othmani's intellectual perspective on the relationship of political and religious affairs takes shape in his 2009 book *Religion and Politics: Distinction, not Separation*,[55] which focuses on two main issues. The first issue is the fact that the acts of the Prophet during the time of his leadership varied. In other words, his actions were not limited to the legislative realm. According to Othmani, some of the Prophet's acts were dictated by divine inspiration (*waḥī*), making them obligatory for Muslims. However, many of his political acts involved his own independent reasoning (*ijtihād*), and thus would not be considered obligatory for all Muslims. The second issue is Othmani's view that political action is an act of *ijtihād* and is therefore subjective. Thus, he concludes that under Islam the state is a civil state, not a religious one. In other words, that the state's decisions are based on individual reasoning, not divine inspiration and that the primary role of the imam or the politician is to manage the daily affairs of people, protect their best interests, and ward off corruption and evil. Accordingly, he concludes that Islamic political thought may seek inspiration from the model of Western democracy, as long as a mechanism to regulate the distance between the religious and the political is established. He describes this model as different from the French model of *laïcité*, which dictates a complete separation, nor does it resemble the theocratic model of absolute integration of religion into politics. Rather, it is a matter of distinguishing[56] between the devotional and the ordinary. This complex relationship is based on the distinction between that which resides in the devotional domain, which is carried out by the clergy through Islamic advocacy (*da'wah*), while the ordinary belongs in the realm of political concern. Othmani recognizes the existence of overlapping areas and the intersection of certain issues across political and religious realms (e.g., the stance on abortion), but at the same time, he argues that legislation can only be adopted through public deliberation and the traditional political process.

4. Morocco's Justice and Development Party

In 2008, at its sixth conference, the PJD presented an institutional response to the issue of the relationship between the religious and the political through the adoption of the "Thesis of the Democratic Struggle," which defined the party as "a civil political party with an Islamic framework that operates according to the rules of democracy." Saadeddine Othmani, the party's secretary general at the time, likened it to Christian Democratic parties.[57] Thus, one could say that the sixth conference marked the transition from the phase of strategic moderation to one of ideological moderation, where the adoption of a separation between the religious and the political was declared on the institutional level. The party also appeared to ease up on the use of religious and identity-based rhetoric in favor of political rhetoric that defended democracy rather than identity.[58]

2. Strategic Moderation

If the pre-2000 stage was one of tactical adaptation and the period between 2000 and 2011 was one of strategic adaptation, then the post-2011 period can be described as the strategic transformation from political Islam to post-political Islam, as distinguished by two characteristics. The first is the party's complete dedication to the national context by differentiating itself from Eastern movements of political Islam. The second is the reinforcement of the process of separation between religious and political realms and the adoption of a more secular political discourse.

The PJD worked to enshrine the notion that it was a national party operating within political institutions and that it represented neither an intellectual nor an organizational extension of any foreign political organization, with a particular emphasis on its distance from the Muslim Brotherhood.[59] It emphasized its distinction from the Muslim Brotherhood through the way in which it managed its position on the June 30, 2013 coup, making sure to distinguish between official government positions and party positions. On the one hand, the Ministry of Foreign Affairs, led by Othmani at the time, issued a statement of neutrality that contained no reference to the military coup, whereas the party cautiously condemned the coup while simultaneously emphasizing the differences between the PJD and the Muslim Brotherhood. Meanwhile, organizations parallel to the PJD (the Unification and Reform Movement, the Justice and Development Youth, and the Students' Renewal Organization) also condemned the coup outright. It appeared to be a distribution of roles among the constituents of the Islamic movement, which alleviated the pressure placed upon the PJD at various levels.[60] In 2015, Abdelilah Benkirane met with Abdel Fattah el-Sisi after the Arab League's meeting in Cairo. The meeting was considered "friendly,"[61] although it sparked criticism of the prime minister on social media.[62]

On the other hand, after 2011, the PJD avoided entering into debates about identity. An analysis of the party's stance on a variety of moral issues, and on women's issues in particular, demonstrates this apparent development in its ideology. After opposing the national plan for the integration of women in development in 2000, and especially the massive ideological battles against the government led by the Socialist Union Party at that time, the party began to soften its political discourse after the March 16, 2003 bombings as a result of external pressures. In the beginning, the party's critiques of the plan centered around an ideological rift, where the party considered the plan to integrate women as representative of a Western agenda to change the cultural and religious identity of Moroccans, which would result in chaos and the destruction of society.[63] After 2003, the party began criticizing specific elements of the plan, especially those that they thought did not specifically address Moroccan society, as well as its exclusionary, top-down approach. This change in its stance can be explained by the party's desire to rebuild its political image amidst sharp criticism that described it as ideologically hidebound and short-sighted.[64] After its rise to power, the PJD took over the Ministry of Family and Development for two consecutive terms, which included a set of policies that ran counter to its previous beliefs. For example, in 2014, the government, with the support of the Ministry of Family and Development (presided over by the JDP), endorsed a United Nations Human Rights Council draft resolution in Geneva that addressed the freedom of religion or faith.[65] The same can be said about the party's position on art festivals and issues of international agreements. Previously opposed to both, the party changed its stance after its arrival to the government, at which time it began to accept them. As for international agreements, the party began to accept them while adopting a conservative doctrine as a tool for adapting local laws to the terms agreed upon in international treaties.[66]

The party has continued to avoid engaging in a discussion of identity issues, especially inheritance, Islamic *jus cogens* (peremptory laws), and abortion. This choice can be explained by the fact that the party believes that engaging in identity discussions is unproductive and polarizing. As Benkirane stated, "If we wanted to fail, we would do it [impose head coverings on all women]. If we are serious about success, we will not interfere in the choices of the people."[67]

3. Cross-Ideological Alliances

The second main ideological shift imposed upon the party by participation in government can be demonstrated through its adoption of cross-ideological alliances. The PJD takes into account two elements of the political environment when building political alliances. The first is whether the policies in question would contradict those of the central authority. The second is whether the policy would have popular support. When a particular policy choice conflicts with the central authority but enjoys broad popular support, it is possible to build loose coalitions and mobilize parties in a straightforward institutional way. When a specific policy choice both conflicts with the central authority and lacks broad support from other political entities, informal alliances are formed between the party and the social movement in support of the policy and carried out by regular members. Finally, in the event that the policy in question does not contradict the state, but lacks popular support, there is no real need to build alliances, so the alliances will be weak and insignificant if they are created at all.[68]

In practice, as noted above, the nature of the electoral system forces political parties to form political alliances in order to build coalitions, both at the national level, as in government coalitions, and locally, in the form of coalitions among municipal councils. The party recognized that avoiding ideological conflicts would be a beneficial strategy for ensuring its continued governance. Some party leaders have explicitly told the researcher that the party "will not be dragged into provocations toward debates related to identity. We realize that they want to drag us into this losing battle."[69] The party benefited from the absence of a "religious right" in parliament. The absence of Salafists in parliament has reduced identity-based polarization and left the PJD with a single choice: to form an alliance with secular parties or face marginalization.

The PJD views engagement with secular parties as an exercise in dealing with difference and an opportunity to restrain the tendency toward domination that Islamist parties are often accused at the time of their arrival to power. For example, the Party of Progress and Socialism was a weak party, but it was awarded more than its fair share of government posts, relative to its size. One PJD minister told the researcher that "even if we win the majority of seats in parliament, we will merge with the other parties for two reasons: to curb the appetite for power and to send a message that the party is not hegemonic." He stressed that his party's failure to win first place in the 2015 local elections was a relief for him because he believed that the state "would slaughter us if we did not leave the opportunity for others to win."[70] Thus, the desire to reduce the thirst for power was not the only motivation for the party's engagement with secularists; a fear of state repression also played a significant role.

4. Gradualism and Flexibility

To understand the PJD's two-term maintenance of power, it is important to consider the way in which the party managed policy constraints before and during its government tenure. In this sense, it is important to consider why the party has resorted to gradualism and flexibility as a way of dealing with the challenges posed by the political environment.

A policy of "gradualism" refers to the seamless participation in the management of public affairs in a gradual and progressive manner. The decision to adopt a policy of gradualism was forced upon the party by pressure from authorities. The state intervened several times in its internal decisions, as was the case in 2003 when Mustafa Ramid was elected president of the party's parliamentary group.[71] This is in addition to the many pressures to which some members of the party were subjected at the local level, such as the dismissal of Abu Bakr Belkoura from the presidency of the local municipal council of Meknes[72] and the arrest of Jama Mu'tasim, one of the party's leaders.[73] As a result of these pressures, Islamists of the PJD resorted to a policy of scaling back in the period between 1997 and 2003.[74] The fact is that that downsizing was the only remaining choice for the party. As previously noted, the JDP, at an early stage, recognized the ability of the royal institution to control the political scene and parties, and that any participation from Islamist parties would need to operate within the conditions set forth by the monarchy.

As a result, the PJD's decision to enact a policy of gradualism as a strategic choice came at the expense of another choice. In other words, the PJD chose not to sweep the election, as this strategy would engender conflict with the palace. The party justified the policy of gradualism by saying that slow and gradual change was the best method for change because it would avoid putting the country's stability at risk. In an interview with the Spanish news agency in 2016, Benkirane explicitly stated that the gradual approach would help Morocco to avoid the instability that other Arab countries experienced.[75]

The process of gradualism is most salient in the evolution of the party's electoral results. The JDP's post-2011 victories were a direct result of its two-decade-long political growth. Since the Islamists joined the political scene in 1996, the party's course has undergone significant developments. In the 1997 election, the party won only nine seats in parliament. That number rose to forty-two seats in the 2002 election, even though the party only had candidates in half of all districts, a self-reductionist strategy it employed out fear of sweeping the stage[76] in response to pressures exerted on party leaders from the Ministry of the Interior at the time.[77] In the 2007 elections, the party won forty-seven seats, a slight increase from 2002, but it remained unable to harness all of its power to succeed in the elections. This followed the trend of Islamist parties in the pre-2011 period, where Islamists largely tried to avoid sweeping the election. Instead, they sought to win a sufficient number of seats that would allow them to pressure the government to make concessions.[78] The party was unable to participate in government prior to 2011 for several reasons. First, because electoral partitioning was engineered in advance by the Ministry of the Interior in such a way that the party could not obtain the majority of seats nor seniority in parliament, despite the fact that it consistently earned a greater number of votes than other parties. The second reason is that none of the most powerful political parties at the time wanted to associate themselves with the Islamists, which meant that the PJD was isolated from political elites at that time.

In reality, the approach of gradualism and flexibility was not associated with the resistance phase alone. In fact, it became a pattern that characterized the PJD throughout the party's government tenure, both during the period of the Benkirane government and later under Saadeddine Othmani. The PJD's restraint is most evident in the fact that it handed over of some of its powers guaranteed by the constitute ion to the monarchy. After the party's rise to power in early 2012, some overlapping areas emerged between the authorities of the king and those of prime minister. To avoid conflict with the palace, the PJD often resorted to a conservative interpretation of the constitution, surrendering many of the prime minister's powers to the king. For instance, after the 2011 constitutional amendment, the prime minister was afforded broad powers of appointment over senior positions in the administrative bureaucracy. The amendment authorized the prime minister to appoint hundreds of senior positions, such as governors and prefects (of provinces), ambassadors, and directors of public administration, among others, with the exception of a limited number of strategic positions that would continue to be appointed by the king. Although these powers were guaranteed by the constitution, Benkirane rarely used them, fearing a strained relationship with the monarchy. Even when an official directly criticized the prime minister on one of the public channels, he did not exercise his power to dismiss her, saying that she had protection,[79] in reference to the royal palace. This has led to criticism from some opposition parties who claim that he compromised his constitutional powers as prime minister. However, Benkirane is clearly aware that the real powers are in the hands of the king. This is enshrined in the constitution, which states that the prime minister of Morocco is a member of the parliament which is headed by the king, while the prime minister leads government meetings. The king is also the de facto ruler, given the vast powers of the palace over the most important ministries, particularly the Ministry of the Interior.[80]

Conclusion

The PJD's experience in government has brought about behavioral and organizational shifts that can be described as practical adaptation. The pressures of the political environment compelled the party to find pragmatic ways of coping in order to maintain leadership in the government and influence as a political actor. In this way, the party worked to establish a clear separation between religious and political action by loosening organizational and intellectual ties with its parent institution, the Unification and Reform Movement. It also worked to build transideological political alliances through coalitions with non-Islamist parties in order to ensure a government majority. Apart from these intellectual transformations, the outcomes of the PJD's political participation on the party's organizational structure were costly. It can be said that the PJD emerged as a victim of its own electoral success. The party recognized that its bipartite mission to appease the palace and simultaneously govern effectively was fraught with many challenges. The PJD's successive electoral victories have raised fears in the palace that the party would build an electoral mechanism that the Ministry of the Interior would be unable to defeat through its standard procedures of controlling elections. The palace, consequently, worried about its ability to control the political scene in the event that the party broke free from the institutional constraints set forth by the state.

It is difficult to predict the fate of the current crisis within the PJD and the future implications for its organizational coherence. There are two possible scenarios, one more optimistic than the other. The first scenario, the optimistic one, arises from the assumption that the PJD has the organizational strength and institutional mechanisms needed to manage internal differences and appease its base in a way will allow the party to overcome the repercussions of Benkirane's dismissal. The party has faced similar trials in the past and succeeded in overcoming them. For example, after the bombings of May 16, 2003, authorities put pressure on the party to reduce its participation in the election. The PJD reacted positively and succeeded in managing the repressive measures carried out by the authorities at the time. In 2011, the party managed to overcome the consequences of the protests led by the 20 February Movement and its institutional structures successfully mitigated and absorbed internal tension.

The second, more pessimistic, scenario is that the PJD, after Benkirane's dismissal in March 2017, will enter a period of organizational decline. Although the leadership of the party managed to recover from the decision to remove him, the process of forming a government under Saadeddine Othmani had repercussions that have lead toward organizational decline, notably Othmani's acceptance of the Socialist Union Party into the government coalition, which Benkirane denied throughout his tenure. His refusal, however, ultimately cost him his position in government. Since that period, differences between members of parliament and Benkirane and his camp have grown. For more than three months, the party's political bureau did not convene. Differences also surfaced via the media and social networking spaces. Signs of decline were again apparent in the aftermath of the eighth national conference, in which none of those who were supportive of a third mandate—not even Abdelali Hami Eddine, one of the party's top leaders— were nominated to lead the party. There have been signs of further division among the party's parallel organizations, especially the Justice and Development Youth. The party's popularity declined after the formation of the Othmani government when it was criticized for its failure to provide answers on a number of key issues, namely protests in rural areas and human rights issues as well as the high cost of living. In addition, the new prime minister was unable to utilize media appearances to frame the public debate to the same extent as his predecessor, who was marginalized within his own party after the eighth conference.

It is difficult to determine which of these two scenarios is more likely to transpire, but the PJD is influenced by the political environment in which it operates. If a climate of control and authoritarianism continues to prevail, the second scenario is more likely. However, in the event that the palace creates an environment of political openness, it is likely that the pace of the PJD's internal erosion will subside.

Chapter 5

TRANSFORMATION OF ISLAMIST GROUPS IN SYRIA

AHRAR AL-SHAM, JAYSH AL-ISLAM, AND THE SHAM LEGION

Hamzah Almustafa

This chapter explores the transformation of Islamists in Syria after the Arab Spring. It critically engages with the inclusion-moderation hypothesis and provides an alternative approach to the study of Islamism in conflict zones such as the case in Syria after 2011. It argues that to understand the transformation of Islamist factions and groups in Syria, one should focus on the dynamics and mechanisms of the transformation process. In other words, instead of asking why a movement becomes radical or moderate, this chapter asks a different question: what is the process by which a movement changes its strategic orientations? It answers this question by analyzing the external political environment in which Islamists are operating, the movements' mobilization structure, and the ideological frames they deploy.

"Killing Politics" was the title Lisa Wedeen chose for the second chapter of her renowned book *Ambiguities of Domination* published in 1999, which worked to unpack the mechanisms of physical and symbolic repression that former Syrian president Hafez al-Assad used against society to consolidate his rule over thirty years. According to Wedeen, the power of the Syrian state "regime" lies not in its control of material resources and the formation of institutions of punishment alone, but in its management of the symbolic order, whereby the community is urged to "worship the ruler" and the image of the opposition is smeared through rhetorical vilification and punitive torture.[1] In comparison with totalitarian or competitive authoritarian regimes in the Arab world, Syria has experienced a unique situation of decades of political desertification. This is due to the fact that the Arab Socialist Ba'ath Party enacted a constitutional provision (Article 8) after it came to power (March 8, 1963), under which it legitimized its "leading" role in state and society in a way that has emptied the multiparty system of all substantive competition.[2]

This is not to say that opposition was nonexistent. Secular political parties and forces, such as the National Democratic Rally and Kurdish parties, have been part of a narrow elite, framed by cultural associations, forums, and political salons that lack effective influence on the ground. On the other hand, the Muslim Brotherhood no longer has any organization inside Syria since its departure in

1982. It was criminalized in 1980 under Law 49, which states: "Any person affiliated with the Muslim Brotherhood is considered a criminal."[3] Although the beginning of the current president Bashar al-Assad's rule witnessed a kind of political openness (Damascus Spring 2001, Damascus Declaration 2005), the promises of political reform and the gradual transition to democracy soon dissipated, and the security crackdown re-emerged as the primary, and indeed the only, way in which the regime dealt with the opposition.[4]

After decades of exclusion and overshadowing, the Syrian revolution, in its peaceful and armed stages, paved the way for opponents of the regime, in general, and Islamists, in particular, to break into the political sphere, creating a public space outside of government control where political and social actors could introduce their ideas and programs.[5] This context led to the founding of a number of armed Islamist movements that have overlapping objectives (such as the establishment of the Islamic state), but vary in the details of how they should be achieved according to their differing schools of thought (Salafi jihadism, Salafi purism, the Muslim Brotherhood, Sufism, etc.). Following the experiences of Islamists in the Arab Spring, the Islamist movements in Syria sought to seize the opportunities available in the revolution to expand their social base and assume a central political position in order to assert their influence in the political dynamics of the country. Subsequently, the movements were exposed to rhetorical, behavioral, and structural changes.

Since mid-2014, Islamist factions have become the leading force in armed action against the Syrian Armed Forces and its supporting foreign factions. At the same time, they have emerged as one of the country's greatest dilemmas. This can be attributed to a gap in the assessment of the Syrian crisis by influential international and regional powers, which has led to a discrepancy in their respective approaches to the problem. Perspectives range from demands to include the Islamist factions on the list of designated terrorist groups and eradicate them militarily to calls for their integration and absorption in oppositional institutions and encouraging them to enter into negotiations for a political settlement.

This study does not intend to present political prescriptions or issue value judgments. In fact, it explicitly aims to avoid the aforementioned two arguments to avoid falling into the trap of their inevitable end, that is, moderation. Instead, this study takes an alternative interpretive approach based on an explanation of the transformations of Islamist movements in Syria during the post-revolutionary period. It focuses on the process or processes of the transformation more than its inevitable ending or its standard provisions. In addition, this study focuses on the tools and mechanisms that contribute to determining the form and quality of the outcomes of the transformation processes.

Thus, the central question of this study revolves around an assessment of the impact of political engagement in the post-revolutionary period on the discourse, behavior, and organizational structure of Syrian Islamist factions. This main inquiry is broken down through a set of questions about the analytical models that explain the transformations of these movements and the nature of these transformations, the quality of the response, and the degree of variation between

5. Transformation of Islamist Groups in Syria

movements. In order to answer these questions, the study uses two research tools: discourse analysis and semi-structured interviews. The majority of interviews were conducted with leaders of these movements, influential opposition figures, activists, and researchers well acquainted with the subject.

Ahrar al-Sham: Gradual Distancing from Salafi Jihadism

Upon their release from detainment in 2011, Salafists in Syria were surprised by the outbreak of the revolution that spread across almost every governorate. They were also surprised by its peaceful nature and sloganeering using phrases like "democracy" and "the state," which did not align with their stance. Despite their early reservations, the revolution was their only gateway to make contact with local communities with differing perspectives. In their discussions about their "imagined" project, which was based on the local-ideological dichotomy, Salafists discussed the reality of the revolution, their previous experiences, especially in the Sednaya prison, and their experience with the regime. This was before Hassan Aboud, the founding leader of the Ahrar al-Sham brigades (November 2011), depicted the project as an armed branch for the "protection of peaceful demonstrations"[6] and a building block of the "local" jihadist project similar to that of the Taliban,[7] but not belonging to the global jihadist movement and its organizational frameworks like Al-Qaeda.

Post-Salafi Jihadism

Ahrar al-Sham has always distinguished itself from Al-Qaeda and the Free Syrian Army (FSA). This has led to the organization's intellectual confusion based on the need to invoke revolutionary rhetoric to differentiate itself from its jihadist counterpart (and vice versa) while acknowledging the prevalence of Salafist rhetoric on the revolutionary beginning of its establishment.[8] During the years of revolution, the movement failed to define itself or to position itself intellectually within a particular school. Instead, its leaders insisted on defining the movement through the denial of its "brothers" and by "exceeding" Salafi jihadism. Hence, the movement is referred to here as post-Salafi jihadism.

Often, jihadist movements do not politically organize through the typical means of process, path, and rules. Rather, they adopt a "violent" revolutionary approach as the only way to establish a "legitimate government." During the early years of their establishment, Ahrar al-Sham was no exception to this rule. The organization's leadership preferred to withdraw into itself for fear of structural imbalances or internal divisions and the defection of its fighters to high-level jihadist movements.[9] This explains their refusal to join the Syrian Islamic Liberation Front (SILF), which was established in September 2012 and constituted the largest Islamist faction at the time. Seeking to assert itself and distinguishing itself from SILF, the organization competed with SILF to attract smaller Islamist factions. This forced the leadership of Ahrar al-Sham to shift to more flexible and general rhetoric in order to find common ground with eleven Islamic factions, with which it formed the Syrian Islamic Front (SIF) in December 2012. SIF's charter contained a rhetorical tone of "renewal" focused on "building a civilized Islamic society" instead of "establishing an Islamic regime." And for the first time, they touched upon problematic issues such as religious minorities, centrism, moderation, and women's rights. The late addition of "Syrian" was important because it formally cemented the nationalist dimension of the faction's "local-national" ideology.

The declaration of the establishment of the Islamic State in Syria (ISIS)—and the resulting changes in the former US administration's priorities in Syria and those of Western countries in general, in terms of combating terrorism rather than focusing on regime change[10]—prompted "Ahrar al-Sham's engagement in politics" for fear of being designated as a terrorist organization. The first step was its transformation into a political movement on January 31, 2013, following its full integration with the Islamic Dawn Movement, the Combatant Vanguard, and the Combatant Faith Brigade.[11] It then abandoned the term "brigade" and defined itself as "a reformist Islamic movement working to build a civilized Islamic society governed by the law of God." The establishment of the Ahrar al-Sham movement in 2013 injected new life into the movement. This, in turn, led to a discussion of the movement's major objectives and priorities. The result was the emergence of a general trend that made it possible to achieve its major objectives (such as the adoption of the sharia law) as long as they were accepted by the community. The movement was also open to accepting outside objectives, provided that they maintained the freedom to conduct preaching work and take an active role in politics.

The aforementioned ideological approaches gave vague indications that the Ahrar al-Sham movement had entered a period of radical intellectual revisions. But the rise of ISIS and its exaggerated discourse in "The Thorn of Empowerment and Spite"[12] and the declaration of the caliphate had a massive impact on the movement, especially after its fighters showed reluctance to fight against ISIS, even in the face of the assassination of its military leaders and its eradication from several areas. At this point, the movement realized the depth of the predicament at the grassroots level. The problem was rooted in the fact that intellectual discussions were restricted to a private elite, while fighters were force-fed lines of religious reasoning that used the Muslim-infidel dichotomy to motivate them to fight the regime and its allies. This approach left fighters without any real philosophical or faith-based motivation to fight outside of this binary.[13]

As a result, the leadership of the movement opted to "bypass" any reply to previous discussions and worked with other Islamist factions on a political-intellectual project to prove to ISIS fighters and those of the Ahrar movement that they were not "Sahawat" (i.e., sons of Iraq) and that the adoption of the sharia law was the main objective.[14] This is the context in which the formation of the Islamic Front was announced on November 22, 2013. Its charter, titled "Project Nation," adopted the goal of "establishing an Islamic state" as a local priority and rejected all other terms (democracy, secularism, nationalism) as incompatible with Islam.[15]

However, this charter, which was full of established positions and rulings, did not last long after the movement's participation in the fight against ISIS in early 2014. Gradually, under the weight of internal debates, as well as Arab and other regional pressures, the movement began to abandon it. In May 2014, the movement adopted the "Charter of Revolutionary Honor," which stipulated respect for human rights within the framework of a state of justice, law, and freedoms, as well as adherence to the diversity of Syrian society in all its ethnic and sectarian variety, leaving the authority of determining the type of government after the fall of the regime to Syrian people.[16]

Two Competing Currents

On September 9, 2014, an explosion at the headquarters in rural Idlib during a meeting of the movement's advisory council took the life of its founder and thirteen leaders from the first and second ranks.[17] After this event, the movement was faced with an existential test. Despite the impact of this deadly event, the movement succeeded in absorbing the first shock. Its solid organizational structure and a unified system helped to heal what remained of the advisory council and, one day later, led to the election of Hashim Sheikh, also known as Abu Jaber, as the movement's leader. The mass murder and its main characters were transformed into a heroic narrative that evolved into a legend of the movement's trials and tribulations and solidified its internal structure.

Following in his predecessor's footsteps, Abu Jaber gradually distanced himself from Salafi jihadism at the beginning of his reign. The adoption of the slogan "The People's Revolution" in place of "Project Nation" offered a preview of new, unfamiliar terms that signaled an emerging political discourse—a government based on the people, a compromise between the government and a people, a constitution guaranteeing the participation of religious minorities—as was evident in Abu Jaber's interview with Al Jazeera in April 2015.[18] The movement attempted to be open to public opinion and decision makers in the West. To this end, Labib al-Nahhas, a member of the movement's political bureau, published an article in *The Washington Post* that posited the movement as a "moderate Sunni" party in the fight against ISIS that "believes in moderation and seeks to play a positive role in a pluralistic state that balances the legitimate aspirations of the majority in Syria and the protection of the rights of minorities."[19] In another article in British newspaper *The Telegraph*, al-Nahhas explained the future strategy of the movement as establishing a government "representative" of all Syrians while taking into account the identity of the absolute majority.[20] On another level, after years of refusing to recognize or cooperate with political bodies of the opposition (i.e. the National Coalition and the interim government), the movement demonstrated openness to these bodies in a way that could be considered an indication of behavioral change.[21] This trend continued until the end of Abu Jaber's era when internal divisions began to appear under the guise of an intellectual conflict, which actually concealed a struggle for power and influence within the movement.

In contrast to external appearances, the new leader, Abu Jaber, tightened his grip on the movement during his term in office. He did so by appointing radical figures, who would insist on a Salafi jihadist identity and reject openness, to important leadership positions, including Abu Saleh Tahan as commander in chief and Abu Muhammad al-Sadiq as general legislator. While former leaders enjoyed direct contact with combatants and took the lion's share of funding earned through military efforts, some figures like Labib al-Nahhas were left with relatively little freedom in terms of external activity in order to present a "moderate," "middle," and "open" appearance, which was the primary concern of the West. Since then, two trends have emerged within the movement, one of which is internally facing and conservative, represented by the tripartite leadership of Abu Jaber, Abu Salah, and Abu Sadiq, and the other outward-facing and open-minded, consisting of the political bureau and the office of foreign relations in Turkey.

With the end of Abu Jaber's mandate and the election of his deputy, Muhannad al-Masri, also known as Abu Yahya al-Hamwi, in September 2015, an internal conflict began to rise.[22] Al-Masri gradually reduced the influence of Abu Jaber by isolating the conservative figures loyal to him before personally removing them from any executive positions within the movement.[23] The preservation of Ahrar al-Sham's "Salafi identity" was the most prominent headline used by Abu Jaber and his peers to oppose the new leader by exploiting his lack of direct contact with the fighters. On the other hand, the outward-facing or open-minded current relied on al-Masri to bring about intellectual changes within the movement. Although al-Masri was closer to the latter trend, the movement did not witness any new intellectual changes in the al-Masri era.[24] The fear of exaggerated rhetoric from the opposition current and the weakness of al-Masri's personal charisma prevented this.

Internal Divisions

Abu Jaber, who on December 12, 2016 established a personal military force within the movement under the name of the "Free Army" after being removed from the leadership of the movement, was keen on returning to lead the movement once again.[25] But the election of Ali al-Omar as the new leader of the movement, replacing Muhannad al-Masri, who engineered the operation within the Shura Council, shattered all hopes and squandered attempts to ease the internal conflict. Under the pretext the leadership's refusal to fully integrate militarily and organizationally with Al-Nusra Front, the former tripartite leadership (Abu Jaber, Tahan, and al-Sadiq) broke away from movement, taking with them 30 military and legislative leaders representing the majority of the Salafi jihadist current within the movement and around 1,500 fighters to form an initial project along with Al-Nusra Front, which was announced on February 9, 2016, as "Hay'at Tahrir al-Sham" (literally: Levant Liberation Committee, abbreviated as HTS) under the leadership of Abu Jaber al-Sheikh.[26]

This new body took Ahrar al-Sham as its implicit enemy, given that it was its only remaining competitor on the Islamist scene. Using exaggerated rhetoric typical of jihadist organizations, defected leaders of HTS tried to pit fighters of Ahrar al-Sham against their own leaders. Meanwhile, the leadership of Ahrar al-Sham was focused on central issues concerning the future of the Syrian conflict, especially the defeat of oppositional forces in Aleppo, the Astana process started under the oversight of Turkey, Russia, and Iran. Defectors succeeded in creating a gap between the leadership and its base of combatants. They refused to implement the command's instructions to counter the attack led by Al-Nusra Front against the movement in mid-2017, resulting in the loss of most of its territory and the Bab al-Hawa border crossing, important strategic areas controlled by the Syrian opposition.

Jaysh al-Islam: From Salafism to the Free Syrian Army

Jaysh al-Islam belongs to what is known as purist Salafism, which originated in Syria in the late 1950s.[27] Sheikh Nasir ad-Din al-Albani is considered the founder of purist Salafism in the style of Wahhabism in Syria. His students Sheikh Abdul Qader Arnaout and Muhammad Eid Abbasi were active in sharia institutes and mosques in Damascus. They succeeded in finding a foothold amidst an environment that was filled with competing movements and schools of thought.[28] Sheikh Abdullah Alloush, the father of Zahran Alloush who was the founder of Jaysh al-Islam, was known most for his preaching work on behalf of the purist Salafist school in rural Damascus, particularly in the city of Douma, which was the only Hanbali stronghold in Syria.[29]

The Test of the Revolution

The revolution was a true test of purist Salafism in Syria. Its sheikhs and advocates had to provide critical and urgent answers to questions of the revolution, which fell outside the principles and parameters of their previous work. The definition of purist Salafism itself, in terms of *da 'wah* (Islamic preaching) and cumulative education, was no longer attractive nor convincing to its followers in the light of the social uprising caused by the revolution. The rejection of politics and political action and the prohibition of deviating from the ruler were no longer realistic within communities that were both horizontally and vertically politicized during the revolution. This new reality prompted the movement to change its view of politics and join the opposition on the basis of religious justifications that Syria's case specifically permitted deviation from the so-called ruling infidel.[30]

With the support of a circle of Salafist scholars in Douma to which Zahran Alloush belonged, the establishment of the "Brigade of Islam" was announced on September 14, 2011. At the beginning of its founding, the brigade included a small group of fourteen enthusiastic, unindoctrinated young people who turned to Zahran Alloush for intellectual and ideological, as well as financial support.[31] It was not long before dozens of smaller civil brigades from the Damascus valley and its southern suburbs joined the Brigade of Islam, bringing its total number of fighters to 1,500 after its first restructuring in mid-2012.[32]

In the early days of its establishment, the brigade backed away from launching a political project of its own, focusing instead on organizing military action while confining the intellectual realm to a narrow elite of Salafist clergy.[33] Focusing on the popular dimension in the intellectual and ideological aspects, they addressed local communities in simple, easily understood language in order to create a robust social incubator around the Brigade of Islam, particularly in Douma and the surrounding regions. The then-commander Zahran Alloush was not the kind of behind-the-scenes military commander who addressed his fighters through recorded statements and audio messages. Rather, he fought alongside combatants and therefore was highly respected by fighters in the brigade.[34] But the intellectual and ideological dexterity associated with the leader's populism deteriorated in his speeches to major sectarian and political ranks.[35] In other words, the model of the Brigade of Islam's founding was epitomized by the rhetoric and behavior of its founder and commander.

Beyond rhetorical populism and intellectual dexterity, Zahran Alloush appeared keen to reproduce the Lebanese experience of Hezbollah in Syria.[36] The most obvious points of similarity include the symbolic significance of their names (Hezbollah: literally Party of God, and Jaysh al-Islam, literally Army of Islam), their shared interest in building a microstate with administrative and organizational independence, and their discourse of sectarian injustice, and the symbolic and authoritative status of their leaders (in terms of Islamic jurisprudence and religious jurisdiction).

The Test of Politics

Having a robust intellectual core supported by both a regional grassroots incubator and organizational cohesion helped Jaysh al-Islam to carry out bold transformations on the same scale as other Islamist factions without the fear of internal fragmentation or defection. Alloush was able to convince his fighters and followers of the righteousness of his decisions even if they were wrong,[37] and to find legal justification for them through the Salafist clergy in Douma.[38] Thus, according to Omar Ashour, Jaysh al-Islam maintained all of the necessary conditions to drive radical groups to "renounce radicalization" to pave the way for their access to political action.

Jaysh al-Islam's battle against ISIS in early 2014 was the movement's first step toward its entry into politics. The long-standing rivalry between Salafism and jihadism hastened the search for a religious justification for Jaysh al-Islam to enter the confrontation with ISIS. Denouncing ISIS as "Khawarij," Jaysh al-Islam managed to expel the organization from eastern Ghouta and isolate it within the suburbs of southern Damascus.[39] In other words, Jaysh al-Islam represented an impenetrable barrier to ISIS's progress toward the capital. The West took note of Jaysh al-Islam as an organized force in the Damascus region with whom they could cooperate in the fight against ISIS. Indeed, channels of communication were opened with American and British officials, after which Jaysh al-Islam received limited military support from the United States.[40] Since then, Alloush recognized that it would be difficult to continue with an isolationist approach based on a holistic ideology that revolved around the goal of rule by Islamic law without providing satisfactory answers to questions of the state and the authority and while refusing to meet with political and military forces.[41]

Zahran Alloush's visit to Istanbul in April 2015 outlined a new approach in terms of political practice: the opening up to political and military opposition, including competition or dissidents, and a commitment to collective positions toward political and military issues related to the Syrian crisis and openness to the outside world in this sense. There was a categorical shift in Jaysh al-Islam's discourse that manifested in the leader's meetings and interviews with American and other Western newspapers. He did away with the touchstones of his former populist rhetoric (i.e., the battle against Zoroastrians and Shi'ites, the crackdown on democracy, and establishing an Islamic caliphate) and instead spoke about a thorough plan to meet public security needs, to protect public facilities and state institutions, and the right of the people to choose the form of their own system of governance. In an advanced position compared to the other Islamist factions, he expressed his desire to be part of a "Syrian army that controls security, gathers arms, and fights against the 'takfiri' project (ISIS) and Iran until their expulsion from Syria."[42]

As a culmination of this approach, Jaysh al-Islam joined the High Commission for Negotiations to represent the Syrian opposition in the negotiation process. In its founding statement (December 10, 2015) the commission affirmed the establishment of a democratic, pluralistic civil state on the principles of equal citizenship and human rights. Jaysh al-Islam made no special demands during the negotiations except the preservation of an article in the constitution regarding Arab-Muslim Syrian identity.[43]

The Sham Legion: Multiple Identities and Changing Alliances

It is difficult for scholars to deal with the Sham Legion separately from the Muslim Brotherhood (MB) for several reasons, namely, their leaders' former intellectual and organizational affiliation with the Brotherhood (Nazir al-Hakim, Haitham Rahma, and Munther Saras), not to mention the Brotherhood's support for the Legion.[44]

The Controversial Relationship with the Muslim Brotherhood

The Brotherhood, by virtue of its weakness and limited activity within Syria, was unable to adopt a clear approach toward the revolution and the regime. However, it birthed a movement that was bolder on intellectual and political levels and emerged independently of the Brotherhood on the ground. Thus, the "New Islamic Youth" sprung up from MB families from abroad. This new movement was very active at the beginning of the revolution, especially on social media. Affiliates and former members of the Brotherhood also tried to organize outside the framework of the group but in coordination with it. Within this context, the establishment of a political body called "National Coalition to Support the Syrian Revolution" was announced in mid-2011. The body was dominated by Islamists, offspring of the MB, and was headed by Nazir al-Hakim, a former member of the Brotherhood.[45] Similarly, in August 2011, another political body was established under the name of the "National Action Group," led by Brotherhood figures from Aleppo, most notably Ahmad Ramadan and Ubaida Nahas. In cooperation with Islamic scholars Imad al-Din al-Rashid and Abdul Rahman al-Hajj, the body aimed to establish a commission representative of the Syrian revolution under the name of "The Syrian National Council."[46]

The former movement was a major subject of debate among the Syrian opposition. Researchers and others concerned with the subject held one of two main viewpoints. The first viewed Islamist movements from the standpoint of "generational divisions," as is the case of Rafael Laufer, who imagined a new movement led by the youth of the Brotherhood figures who were dissatisfied with traditional sheikhs and aspired to play role in the future of politics through participation in the revolution. The second camp—that of Aron Lund—viewed the subject as an extension of the Brotherhood's internal policy which has, since the beginning, aimed to lead oppositional revolutionary action without publicly announcing those intentions.[47]

"Democratic" Revolutionary Organization

The Civil Protection Authority (CPA), which was founded in January 2012, was the first organizational iteration, or the "revolutionary version" of the Sham Legion. The body reflected the implications of its name: the end of the stage of peaceful protests in the Syrian revolution and the beginning of the stage of armed action. Accordingly, the CPA, headed by Haitham Rahma, presented itself as a political and military revolutionary body whose aim was to provide financial and military support to the brigades fighting under the name of the "Free Syrian Army."[48] The organization tried to differentiate itself from other Islamist factions and to highlight its revolutionary identity focusing on the inclusive nationalist dimension of the Syrian revolution. It also made use of slogans that evoked freedom, dignity, the "democratic state," and framed its political and military action within the National Coalition and its military councils.[49] Despite their authority in the realm of Islamic thought, CPA leaders were keen to avoid the religious ideological tone that began to overwhelm the armed action at the time. Moreover, compared to the rest of the factions, they took a bold stance against jihadist groups including "non-Syrian fighters" (i.e., Al-Nusra Front).[50] However, the CPA did not achieve its desired goal of securing an umbrella organization to carry out domestic military action and frame it within a harmonious format that would produce a military leadership representative of the armed revolution alongside the political opposition. Failure to achieve this objective can be attributed to several factors, such as the absence of a popular base of support, its ambiguous relationship with the Brotherhood, and its selective manner of providing military support.

5. Transformation of Islamist Groups in Syria   61

In fact, the "revolutionary" identity that the CPA demonstrated during 2012 and 2013 was not an authentic reflection of leaders' intellect and conviction as much as it was a pragmatic response to internal and foreign contexts. Faced with this reality, particularly after the failure to find a political solution to the Syrian crisis during Geneva II, the CPA began to look for another method outside of its "revolutionary" path and highlight its "Islamic" identity, especially after it was joined by the "Shields of the Revolution Council." The movement was in need of a new name to reflect its new orientation. Hence, the name "Sham Legion" was adopted.

The Sham Legion was established in Aleppo on April 9, 2014, after some nineteen brigades and squadrons had been operating under the banner of the CPA in the governorates of Aleppo, Idleb, Homs, Hama, and the countryside of Damascus. In order to overcome the mistakes of the CPA, the military leadership of the Legion was entrusted to defected officers from the former army, notably Yasser Abdel Rahim, who served as the military commander of the Legion. The leadership designed a "disciplined" military experiment following rules similar to those of the national armies, focusing on the quality of fighters rather than the quantity, and the formation of a legal office to prepare them ideologically and tactically, and to organize them in light-movement battalions. They also formed a "central force," along the lines of special forces, which would be able to move according to the frontlines and the demands.[51]

In terms of transformations, the Legion adopted an Islamic approach on the level of rhetoric, symbolism, and political alliances, giving up the "flag of the revolution" years after it was adopted by the CPA and replacing it with a white Islamic flag with black letters reading "There is no god but God." In the same context, the Legion has issued its statements in isolation, separate from the other Free Army factions, which contain a great deal of Islamic vocabulary and Quranic verses.[52] Unlike the CPA, which, as noted earlier, refused to cooperate with jihadist groups and issued statements against Al-Nusra Front and ISIS together, the Sham Legion entered into a strategic military alliance with Al-Nusra Front and Ahrar al-Sham on April 30, 2015, in what became known as Jaysh al-Fatah (literally "Army of Conquest," abbreviated as JaF) after its constituent factions succeeded in gaining control of the city of Idlib in the north of Syria on March 30, 2015.[53] Despite the great ideological gap between the Sham Legion, which was dominated by those close to the school of thought of the MB, and the other JaF factions, which belonged to the Salafi jihadist movement, the alliance endured for about a year and a half before the Sham Legion announced its withdrawal from the alliance on January 3, 2016. Their withdrawal was justified by the completion of the JaF's mission to defeat the regime forces in Idlib and the need to devote themselves to supporting the opposition factions in Aleppo, which were under attack by ISIS and its allied militias.[54]

In the researcher's opinion, the Sham Legion cloaked itself in an "Islamic" identity in both discourse and in practice for purely functional reasons. These included the need to find common ground with Salafist factions in order to work together to achieve the common goal of Arab and other regional powers (namely,

Qatar, Turkey, and Saudi Arabia). In 2015, these powers agreed to provide the necessary military support to Syrian opposition groups in order to help oust the Syrian regime forces from the northern governorates, to upset the balance of military forces in favor of the opposition, and to thwart direct and indirect Iranian military intervention (militias) in Syria along the lines of what happened with "Operation Decisive Storm," the Saudi Arabia-led intervention in Yemen. This is indeed what happened in mid-2015 in the form of Russia's push to intervene in order to save the regime.[55]

With the completion of the JaF's mission in Idlib, the Sham Legion began to shed its "Islamic" appearance and returned to its "revolutionary" identity both intellectually and behaviorally. After its withdrawal from the JaF, the Legion joined the Aleppo Conquest (Fatah Halab), which included groups of the FSA, refusing to join former alliances (i.e., Al-Nusra Front and Ahrar al-Sham) who were affiliated with Ansar al-Shari'a. The Legion also readopted the "flag of the revolution" before joining the Military Operations Centre (MOC) in 2017 and participating in the negotiation process including peace talks in Astana and Geneva.[56]

Determinants and Mechanisms of Transformation

The most significant conclusion that can be drawn from this overview of Islamist groups and the evaluation of their engagement in Syria is the absence of a single determinant or factor governing the interactions and changes taking place within the movements over the course of their engagement in politics. Rather, transformations within these factions are governed by a set of interconnected determinants and variables that this study has tried to identify and disentangle. These determinants can be broken down as follows.

Internal Drivers

This refers to factors related to the movement itself and its interrelational interactions that impact the management of its members' behavior in one way or another and solidify its intellectual vision. Perhaps the most common of these in the Syrian case include:

The Leader's Charisma The leader occupies a prominent place in radical movements that are established during times of civil war and disorder. Sometimes, it reaches a point where the leader becomes synonymous with the movement. In light of this, the leader's absence may lead to the collapse of the movement or the decline of its influence. Syria's case is full of examples of radical Islamist movements that have been completely disrupted by the death of their leaders. As for Ahrar al-Sham, its leader and founder played a pivotal role in the course of its transformations until his assassination, from the group's break with global Salafi jihadism to its transformation from combat brigades into a movement that offered more realistic political visions and programs. As a result of weak leadership or lack of unanimity regarding its leadership after the assassination of its founder, Ahrar al-Sham launched into a series of divisions that led to its defeat or "humiliation" at the hands of Al-Nusra Front. The movement's leaders recognized this and worked to address it by entering into prisoner exchange negotiations with the regime, which eventually led to the release of Hassan Soufan from the Sednaya prison, who took command of the movement in August 2017. Soufan managed to reorganize the movement and made bold decisions, such as the declaration of Ahrar al-Sham as a "revolutionary" movement and the adoption of the "flag of the revolution" for the first time, without resulting in a major conflict. This is more or less true of Zahran Alloush, commander and founder of the Jaysh al-Islam, in terms of determining the identity and nature of the movement and his role in the development of changes to its political and intellectual script over in past years. Although Aboud's killing and Alloush's assassination did not lead to collapse or dissolution of either movement, it created a dynamic that led to the emergence of underlying conflicts and clashes that resulted in the division of the movement in the case of Ahrar al-Sham and the regression of military power in the case of Jaysh al-Islam. The Sham Legion was also known for the personalities of its leaders, Nazir al-Hakim and Haitham Rahma. These leaders solidified all the transformations and changes that the movement witnessed since its initial founding in 2012 with a revolutionary identity under the name of the CPA, through its impersonation of an Islamist identity in keeping pace with the "Salafist tide" in the Syrian revolution, and finally the reclaiming of its revolutionary identity after its withdrawal from Jaysh al-Fatah and its participation in the political negotiation process.[57]

Internal Conflicts and Balances The effects of internal conflicts varied widely among the three movements. Their impact was minimal in the transformations of the Sham Legion. In the course of Jaysh al-Islam's transformation, internal conflicts emerged dimly after the death of Zahran Alloush. Meanwhile, internal conflict was a major determinant in bringing Ahrar al-Sham's transformations to fruition. The conflict over the movement's leadership and new leaders' domination of the decision created confrontational dynamics between two competing currents that, over time, have positioned themselves in a radical-versus-moderate intellectual dichotomy, which was not native to the movement, but rather, emerged as one of the tools of the conflict. This, in turn, ended with the partial division of the movement and the emergence of what was described as the "conservative current" in February 2017.

Generational Divisions The leadership and constituents of Ahrar al-Sham and Jaysh al-Islam can be considered part of the new generation (based on their age).[58] Hence, there is no significant difference between the age of the movement and the generation of its leaders[59] within these two movements. Thus, the establishment of CPA (2012) and the Sham Legion (2014) in some ways reflected the generational polarization between MB sheikhs who controlled the group's leadership positions and later generations who grew up outside of Syria and took the revolution as an opportunity to engage in political action independently, or without direct affiliation with the Brotherhood, as was the case with Haitham Rahma and Nazir al-Hakim, the founders of the Sham Legion.[60] Their liberation from the organizational affiliations and their rush to assume a prominent political position in the revolution and among the Syrian opposition led to the adoption of a pragmatic reformed approach that had a profound impact on the Legion's intellectual transformations, the nature of its political practice, and its relationship with other factions with differing intellectual and ideological orientations, as well as the social incubator that stretched along the northern region of Syria, outside of the regime's control.

External Drivers

External drivers are those factors that are related to the external environment in which these factions operate. These determinants played a role in shaping the groups' transformations during the period of the study. In this context, they can be distributed across three levels.

The Local Level The increase in armed action forced Syrian Islamist factions to compensate for the absence of a state and its administrative functions. As a result, Islamist factions were forced to contact local communities, determine their demands and priorities, and measure them against current and future goals that would be adopted. It is true that the inhabitants of the regions rebelling against the Syrian regime (the Damascus countryside, Hama, Idlib, and Aleppo) formed a social incubator for the armed Islamist factions and influenced their ideas. The influence was mutual in that the community's demands and differences between theory and practice pushed Islamist factions to base their intellectual and political ideas on the existing reality instead of they thought it should be.[61]

The Regional Level After the expansion of armament, armed action became almost entirely contingent upon the regional and international forces supporting it. This gave regional and international forces the ability to exert pressure and influence the political and armed opposition, including the Islamist factions. The "Charter of Revolutionary Honor" signed by all of the Syrian armed factions, including Ahrar al-Sham, consisted of a new flexible political rhetoric as compared to the "Project Nation" charter. It is, therefore, one of the most striking examples of the influence of the regional context on the intellectual and behavioral transformations of Ahrar al-Sham and Jaysh al-Islam.[62] In the same context, the continued Turkish pressure on Islamist factions was one of the factors that led the factions, excluding Ahrar al-Sham, to participate in the Astana peace negotiations after the fall of Aleppo in late 2016 despite Russian sponsorship and dominance in these negotiations.[63] As for the Sham Legion, it operated politically according to its backers, showing great flexibility in adapting its behavioral practices according to their will.[64]

In short, Islamist factions, by virtue of their need for support or geographic proximity, found themselves forced into an asymmetrical relationship with regional powers, which gave the latter influential power over them. In the same context, regional dynamics associated with the Syrian crisis had a relatively influential impact on the Syrian Islamist factions, especially after the 2013 military coup in Egypt, where Islamists' aspirations and goals clashed with the interests of some of the region's states involved in the crisis. This is what led them to reconsider some of their behaviors and ideas in order to avoid entering into a side conflict that would distract from their primary battle against the regime.[65]

The International Level The impact of the international context is twofold. The primary influence of international actors relates to incentives, most importantly in the form of military support. The second relates to restrictions imposed on these incentives. Western support classifies factions based on the criterion of "moderation" to distinguish between those who receive military and logistical support from the two existing centers of international coordination (MOM in Jordan and MOC in Turkey) and those who do not receive support but are also not included in the list of terrorist organizations.[66] Until the end of 2016, the three factions were placed in the latter group, which did not qualify them for "qualitative" military support. This prompted some, especially the Sham Legion and Jaysh al-Islam, to make changes to their rhetoric and practices in order to influence international actors to cooperate with them and provide military support. With this understanding, Sham Legion's withdrawal from the JaF (Idlib), the largest gathering of Salafist factions in Syria, can be interpreted as a move that allowed the faction access to support from MOC. The change in Jaysh al-Islam's rhetoric came in more or less the same context, as it sought to present itself as a party that believed in pluralism and could be a partner in the confrontation with ISIS and could be part of a future Syrian national army. In contrast, the restrictions imposed on Islamist factions by international forces were of great importance in pushing factions to make changes in line with reality. For example, since its inception, Ahrar al-Sham has been preoccupied with the issue of "avoiding international classification" (i.e., being placed on the terrorism list) with the likes of Al-Nusra Front or ISIS.[67] Within this framework, the movement has always emphasized its nationalist affiliation and its separation from the internationalist trends, which was undoubtedly a starting point in the series of transformations experienced by the movement.

Intra-Jihadist Conflicts and Competition

Radical movements are not concerned with those who might be opposed to them precisely because they are defined as their ideological and intellectual adversaries. On the other hand, they assign great importance to models that are ideologically and intellectually similar, driven by this "competition" on a social basis. Over the past years, the Syrian conflict has been fertile ground for intellectual and behavioral developments among Islamist factions, which has had direct repercussions on the transformation process and its outcomes, especially on the intellectual side.[68] Since its founding, competition has been one of the most prominent determinants of the relationship between Ahrar al-Sham and Al-Nusra Front, which escalated to the point of armed clashes and full-scale confrontation.

It is true that Ahrar al-Sham has always distinguished itself from traditional jihadism. Until the end of 2012, the movement's political discourse drew upon jihadi Salafist literature as a tool to combat Al-Nusra Front's exaggerated rhetoric about the movement. However, Ahrar al-Sham was unable to emphasize this distinction until after the establishment of the SIF in late 2012 when the Front was presented Ahrar al-Sham fighters as an alternative to Al-Qaeda and the Free Army that shared their overall objectives while also taking into account the conditions of reality. This, in the researcher's opinion, gave the Ahrar al-Sham's leaders greater confidence and a wider margin of freedom to demonstrate flexibility in its intellectual assertions and behavioral practices.[69]

But the alternative model put forward by Ahrar al-Sham was undermined after its defeat in 2014 by ISIS, which adopted an approach of "ideological outbidding" that led to the neutralization of its Ahrar al-Sham's fighters.[70] In order to confront this competitive approach, the movement, in cooperation with other Islamist factions, issued the charter of "Project Nation," which, as noted earlier, was viewed as a retreat from the discussions and transformations that the movement had witnessed. In contrast with Ahrar al-Sham, this intra-jihadist competition gave Jaysh al-Islam a positive impetus to approach the revolutionary line where its leaders were convinced of the futility of the dialogue with ISIS. Jaysh al-Islam adopted a script opposing ISIS early on using the same competitive methods, describing ISIS fighters as *Khawarij* and proceeding to eradicate them completely from Ghouta and the areas surrounding Damascus. This gave Jaysh al-Islam incentives to open up to the opposition and external states.[71] In a similar context, the founding of the Sham Legion came as one of the repercussions of the competition between Islamists and jihadists. The decline of the FSA's presence and the dominance of the Islamist nature over armed action was one of the factors that led the leadership of the CPA to leave its "revolutionary" identity behind, replacing it with the "Islamist" identity that allowed it to join forces with JaF in late 2014.[72] In terms of symbolism, the name of the Sham Legion was derived from the names of the Salafist factions such as Ahrar al-Sham, Al-Nusra Front of the Sham, and Suqour al-Sham.

Conclusion

It can be said that Syrian Islamist factions' engagement in politics led them to undergo a complex process of intellectual, behavioral, and organizational transformations that brought about fundamental changes as follows:

Ideological Changes: The intellectual changes in Jaysh al-Islam and Ahrar al-Sham were more radical than those of the Sham Legion, whose intellectual transformations could be classified within the realm of political pragmatism of its leaders rather than profound strategic transformations. After its engagement in politics, its accession to the High Commission for Negotiations, and its participation in the political negotiation process, Jaysh al-Islam adopted bold new visions and ideas regarding the acceptance of the civil state and a democratic system of government.[73] For over a year, its leaders have promoted an alternative model that viewed the experience of the Turkish Justice and Development Party (AKP) as an inspiration to be applied in Syria with minor differences that would give Islamic law a greater role and higher status than in Turkey.[74] In addition, Jaysh al-Islam, after participating in the negotiating process, officially adopted the "flag of the Syrian revolution" after refraining to do so for a period of about six years. In short, Jaysh al-Islam is no longer distinguishable from Free Army factions in any way other than its name.[75] These transformations, however, did not prevent Russia from pursuing military operations until it succeeded in defeating Jaysh al-Islam in April 2018 and forced it to sign a document of surrender that guaranteed its transference from its primary stronghold in Duma to the areas of the "Euphrates Shield," controlled by the Syrian opposition and the Turkish army. This entered the organization into a chaotic series of divisions with the resignation of most of its political leaders. Mohammed Alloush, former representative of the delegation of the High Commission for Negotiations, resigned last.

After a long course of discussions, Ahrar al-Sham also reached a consensus regarding its intellectual transformations, which preserved its founding slogans and overall goals of establishing the Islamic state as a firm ideology of the movement. Its implementation did not constitute an urgent priority, but rather an achievement contingent upon community approval. In this case, the movement is willing and capable of cooperating with other models of governance and power, provided that it is guaranteed general liberties and the right to religious preaching (da'wah) activity in society and that its constitutions do not conflict with the principles and values of Islamic law.[76]

Behavioral Changes: The revolution forced Syrian Islamist movements to consolidate their political perceptions for the first time within organizational frameworks or military-political coalitions that could provide a comprehensive vision for the future. After long experience in establishing organizational, political, and military frameworks, as well as contact and context on local, regional, and international levels, all of the Islamist factions have become more open or less isolated in terms of accepting and cooperating with dissimilar entities.

Changes in Organizational Structure: Engaging in politics and political action led to a remarkable development in the organizational and administrative structure of the majority of the Islamist factions, especially Ahrar al-Sham and Jaysh al-Islam. Beginning its course in the revolution as an armed brigade, Ahrar al-Sham soon became a movement of administration, services, and political and media offices, framed by an internal system. In the same vein, Jaysh al-Islam began its course with the underground establishment of a force of only fourteen people. It later evolved into a brigade and then an army of around 10,000 people supervised by an administration of about one million people crammed into eastern towns and villages of Ghouta until its defeat by the Russian military campaign. If the international and regional approaches to the Syrian crisis remain unchanged, it seems that the Russian campaign will play a major role in shaping the characteristics and transformations of Syrian Islamist factions in the coming years.

Chapter 6

ISLAMISTS IN TRANSITION

THE YEMENI CONGREGATION OF REFORM—ISLAH PARTY

Taha Yaseen

The aftermath of the 2011 Arab Spring is distinguished by the emergence of Islamist political forces. However, these Islamist forces have largely been unsuccessful, leading to a decline in their influence and the rise of anti-Islamist politics in the Arab geopolitical world. In the seven years since the Arab Spring, regimes have fallen in Egypt, Tunisia, Libya, and Yemen. During this time of significant upheaval, these countries' transitions have both been impacted significantly by Islamist politics and directly impacted the internal and external dynamics of Islamist politics themselves. This chapter explores the transformation of Islah (Yemeni Congregation for Reform, or al-Tajummu' al-Yamani lil-Islah), the major Islamist political party in Yemen, during the Arab Spring, and the transition from revolution to civil war. It examines the reciprocal influence of the party on the post-revolt political and social shifts and equally the impacts of such vicissitudes on the party's political behavior, strategy, agenda, and discourse. The chapter argues that Islah party was significantly affected by the post-revolution events in Yemen. It witnessed several political, organizational, and ideological changes over the past few years.

Islamists in Yemeni Political Landscape

The Arab Spring has drastically reshaped Islamist politics in the Middle East. New Islamist actors are emerging, while existing actors are forced to alter their tactics and ideological views.[1] The 2011 uprising in Yemen marked a historical turning point, creating dramatic political and social dynamics, which have lasted for more than seven years. Islamists in Yemen are of various organizational structures, sizes, and doctrines, and have shaped the political and social landscape from revolution to war. The three primary Islamist movements in Yemen are the Islah party, Houthis, and Salafists. These groups differ in terms of structure and behavior on issues of in-party politics, loyalty to the ruler, significant episodes of confrontation with the state, and overt stigmatization of other religious and political identities.[2] However, they all show adaptive behavior, altering it to preserve their interests in the new landscape shaped by the uprisings, the transition that followed, and in accordance with the dynamics of the political atmosphere.

The Islah party was established in September 1990 and is the largest Islamist party in Yemen with the most political experience, bringing together Islamist figures, tribal leaders, and businessmen. The party was founded by Sheikh Abdullah bin Hussein al-Ahmar, who served as the speaker of parliament and chief of the Hashid, the most prominent Yemeni tribal confederation in the north, up to his death in December 2007. The second prominent Islamist movement in Yemen is the armed Houthi movement (Ansar Allah), which emerged as a key force in the 2011 uprisings, has been a major determinant of Yemen's political conflict scene.[3] The Houthis were established in 1992 as the "Believing Youth" Zaydi revivalist movement in the northern Sa'ada Governorate and aimed to reactivate the main tenets of the Zaydi belief. The Houthis led six rebellion wars against the state from 2004 to 2009. While the Islah party includes Zaydis and Shafi'is in both its membership and leadership, the Houthis adhere to strict Zaydi membership and leadership and the deeply held belief of the Hashemite social group's innate right to rule.[4] The third prominent movement is the Islamist Salafists. The Salafist movement emerged in Yemen in the early 1980s with the rise of Muqbil al-Wadi'i. At the time, the Yemeni Salafists adhered to principles of complete loyalty to the ruler and disavowed political participation at any level. Despite rejecting participation in the 2011 revolution, the Yemeni Salafists formed a political party—Al-Rashad Union—in Yemen's capital city of Sana'a in July 2012 to adapt to the new context of political change and preserve their interests.

Islah Party and Prerevolution Politics: Few Particularities

In contrast to Islamists in Egypt, Tunisia, and Jordan, the Islah party in Yemen did not emerge into political activism following the 2011 revolution—it participated in politics since its inception, and the revolution only brought it further to the fore. Islah was an ally of the ruling General People's Congress (GPC) between 1990 and 1997 and participated in the coalition government from 1994 to 1997. While certain elements within Islah responded with limited criticism to the president, Islah's senior leaders kept close relations and maintained interests. This continued for decades even when the party's relations with the regime reached an impasse in 2009. As an opposition party, Islah sought political alliances even with rival leftists and nonreligious parties against which the party used to take ideological and less politically contending positions. The year 2006 marked a turning point where Islah and five other nationalist and leftist parties established the Joint Meeting Parties opposition bloc to create a joint force in confronting the regime's authoritarian conduct and pressuring for political reforms. The fact that this coalition was created among groups with rivalries and ideological antagonism was inspired not only by the regime's exclusionary behavior toward opposition groups but also by the opposition groups' inability to enact change on their own, Islah's realization that the regime would no longer consider an alliance

6. Islamists in Transition   71

with it, and attitudes toward Islamists and terrorism following the September 2011 attacks in the United States.

Nonetheless, Islah's participation in this alliance with political rivals and use of modern slogans of democracy and political reforms was a significant alteration in Islah's activism, moving from ideology to politics. It was a unique experiment in the region—the political alliance between two heterogeneous ideologies such as Islamism and the Left. The result of this experiment was increased political openness within the Islah party. It helped the party to start removing conservative leaders from the decision-making process within the party structure, especially those who were highly ideological such as Abdulmajed al-Zendani, who criticized the party's decision to ally with non-Islamist parties.

The corruption of the regime, deteriorating living conditions, and especially increasing unemployment mobilized people against the political status quo. Islah was able to garner wider constituencies given its social activism, which relied on affiliated charitable, religious, and educational institutions to enlarge its power base through the delivery of social services. For example, Islah Social Welfare Society engages in health awareness campaigns, religious education, eradication of illiteracy, and relief donations, mostly in urban poor areas. While businessmen and tribal leaders provided charity for social services in their areas, religious clerks took advantage of preaching in mosques, Islamic schooling, and university education to garner supporters and influence.

During and Post-Yemeni Revolt

The Islah party's response to 2011 anti-regime popular protests in Yemen was quick. The party pushed its grassroots to join the demonstrations from the beginning, prior even to its official announcement with other Joint Meeting Parties to support the protests and promote demands for regime change. Islah members played a key role in organizing the provision of security, food, medicine, and other logistics. The party's involvement in the uprisings was characterized by its significant, well-organized, and cohesive presence. This was in stark contrast to unruly and disorganized crowds of revolutionary movements and other political forces.[5] As a result, the party maintained considerable influence in the decision-making process among those protesting in the city squares.

In particular, the party viewed the revolution as an ideal chance to improve its negotiating position with the regime and raise the ceiling of political reforms. However, as demands from revolutionary forces (particularly the youth) changed from political reforms to regime change, the Islah leadership was obliged to adapt to keep pace with the mainstream protesting wave across the country.[6] Islah's dominating presence and influential role in the protests was used to impose the party's vision for the internal organizational structure of the protests' camps, administration of activities, and selection of voices in the revolutionary platform. This created tensions with the revolutionaries, pushed the party to understand others' concerns, and changed its exclusionary strategy to keep the protests united.

By providing younger party leaders the opportunity to assume a higher profile in place of traditional leaders, Islah provided an opportunity for new voices to enter the revolutionary discourse, particularly independents and women. This inclusive approach enabled the party to maintain good relations with other entities at the protest squares.

The party leadership initially took the youth revolt as a chance to enhance its position in negotiating reforms with the regime or interests with political elites and had employed the adopted revolutionary tactics to serve this objective. The party, with other allied forces, therefore, kept pace with raising the ceiling of the revolt's demands with the goal of reaching a mediated political deal with the regime, in contrast to the revolutionary youths' aspirations of regime change. Islah employed its dominant role in the opposition to influence political opinion toward a deal brokered by the Gulf Cooperation Council (GCC), which offered President Ali Abdullah Saleh immunity from domestic prosecution in return for stepping down in 2012 and transferring power to his vice president.[7]

Islah's inability to refuse the deal was driven by its interests and deep-rooted relations with Saudi Arabia, a key sponsor of the proposal, and other Gulf states. This was the case with the party's overall approach of foreign policy during the revolution. Owing to its interests with regional powers and fears from Western powers over terrorism and Islamism, the party introduced itself through further understanding and cooperation with those powers in terms of their interests and concerns. The party's leadership frequently engaged in meetings, talks, and visits with Western actors. More importantly, this international challenge pushed the party to begin expressing its stance on terrorism and call for combating terrorist organizations, despite the fact that it was maneuvering this issue for decades and repeated its insistence on the need for defining terrorism, its applications, and the dichotomy between terrorism and religion.[8]

During this time, Islah embraced a greater emphasis on the concept of the institutional state that provides public services to the people and guarantees equal citizenship. It showed a greater readiness and openness to value partnership through close work with key forces of the revolution and acceptance of sharing power with the regime's party during the transition. Although this was part of its responsive strategy to the situation's challenges and demands, it was also among its tools to avoid sparking tensions with other political and social or even religious forces in the revolutionary camp. According to this, the party formulated its rhetoric and notions to come a long way. Seizing the chance created by the atmosphere and its dire need for new strategies to work, the party decreased its conservative wing's influence on the decision-making process to adapt to modern politics. This resulted in the party toning down its traditional religious and ideological rhetoric, and the rise of a new political discourse.[9]

However, Islah did not discard its religious discourse entirely. Unlike similar Islamist parties in Egypt, Islah's discourse has been always varied and not restricted to merely religious or political statements. The party utilized the religious discourse to advance its political agenda. Many prayers and Islamic slogans were introduced and chanted at the protest squares by the party members. The party kept close to the community through its control of mosques, religious preaching, and philanthropic activities.

Although Islah's rollback of its religious agenda can be viewed as a tactical move intended to maintain positive relations with opposition forces, it was more importantly pursued to challenge the influence of its conservative currents and improve its ability to advance its political positions.

To this day, Islah's religious agenda is not recognizable in a country whose laws and community have not been exposed to secularism and modernization, and the party has not run into conflicts with liberals over religious issues, as is the case in Tunisia, Egypt, and Syria.[10] In terms of democracy, the party adhered to promoting the discourse of peaceful transition of power through democratic and fair elections. Islah remained silent on other controversial issues such as Yemeni unification and the future of the state regime, and deferred these issues to the post-elections era.

In addition, Islah demonstrated more openness on women's political rights. It accepted that women play a political role, and thus, mobilized its female members to the squares, a feature of the revolution, despite challenges from religious parties and conservative aspects of society. This openness toward women was not a new element of Islah's discourse. In March 2009, Islah amended its bylaws at its General Congress (Article 36) to allow for greater female representation, and also added a department for women to the general secretariat. A significant example of this was manifested by the role played by Tawakkol Karman, a Nobel Peace Prize laureate and member of the party's Central Shura Council. Tawakkol received the Nobel Peace Prize in 2012 for her active participation in the popular uprisings and promotion of peaceful political change and social reforms. Tawakkol is unique in that she is the only female figure to openly disagree with the party's conservative wing prior to the 2011 uprising over issues such as women's participation and early marriage age. This type of activism has not otherwise been promoted by the party. Tawakkol's activism is therefore still a special case that does not necessarily reflect Islah's stance on women's political rights as a whole.[11]

On February 4, 2018, Islah suspended Twakol Karaman's membership in the party after she publicly criticized Saudi Arabia and the United Arab Emirates (UAE), accusing them of backing a campaign to divide Yemen. To ease the worries of Gulf Arab states about its leanings among regional division after both countries severed relations with Qatar in July 2017, Islah froze her membership and justified the decision by declaring that her statements do not represent the Islah party's policies and positions.[12]

The party's stances and strategies during this period can be explained by two factors: first, the challenges of the situation and its requirements to adapt nationally, regionally, and internationally. Second and more importantly, the events of this period provided the party with justifications and the influence needed to overcome its hard-liners in favor of its political moderates. Moreover, on democracy, it was the party's conviction that democracy is an effective tool to reach power given the party's cohesive organization, resources, and popular support from its grassroots, even if the party does not believe in democracy[13] or experiences internal challenges over accepting it. This pragmatic approach will keep the party away from long and unsettled conflicts with other forces if it decides to seek power through traditional religious ways. However, Islah's leadership view these changes as a result of "awareness of the party, its self-realization and realization of national causes have changed. A party that managed to be part of a coalition included its ideological rivals is not the same as it was the moment of establishment."[14] Participation in uprisings has also unlocked the awareness of the party's youth members. Since then, there has been increasing disagreement among the youth seeking a renewal within the party's organizational structure and leadership based on actual democratic mechanisms in place of old-fashioned tools that are contingent upon organizational recommendations for those with absolute organizational and partisan loyalty.[15] The outcomes of such internal movement and demands are yet to deliver results.

Transition and War

The transition process ran in effect from November 2011, when Saleh stepped down and was followed by the interim president Abd-Rabbu Mansour Hadi, to September 21, 2014, when the Houthi armed group Ansar Allah allied with Saleh and seized power in Sana'a. Following the February 2012 elections that resulted in Hadi's rise to power, Islah partially moved from the opposition to power in a consensus government. The party showed strong commitment to the newly formed authority under Hadi and tried to make use of its close relations with the president to fill senior public-sector posts, which were ultimately limited and did not provide Islah with significant political power control. Attracted by the opportunities afforded by its political influence, Islah did not honor its political alliance with groups in the Joint Meeting Parties bloc, creating tensions with its allies instead of maintaining a joint agenda to face the transition's enormous challenges and deliver on the aspirations voiced by the revolutionaries. The party did not seriously consider its alliances during this period, so its politics were marked by tensions and political cleavages with these key actors. Both sides are to be blamed for contributing to the failure of preserving a united front in the face of the state and emerging anti-revolutionary forces. However, Islah's political competence and overall participatory or exclusionary comportment cannot be fairly evaluated during this period because it had only a limited share of power.

Nevertheless, Islah's political foes capitalized on some of Islah's tribal sheikhs' employment-related cronyism, nepotism, and misconducts to tarnish the party's image and mobilize against it. At the same time, Yemen experienced rampant corruption, security vacuums, and deteriorating living conditions during the transition. Ultimately, although Islah was one of many actors contributing to political failures during this transition period, it was the most negatively impacted because it was the focal point of popular discontent and outrage. Politically, Islah lacked awareness during this time to realize its impending peril as the Houthis advanced militarily and built alliances with their adversaries. The rise of the Houthis came as a surprise to Islah who continuously underestimated the power of the movement to rebalance the political landscape. Mohammed Qahtan, a member of the Supreme Committee of Islah, stated in 2013 that the Houthis did not pose a threat and that it could easily counterbalance it if needed.[16]

The greatest achievement of the transition period was the National Dialogue Conference in which Yemenis from all walks of life gathered and comprehensively discussed and agreed upon the outcomes that outlined the details of their future state. Moreover, the national dialogue provided an arena for Islah to examine its stance on controversial issues such as democratization, women's and minorities' rights, and other sensitive issues such as national unification, Houthi armed groups, and Herak secession movements.

The outcomes, which the party approved, stated that Yemen is to be a federal state of six regions, two in the south and four in the north. It stipulated that women be given a 30 percent quota in representation in all state bodies and structures, as well as leadership in political parties, and ensuring all women possess political, social, and economic rights. For the issue of personal rights and minority representation, the outcomes clearly included articles that ensure full rights and freedoms of individuals, including political rights and rights of belief, speech, and thought. The state regime is stated to be republican, constitutional, and selected through democratic elections. All participants except the Houthis agreed that Islamic teachings would be the main source for legislation.[17] Finally, the dialogue ensured minorities possess full rights and the freedom to practice their beliefs, faith, and special occasions.

These advanced views of political practice in the party have not been a result of strategic review and planning, but a response to compounding challenges, risks, and opportunities in a political environment characterized by a strong presence of antagonistic forces to the party. Apart from the conventional adversity characterizing the relationship between Islah and the GPC, new political powers with old scores to settle with the Islah party emerged in the post-2011 period. These forces included Salafists, the Houthi armed group, and Herak secessionist movement in the south.

In foreign policy, Islah's rise to power in parallel with that of the Muslim Brotherhood in Egypt and Tunisia strengthened the party's regional alliances with Qatar, Turkey, and Egypt, a trend that was interrupted shortly after Egypt's president Morsi was ousted in July 2013.[18]

The rise of the Islah party to institutional power was interrupted by the Houthis' expansion during the second half of 2014. The fall of Amran in July 2014 and then of the capital Sana'a two months later shattered Islahis. Islah lost not only its military and tribal allies in both cities, but also its military might, financial resources, and leaders, who either fled or were arrested.[19]

Conflict and Reversed Implications on the Party's Gun Politics

Riding the wave of massive protests against the government, the Houthis and Saleh[20] seized power in Sana'a and beyond in September 21, 2014, undermining the transition and putting the president and his government members under house arrest. This raised concerns among regional neighbors, mainly Saudi Arabia that had remained silent and did not act over earlier months of Houthis' advance and territorial expansion from the Saada governorate to Amran on their way toward Sana'a under the pretext of fighting Islah party. Such silence seemed to explain Saudi Arabia's concerns and consideration of Islah party as an affiliation of Egyptian Muslim Brotherhood with whom Saudi Arabia had tensions and supported a military coup that removed them from power in July 2013. Since the Houthi-Saleh alliance posed a threat to Saudi interests, Saudi Arabia organized a coalition and intervened against Houthi and Saleh forces with the announced objective of restoring former president Hadi to power. Islah found itself mired in political oppression and media-driven animosity domestically, and an emerging wave of anti-Islamist sentiment pushed by regional and international powers internationally. They realized that they were a target and their existence was at stake. The shocking events for the party came with the fall of President Mohammed Morsi in Egypt in July 2013 and the resulting crackdown on Muslim Brotherhood members, as well as the coup in Libya on February 14, 2014.

As a result of these events, the party's leadership understood it was a target and how little protection it had with its existence at stake. With the onset of war and the intervention of the Saudi-led coalition, Islah declared its support for the Saudi-led military campaign.[21] With this move, the party sacrificed all political gains and the legacy it built and envisaged for itself since 2011. Beyond the announced support for the war, the party joined the fight against Houthi-Saleh alliance in different areas of the country. Confounding political conditions coupled with the emerging hostile status quo and the lack of political options impacted the party's decision of joining the war; this decision was also ripped by the previous conditions in addition to other calculated drivers.

Lacking options and influence amidst the emerging political and military mobilization, Islah realized that the Houthi group would never accept its existence as an ideological and political rival. In addition, the time was ripe to restore deep and historical relations with Saudi Arabia on the heel of Morsi's downfall and the new anti-Muslim Brotherhood sentiment in the Saudi and UAE political approach of dealing with the uprisings in the Arab world. As a result, under the banner of the internationally recognized government led by resident Hadi, Islah played a key role in the armed resistance against the Houthis, starting from the south and Marib, in addition to spearheading a military operation against them in Taiz. Despite the party's major existential dilemma, it did not use religious rhetoric or fatwas to justify their decision to join the fighting against the Houthi-Saleh forces. The official statements included the legitimacy of the Yemeni state, the elected president, and communal fate with a security threat to its regional neighbors.

In response to its stance in the conflict, hundreds of Islah's members were arrested and tortured, headquarters were shut down, and its properties were confiscated. Members were tortured to death in jails and killed and injured on the battlefields.[22] The party secured its positioning with a strong political and military presence in both Marib and Taiz after its presence was dramatically reduced in the north because of the Houthi crackdown, as well as in the south because of the UAE-supported secessionist Southern Transitional Council. Wary of future political and legal accountability, Islah avoided appearing as a militia or paramilitary. It mobilized its supporters and kept its positions under the umbrella of and in line with the legitimate government. A number of its members rolled into legitimate military brigades.[23]

Islah maintained a calm, collaborative attitude toward other political parties, especially after the killing of the former president Saleh and the disturbances by the GPC party. It aspired to be engaged further in a broader national coalition but also set hard lines that prevented any potential relations with illegal movements in a clear message to Heraks, Salafists, and Houthis.[24] However, Islah has more recently adopted a more hostile position toward the Heraks and the UAE-supported Southern Transitional Council. This came after the Herak movement grew into a fully fledged UAE-supported military force that controls much of southern Yemen. Islah's relationship with the Houthis is based on mistrust and concealed animosity, despite the party's endeavors to show otherwise during recent years. This relationship dynamic is likely to remain for the foreseeable future, especially after the wars fought between the two rivals and all damages and losses incurred by Islah at the hands of the Houthis. For the Salafists, it is likely that this relationship will become an intense rivalry. The political offshoot of the Salafists, Al-Rashad Union, has made great strides in its competition with Islah in areas that were predominantly dominated by Islah, especially in the field of social activities.

The case is different with fundamental Salafists with whom the party is in a constant state of confrontation after fighting side by side against the Houthis at the beginniing of the conflict. This confrontation seems to vary according to the scenarios of war and peace in the country. A living example of the prospective relationship between Islah and fundamental Salafists is the current dispute between Islah and the Taiz-based, UAE-backed Salafist group led by Abu al-Abbas, as well as the Salafi-dominant Security Belt military brigade in the south. August 8, 2018, witnessed the latest example when fierce fighting erupted between Islah-affiliated national army units and Abu al-Abbas brigades inside the city of Taiz. Clashes that led to considerable casualties in both sides and civilians ended with a deal that relocated Abu al-Abbas's brigades outside Taiz city and consolidation of an Islah-affiliated state authority inside the city. In Aden, the party's members faced a campaign of assassinations, arrests, and forceful disappearances.

Internal Cohesion and External Ties: Further Divides

Since its foundation, Islah has been a party of diverse membership that includes moderates, conservatives, ultra-conservatives, tribal sheikhs, and businessmen. This is among the main features of the party that distinguishes it from other Brotherhood organizations that have maintained greater internal coherence and discipline.[25]

These internal divisions are manifested at times via the party's external outlook and behavior but have not yet led to deep fractures and the formation of new rival movements. Despite the significant domestic instability caused by the Yemeni civil war as well as political and ideological differences over key issues within these internal wings, Islah has maintained its cohesion and does not appear headed for structural challenges. Islah maintained its adaptability and cohesion in the face of events where it could have fractured and split. In fact, the emergence of internal differences may have been essential to the party's adaptability, allowing it to be many things to many people in a time of great uncertainty.[26] At the same time, however, Islah's experience in handling internal differences also demonstrates the party's weakness in controlling opposing voices that may endanger its survival when such voices raise concerns over the party's activism and agenda, especially as it relates to its relations with Western and regional powers.

Islah's communication with the community has been constrained to a great extent in both the north where the party's presence has been curbed by Houthi control and the south where a campaign of oppression has been in place against its members. The continuous demonization campaigns against Islah in these areas has significantly impacted its members in these regions as it has restricted their freedoms and even put their lives at risk. The distance created between the party and its members in these regions remains uncertain as the party may still be able to communicate with these pockets of membership despite the tumultuous conditions.[27] However, the war blocked Islah's ability to proceed with its social, religious, charitable, developmental, cultural, and organizational activities in these areas. Despite the fact that the conflict has damaged the party's ability to recruit new members and proselytize in these regions, it still remains active and manages to have influence in other areas such as the Marib and Taiz governorates.

The conservative radical branch of the party returned over the last two years with a discourse that contradicts the party's embraced stance on many issues. The party became increasingly frustrated and embarrassed by its inability to manage this messaging, as it was unable to curb the influence of such messaging. For example, the controversial Islahi parliamentarian figure, clerk, and preacher Abdullah al-Udini in Taiz frequently appeared to announce Islah's refusal to accept the principle of the civil state and outcomes from the National Dialogue Conference, stating they are forbidden by Islam and a product of Western immorality and corruption to the community. The clerk based in Taiz lashed out more than once regarding the coexistence of both men and women in public places, stating this violated Islamic principles and basic societal norms. This trend led by al-Udini is said to follow a wider branch within the party led by Abdul Majeed al-Zindani, a conservative party leader who was designated as a terrorist by the US Treasury Department.[28] This aggressive stance contradicts the party's current political position and its claims of vanishing impact of Islamic movement on its political entity.[29]

In addition, the civil war impacted Islah's internal dynamics by supporting the emergence of influential leaders on the ground that established foreign relations with powers outside the party's framework. For example, the governor of Marib, Sultan al-Aradah, maintained good relations with the UAE and visited the country more than once to garner support for his governorate despite the fact that the UAE is an opponent of the Islah party. The rise of such influential military leaders may create a state of superiority within the party's leadership between those who sought refuge outside for safety and security during the war and those who sacrificed at home and made gains. Ultimately, Islah is facing significant challenges due to the current vicissitudes of Yemeni politics and the inactivity of its leadership at home. The greatest challenge facing Islah's leadership will be their ability to maintain the party's organizational structure, hierarchy, and relationship with its rank and file if the war continues for years to come. This challenge will be particularly acute given the fact that its supporters' interests may have changed during the war or they may have experienced significant oppression if they live in areas under the control of Houthis or other armed groups hostile to Islah.

Islah and the Region: Tensions and Muslim Brotherhood's Dilemma

Externally, the party's attitude toward regional powers is changing according to its short- and long-term interests and objectives. However, the Saudi-Qatari divide[30] triggered internal division within the party, particularly between the leadership residing in Saudi Arabia and other leadership figures who settled in Qatar and Turkey. While Saudi-Islahi relations have been historically strong and well established, they have become shaky and uncertain since the Arab Spring. Up to 2007, the alliance between Saudi Arabia and Islah was bolstered by the leadership of Sheikh Abdullah al-Ahmar who mobilized and co-opted Yemeni tribes to serve Saudi interests. Although Islah assisted Saudi Arabia with containing the Yemeni revolution and sharing power with Saleh in 2011, it became clear that the relationship was deteriorating when Saudi Arabia turned a blind eye to the Houthi advances against Islah's military and tribal allies in Amran in 2014 before reaching Sana'a.

In addition, Saudi Arabia and the UAE effectively supported the 2013 military coup in Egypt. Despite this action against the Muslim Brotherhood in Egypt, Saudi Arabia and Islah continued to support one another to support their mutual interests in a cautious temporary alliance of necessity, which was contrary to their old strategic alliance. For example, Islah declared support to the 2015 Saudi-led military intervention against the Houthi-Saleh forces. Moreover, Saudi Arabia welcomed and hosted Islah's leadership and members who needed to flee Yemen during the war, including the conservative clerk Abdulmajed al-Zendani. However, this return of relations did not emanate from desires to reform the ties and resume a strategic alliance, but rather from necessity as both Saudi Arabia and Islah faced communal threats and shared the objective of fighting against the Iran-backed Houthis in Yemen. Also, Islah's ability to avoid Saudi Arabia's anti-Muslim Brotherhood politics can be traced further to two main drivers. First, Saudi Arabia's view of Islah is not governed only by religious ideology, but transcends to a tribal dimension of the party that Saudis do not want to lose as part of their influential card to play in influencing Yemeni politics. Second, Islah has demonstrated a pragmatic ideological flexibility, similar to the Muslim Brotherhood in Egypt.

During the conflict, Islah has been keen to preserve its relationship with Saudi Arabia and trying to repair it by easing Saudi concerns. In 2017, the party's leadership declared it cannot be designated as an extension of the Muslim Brotherhood.[31] Furthermore, Islah suspended the membership of Tawakkol Karman in 2018 in the backdrop of her criticism of the Saudi kingdom, and recently, a leader in the party publicly condemned Qatar for its alleged support of Houthis.[32] Both attitudes of Islah and Saudi Arabia are governed by their pragmatism and fears of each other as well. While this relationship continues for the shared purpose of fighting the Houthis, as long as Islah continues to find refuge in Saudi Arabia when it lacks options domestically, it will seek to keep up a strong relationship with Saudi Arabia even if ties between Saudi Arabia and Yemeni government hit rock bottom.

Islah tried more than once to maintain good relations with the UAE, but these attempts have been unsuccessful. For example, Islah's top leaders met with UAE state leadership in 2018[33] without tangible outcomes on the ground or discourse. In contrast to Saudi Arabia, the UAE does not want to align or meet with Islah under any circumstances and has a clear-cut rivalry with the party. As a whole, Islah continues to struggle to strike a balance between a committed national course, strong relationship with Saudi Arabia, and states that are skeptical of its intentions, such as the UAE.

Conclusion

Islah's future is inextricably linked to and contingent upon the future of the country and its chances of peace as a whole. If the war continues to go on with no end in sight, the party will be threatened by aging and may lose its presence on the ground. However, based on this analysis, Islah may be able to avoid the fate of the Muslim Brotherhood in Egypt because it is battle tested and demonstrated its ability to be flexible to preserve its survival. In this author's opinion, it is highly unlikely that the party will reach the point of being completely eliminated. In order to survive, Islah must bring new blood to replace its aging leadership, and it must reconcile discourse with practice. Furthermore, the party needs to maintain a strong and distinctive influence in its areas of historical influence and be careful not to mobilize its rank-and-file masses and supporters for negative agendas. As a result of the civil war, Islah's most important strategies for mobilization have been drained. Specifically, it has lost its ability to recruit youth through educational programs and its mobilization for mass demonstrations and elections were proven unsuccessful when the Houthis took over Sana'a. This highlights the need for the party to streamline an alternative political model for the public that addresses its actual problems.

Chapter 7

ISLAMISTS IN JORDAN

THE LONG JOURNEY OF THE MUSLIM BROTHERHOOD'S CHANGES

Mohammad Abu Rumman

Since its founding nearly seventy years ago, the Society of Muslim Brothers ("Muslim Brotherhood," "MB," or "Brotherhood") has played an active role in the Jordanian sociocultural and political life. Since 1989—which marked the return of parliamentary life to the country after a decades-long break followed by the establishment of the Islamist Action Front (IAF) party in 1992—the Muslim Brotherhood occupied the country's first political and legal opposition bloc, and its popularity has exceeded that of other political parties in the majority of the parliamentary, student, and union elections. At the same time, it has acquired many economic, social, and charitable institutions which, over the past decades, have enabled it to build a wide-ranging social network across a range of sectors and to build channels of interaction and communication with the society. However, things did not remain this way. Since the 1990s, the Brotherhood's relationship with the government began to shift. The movement took on the role of the political opposition, boycotting parliamentary elections on many occasions. Since 1999 (after the death of King Hussein and the accession of King Abdullah II), the relationship between the two sides—the Brotherhood and the regime—entered a phase of ambiguity and uncertainty, punctuated by numerous crises and limited periods of openness. This went on until 2006, which, practically speaking, marked the beginning of a period of "open crisis" between the two sides. This crisis was made worse by the events of the Arab Spring in 2011, which underscored the breach of trust between them. In the meantime, the Brotherhood lost the Islamic Centre (founded in 1963), which previously constituted an important financial resource, when the state took control of it. The most prominent developments occurred a few years ago when the Association of the Muslim Brotherhood was officially founded, pulling the rug out from under the feet of its parent organization, which became illegal for the first time in the kingdom's history. Hundreds of leaders and youth left the Muslim Brotherhood to form new political parties, including the National Congress (Zamzam) and the Rescue and Partnership Party.

This chapter explores the transformation of the Muslim Brotherhood in Jordan. It discusses the most important changes that the group has undergone, both ideologically and politically, and the repercussions of these changes on

82 *Islamism and Revolution Across the Middle East*

organizational polarizations and internal mobilization through an analysis of the stages that the group experienced from its establishment until today and the founding of new political parties. The chapter argues that the Arab Spring has significantly impacted the movement's structure and organization and led to divisions and factionalism within the movement. These divisions have greatly affected the social, political, and mobilization capabilities of the Brotherhood over the past decade, and it will continue to impact it for years to come.

The Brotherhood in Jordan: A Brief History

The Muslim Brotherhood's work in Jordan dates back to the time of the kingdom's independence in 1946. At that time, its work was more akin to that of a charity or Islamic preaching organization. Its founding leaders were mostly merchants and enjoyed a friendly and amicable relationship with king, as did the Brotherhood's leader, Hassan al-Banna. However, at a later stage, beginning in the 1950s, elements of change began to have an effect on the Brotherhood, its role, and its organizational structure, including the consequences of the war on Jordan in 1948, the annexation of the West Bank, the emergence of the Palestinian cause in Jordanian and Arab political life after the Nakba, and the rise of Nasserism, nationalism, and leftist movements throughout that period. From the 1950s until the beginning of the 1970s, the Brotherhood lacked a broad social base compared to nationalist and leftist parties, as well as Palestinian forces and organizations in the Jordanian arena. Thus, the followers of the group and its activists were more engaged in religious preaching (*da'wah*) and education than they were in political activism, even at the declaration of martial law (after Suleiman al-Nabulsi's government) from which the Muslim Brotherhood was exempted. This stage was one of constructing social norms. The Brotherhood established the Islamic Center in 1963, which spread and expanded until it formed a web of the group's activities and channels of communication with various social groups as well as mosques. Brotherhood members considered the activities of the mosque to be an important tool for recruitment. Indeed, none of the political or even religious forces could begin to compete in this regard, although they did increase at a later stage. The Islamic Center took over a large part of the mosque's activities, such as Salafist currents and Islamic preaching, and reporting, and others.

The Six-Day War of 1976 was a turning point in the history of the Muslim Brotherhood, or, more precisely, a starting point for popular expansion. This expansion took place within Arab society first, and later at the local level. This transformation occurred in parallel with the events of the 1970s, in which the Brotherhood's activism increased and expanded further and further into society. At this stage, the ideas of Sayyid Qutb (who was executed by Gamal Abdel Nasser in 1966) continued to dominate the group. Despite its coexistence with the regime, the intellectual and ideological leadership of the Brotherhood represented ideas closer to the concepts of governance—*jahiliyya* (the pre-Islamic period), separation, and the superiority of the Muslim community, and others—that reinforced its influence on Brotherhood members according to two main factors. The first is students abroad in Saudi Arabia, Egypt, and other countries who were impacted by these concepts, and the second is the lack of democratic life, which eliminated any real consideration of the seriousness and usefulness of these concepts. At this time, the most prominent names were those close to leaders such as Abdullah Azzam, Ahmed Nofal, and Mohammed Abu Fares, among others. In his review of the Muslim Brotherhood's history and intellectual milestones, Dr. Gharaibeh, one of the most prominent former leaders of the Brotherhood, pointed out that the 1970s witnessed the formation of a secret society within the Muslim Brotherhood. It was eventually exposed and consisted mostly of a group of students in Egypt, from the Muslim Brotherhood youth, who were affected by the events there. They were especially impacted by the ideas of Sayyid Qutb and what is called the idea of *mihna* (literally: "ordeal"). Some members of this elite were among those who took control of the Muslim Brotherhood from the 1970s until the end of the 1980s.[1] The 1970s was also a golden period for Islamist student action. The Brotherhood was active in student unions and student associations. Dr. Abdullah Azzam played a major role in the establishment of student action, and the luminary Dr. Ahmed Nofal rose to prominence during this period, followed by Hammam Saeed, Mohammed Abu Fares, and others.[2] Gharaibeh calls this stage, from the 1970s to the end of the 1980s, a "wave of Qutbist thought," which began to decline later in the 1990s. It gave way to a new wave in the Arab world that had begun to emerge in the mid-1980s led by Hassan al-Turabi and Rached Ghannouchi. It was a period of pragmatic and democratic thought that was far-reaching in Jordan in the 1990s.[3]

From Religion to Politics

The year 1989 served as an important turning point in the Brotherhood's internal debates and organizational mobility. The faction known as the "Doves" clearly exceeded the "Hawks" in terms of their vision and leadership. The former was a more pragmatic and realistic trend, while the latter tended toward ideologism and Qutbism. Nevertheless, the two factions both took part in parliamentary elections, and the leaders of both parties were elected to the House of Representatives. The most prominent issue of internal debate was the factions' stances on democracy. While the Doves began incorporating the concept of democracy into the Brotherhood's discourse, and created, along with other Islamists, the term "shuracracy," to emphasize a certain unity between democracy and the *Shura* (consultation). They began to see the need to accept the democratic game and what came along with it, such as pluralism, the rotation of power, and general freedoms. In this regard, there was some hesitation among the Hawks, as well as an attempt to restrict the participation of the group, its objectives in the electoral process, and their roles in the House of Representatives. The Brotherhood put forward a set of fourteen conditions required to give their confidence to Badran's government. Looking at these fourteen conditions, it is clear that the majority of them were related to the government's noninterference in the Brotherhood's

Islamic preaching and organizational activities. Some traditional issues were also included in the conditions, such as the implementation of *shari'a*, the prohibition of the wine industry, the establishment of a private Islamic university, support for the intifada (literally: "uprising," in reference to the Palestinian resistance), and the cancellation of interest on state loans to small farmers, along with issues of reinstatement and elimination of repercussions of emergency law, and martial law, and so on.[4] The Muslim Brotherhood contributed five members to the National Charter Committee in the early 1990s, which was formed by the king in order to reach internal understandings among the various political forces on shared political ground. It included representatives of Islamist, nationalist, leftist, conservative, and liberal factions. The inspector general sent a letter to the prime minister based upon the fatwa about the national charter issued by a committee formed by the Brotherhood's Shura Council that predominantly addressed the Islamic identity of the state and society.[5]

The participation of the Muslim Brotherhood in Mudar Badran's government increased the schism between the two factions. Muhammad Abu Fares published a well-known book on the Brotherhood's participation in governance as a source for a fatwa to deny the Brotherhood's participation. The Muslim Brotherhood, in turn, withdrew the book from the market. This pushed a number of religious sources, including Dr. Omar Al-Ashqar and Dr. Ali al-Sawa, both members of the Muslim Brotherhood, to issue a fatwa against government participation.

In parallel to their differences in the intellectual approach (their attitude toward governments, the regime, and political action, etc.) and in political vision (ideology versus pragmatism), differences between the Doves and Hawks emerged in regard to oppositional discourse against the regime. Especially with the rapid deterioration of the democratic process (since 1992, beginning with Jordan's entry into peace negotiations, followed by the "one-man, one-vote" law and the signing of the Wadi Araba Treaty), the Hawks attacked the Brotherhood's official position in an effective and powerful manner. They raised criticisms in their rhetoric, while Doves acted to contain the regime's reactions in an attempt to defuse crises, as mentioned earlier. This was the signature role of Doves in the Muslim Brotherhood's trajectory, especially under King Hussein.[6]

The Islamic Action Front

The Islamic Action Front party was established in 1992 after the passage of the Political Parties Law and the process of screening the legislation related to the state of emergency and martial law. The party's founding was surrounded by a wide debate among the Muslim Brotherhood about its anticipated relationship with the party. The Brotherhood's planning arm, whose members were mostly young, presented a vision for the scenarios of the relationship between the Brotherhood and the planned party. This plan suggested that the group would remain and that the party would be established with a high degree of organizational independence. This is what happened but only after serious internal differences and mutual

7. Islamists in Jordan 85

accusations between the two sides and their leaders regarding this new phase in the Brotherhood's history.[7]

The year 1994 witnessed the announcement of the rise of a new trend of organizational mobility within the Brotherhood, which was later referred to by the media as the centrist movement. In practice, it represented the younger generation of the Brotherhood, which had its own perceptions of both the Hawks and the Doves. This new trend viewed the Hawks' fiery discourse that lacked practical and realistic content as its main problem. Such an approach appealed to the emotions of members only to fall short of expectations, coming to an abrupt standstill when the group was unable to cross a certain line in its relationship with the regime. It also contradicted the premise of Sayyid Qutb's ideas by participating in the political process. The Doves, on the other hand, had allowed personal interests to preside over other considerations in their relationship with the regime. They did not take into account the state's retreat from the democratic process, nor did they consider alternative options—such as boycotts—in their relationship to the state in protest against the retreat from democracy and the crackdown on the Muslim Brotherhood.[8]

The centrist movement—which took Ahmad Qutaysh al-Azayida[9] (the Brotherhood's leader) as its intellectual and political inspiration—was convinced that the state was indifferent about its relationship with the Brotherhood as well as the political opposition because it believed that it held the keys to dealing with the group through its relationship with prominent figures in the Doves. The new generation wanted to deliver a blow to this conviction, which had taken hold in decision-making centers, in order to demonstrate that there was a new generation that had become influential in the Brotherhood's trajectory and its leadership.[10] In 1994, the executive office changed hands and Abdul Majid Thunibat became inspector general of the Muslim Brotherhood after nearly four decades of Abdul Rahman Khalifa's leadership. The executive office under Thunibat was a mix of Doves and new young leaders from the centrist movement (Imad Abu Dayyah, Salem al-Falahat, and Jamil Abu Bakr).[11] The new members of the executive office who represented the younger generation of the centrist movement contributed to the Brotherhood's decision to boycott the 1997 elections. This decision led to the blocking and exclusion of those members who were against the decision and the departure of others, most of whom were Doves, such as Abdelrahim Al-Akour,[12] Abdullah Al-Akaily,[13] Dr. Bassam al-Amoush,[14] and a group of young people from Salt (Marwan al-Faouri, Asaad al-Qariuti, Malak al-Amariyya, and Husayn Hiyasat).[15]

In 1998, the executive office was reconstructed and the centrist movement, under the leadership of Imad Abu Dayyah, increased its presence within the Brotherhood. But the trend was dealt a severe blow with the departure of large swaths of the group, as mentioned earlier, as well as the expulsion of Hamas's leadership from Jordan in 1999 and the impact of media leaks, which tried to imply that some leaders of the centrist movement were previously aware of this decision.[16] As a result, the young centrist movement split into two directions. The first led was led by Imad Abu Dayyah and included members such as Salem al-Falahat, Nimer Al-Assaf, Rahil Gharaibeh, and Nabil Kofahi. On the other hand, there was a group closer to Hamas, which was opposed to Abu Dayyah and his faction, including Saud Abu Mahfouz, Zaki Bani Irsheid, Muhammad al-Attar, and others. During the 1990s, a group of young Hamas leaders returned to Jordan from Kuwait after the events of the First Gulf War in 1990. They formed the political bureau of the movement, made a "gentleman's agreement" in 1993 with the Jordanian government, and expanded their political and media activities. Leaders of the centrist movement in Jordan criticized Hamas's political bureau of reaching into the Brotherhood's ranks in its expansion of recruitment for newcomers to the movement and of confusing the two organizations to the extent that the Hamas movement within the Jordanian Muslim Brotherhood grew until it became a so-called "shadow organization." In his review of the Brotherhood's transformations, Rahil Gharaibeh points out that the Gulf crisis was a major turning point in Muslim Brotherhood's internal structural development. Many Brotherhood members with Palestinian origins returned from Kuwait, which first brought about demographic changes in its organizational structure. Second, it led to a shift in the tone of its rhetoric on both national and local issues toward greater involvement in the Palestinian issue and hostility with the United States. Their return also contributed to the rise of the Hamas group, which was later referred to as the Brotherhood's "shadow organization."[17]

The Debate over the "Issue of Nationalism"

The intensity of internal differences between the Jordanian centrist movement and the centrist movement close to Hamas escalated, which led to a change in the executive office in 2002 (leaders of the centrist movement decided not to return to the leadership positions later, especially Imad Abu Dayyah, who was considered the architect of the centrist movement during its rise in the mid-1990s). The new office consisted of the inspector general (Abdul Majid Thunibat) and a mixture of Hawks and Doves. In the following years, two major alliances took root in the Brotherhood and the party, which brought the groups into a state of internal polarization, debates, and personal disputes that extended into the following years. The first faction was made up of the Doves and the centrist movement in Jordan and was categorized as the moderate wing of the Brotherhood. Its most prominent leaders included Salem al-Falahat, Rahil Gharaibeh, Nabil al-Kofahi, Nimr Assaf, Abdul Latif Arabiyat, Abdul Majid Thunibat, and Abdul Hamid al-Qudah. The second wing was described as extremist and was borne out of the alliance of the Hawks and the movement that was considered closely related to Hamas. Its most prominent leaders included Hammam Saeed, Zaki Bani Irsheid, Ahmad al-Zarqan, and Ali al-Atoum.[18] It would be inaccurate to say that the first wing, the moderate wing, represents the eastern Jordanians while the second, extremist wing represents Jordanians of Palestinian origin in the Brotherhood, because the leadership of both wings was mixed. However, at the same time, it would be unreasonable to deny the fact that the issue of nationalism, the relationship with

7. Islamists in Jordan

Hamas, the definition of the Brotherhood and the party, and the determination of priorities were the key factors in the debate between the two former wings, which began to compete for leadership positions in the Brotherhood and the party.

The moderate movement, which has been described as the Jordanian current and has its backbone in the eastern region of Jordan, sees a need for a clear organizational separation from Hamas and had its suspicions about the existence of a "shadow organization" loyal to Hamas within the Jordanian Muslim Brotherhood. The movement believed that priorities should be linked to local affairs and political coordinates, meaning that the relationship between the state, the party, and the Brotherhood should not be subordinate to a relationship with Hamas. They see the Brotherhood, and therefore the party, as a Jordanian movement with an Islamic framework. On the other hand, the second movement, which was closely tied to Hamas, gave importance to the issue supporting Hamas in its discourse, popular mobilization, and its organizational process. In contrast to the moderate wing's focus on the subject of domestic political reform, the second movement considered its priority to be supporting the struggle of the Palestinians and the preservation of Palestinian land. It can be said, therefore, that the controversy of the "issue of nationalism" as it relates to internal political reforms and the relationship with Hamas became the focus of the Brotherhood's internal debates and organizational alignments. Their stance on democracy, for example, was no longer controversial between the two factions. Both agreed to accept democracy in its entirety, but the tendency toward either moderation or extremism was linked to each faction's attitude toward the regime. While the moderate wing wanted to create a buffer against crises, the other was escalating the political discourse. However, it will be noted below that the positions vis-à-vis the regime later traded places between leaders of the two factions.[19]

In 2005, the Brotherhood issued its vision for political reform and democracy, which clearly represented a qualitative shift in the Brotherhood's thinking. The group definitively decided its position on democracy, accepted political pluralism, and took a position similar to the Muslim Brotherhood of Egypt and Syria in what was considered a universal answer from the Brotherhood to a question that resonated in political and Western research circles at the time, that is, after the events of September 11. The question was whether the Muslim Brotherhood would accept the democratic game and whether they could form an alternative to the Arab regimes. Whether the drafting of these documents was internally or externally motivated, they constituted a clear break from the state of reluctance to accept democracy, at least in the official position of these Islamist movements. There remained some ambiguous areas in the movement's position on many issues related to the acceptance of democracy. Indeed, issues such as religious freedoms, minority rights, women, and many other questions remained open and on the table.[20]

In 2006, the executive office of the Brotherhood was reconfigured and Salem al-Falahat, belonging to the Jordanian centrist movement, became inspector general of a mixed executive office with centrist ideas prevailing. On the other hand, Zaki Bani Irsheid, one of the most prominent leaders of Hamas, was chosen as secretary general of the Islamic Action Front, which intensified the dynamic of the crisis with the state. In the same year, the issue of regional coalitions (the two axes of resistance and moderation) came to the fore and the Brotherhood fell into the resistance camp. Hamas won the Palestinian elections, which fueled the crisis with the Brotherhood at home, as was mentioned earlier. Then, leaders of the Brotherhood were arrested while visiting al-Zarqawi's home for his funeral.[21]

In the meantime, to contain the crisis with the state, Inspector General Salem al-Falahat signed a document underscoring the group's belief in tolerance between sects, its rejection of violence, extremism, and terrorism, and emphasizing its loyalty to the king and the state. That document sparked a large amount of internal discussion and debate between the two factions. The executive office and the moderate wing were accused of conspiracy against the Brotherhood, and a *shari'a* committee formed by the group was forced to issue a fatwa forbidding any violations of the tenets of that document and, in general, of the group's positions and approach. The document was used in an attack launched by the hard-line movement against the moderate wing after the 2007 elections were rigged. The moderates were accused of being easily deceived by the state. The scenario ended with the resignation of the executive office led by Salem al-Falahat, followed by increasing differences within the Brotherhood's Shura Council.[22] In 2008, a Jordanian of Palestinian origin, Dr. Hammam Saeed, assumed the position of inspector general for the first time. This shift was reflected in the moderate movement of the Brotherhood and in the policies of the state, which then took a confrontational approach in its dealings with the Brotherhood.

From these realities, the "constitutional monarchy" initiative of the moderate movement (in particular, Rahil Gharaibeh and Nabil al-Kofahi) was born. It was an unprecedented initiative among the Muslim Brotherhood and in its relationship with the state. It consisted of rhetoric that emphasized the importance of reducing the king's powers, curtailing his constitutional role, and of crafting a constitutional monarchy that resembled that of Britain and other European countries.[23] The state was shocked by this initiative and fought it by all means. The new rhetoric constituted an exceptional turning point between the Brotherhood and the state. Paradoxically, the Brotherhood's extremist wing renounced the initiative and denied the Brotherhood's connection to it. This led to a great controversy between the hard-line leaders, the executive office of the Brotherhood, and the party about whether or not the group endorsed the initiative.[24]

In 2010, an important conference of internal meetings was held within the Muslim Brotherhood. Working papers on the main themes of the Brotherhood's approach were presented for discussion. A review of these themes demonstrates the transformations in the focus of the Brotherhood's internal debates and discussions. The debate and differences between the two factions (moderate and extremist) were replaced by the issue of the Brotherhood's relationship with Hamas (organizational duality) and the issue of domestic reform associated with "the issue of nationalism," with the moderate movement focusing on the need to uphold the 1988 decision of Jordanian disengagement and the Brotherhood's acceptance of this resolution.[25]

Since the resignation of the executive office and the inspector general and the dissolution of the Shura Council after the 2007 elections, the Brotherhood had fallen prey to the internal crisis and its dynamics. The crisis itself has become the main concern of the Brotherhood and its members, as well as the media. The former inspector general Salem al-Falahat monitored the details of the crisis, its resulting problems, resignations, media coverage, dozens of initiatives, and the group's leadership figures in an effort to resolve the internal crisis until 2015, when these crises erupted. This led to the announcement of the National Reform Initiative (Zamzam) in October 2013, led by the two most prominent leaders in the moderate wing, Dr. Rahil Gharaibeh and Dr. Nabil Kofahi, along with Dr. Jamil Dheisat and Dr. Nael Zaidan Musallah and dozens of leaders and young people from the Brotherhood, specifically from the moderate wing.

Repercussions of the Arab Spring for the Jordanian Muslim Brotherhood

In an effort to emphasize the moderate wing's departure from the Brotherhood, former inspector general Abdul Majid Thunibat registered a new association of the Muslim Brotherhood with the blessing of official institutions, especially after the separation of the majority of the leaders who participated in these two steps (Zamzam and the new Muslim Brotherhood Association). Then, in 2016, an internal initiative led by a committee of elders transformed into a plan for a party, with most of its members also from the moderate wing, under the name Rescue and Partnership Party (RPP).[26] In the meantime, Hamas reiterated its demands for separation from the Muslim Brotherhood in Jordan and independence within an organization dedicated specifically to Palestine.[27] This was rejected by the Brotherhood's executive offices more than once until the intervention of the Egyptian "Guidance Bureau," which sparked the process of separation between the two organizations (Hamas and the Muslim Brotherhood). The Palestinian Muslim Brotherhood came to include Palestinians in Palestine as well as those in the global diaspora, whereas the Jordanian branch included Jordanians. However, the question of Jordanians of Palestinian origin (those with Palestinian national numbers and Jordanian passports) remained. Should they join the Jordanian Brotherhood or Hamas or should they have the option to choose? There was also the issue of foreign administrative offices, especially in the Gulf countries, since there was a large number of members in the expatriate community there.[28]

In recent years, the Muslim Brotherhood has begun to review its statutes (especially after the establishment of the New Muslim Brotherhood Association) and outlined a new system separating the group from its parent organization in Egypt. This came in conjunction and in parallel with the preparation of a new draft of the IAF's statutes that promotes independence from the Muslim Brotherhood and pushes toward greater participation of women and youth and the development of the party's political discourse. The Muslim Brotherhood in Jordan, in a state of shock after the military intervention and the overthrow of President Mohamed Morsi (July 2013), denied any need to review the Brotherhood's trajectory and learn from the mistakes made by the Egyptian Brotherhood. However, in the last two years, the Brotherhood made attempts to develop their rhetoric, to return to political life, and to overcome the repercussions of what happened in Egypt, hinting at its readiness to legally register again. The Brotherhood began secret talks about its relationship with the regime and the need to separate *da 'wah* (Islamic preaching) from politics and raised a debate within the group about the civil state and its stance in that regard.[29]

Divisions of the Brotherhood

Since 2013, the movements of departure, division, and separation within the Muslim Brotherhood have witnessed a clear and tangible evolution. This evolution began with the announcement of the Zamzam initiative in the same year, followed by the establishment of a new association named after the Muslim Brotherhood under the leadership of the former inspector general Abdul Majid Thunibat in 2015. Later came the declaration of the intention to establish the RPP, led by another group of leaders from the Muslim Brotherhood, including Salem al-Falahat, who also formerly served as the Brotherhood's inspector general. It was previously mentioned that three new structures (the Association of the Muslim Brotherhood, the Zamzam Party, and the RPP) all emerged from the moderate wing of the Muslim Brotherhood and the Islamic Action Front. Although, organizationally, they are three distinct structures, it is difficult to distinguish between them intellectually and ideologically. They present similar intellectual rhetoric on subjects of democracy, civil state, human rights, general freedoms, and attitudes toward women and minorities. Their views are also comparable with regard to the "issue of nationalism," an issue that dominated many of the Brotherhood's debates in recent years and the dynamics of its organizational crises, as mentioned previously. It can be said that what brings the three structures together is that they exceed categorization within classical political Islam, belonging more to an era of "post-political Islam." Even the Muslim Brotherhood (the Association) acknowledges the separation of the religious from the political, and independence from the Brotherhood in Egypt. The Association also leaves political action to the new political parties and, as a civil society organization, restricts its work to religious preaching, and social and cultural activities (although its system includes political activities, it appears to be confined to supporting one particular party, similar to the concept of a "pressure group," that is, an indirect political role). Likewise, the subject of the Islamic state and the application of *shari 'a* law is no longer raised in the literature of these new structures, having been replaced by a vague expression of the concept of a framework of Islamic values. However, there appear to be differences in the political orientations of the new structures, particularly in terms of proximity to the state and the relationship with state institutions. Both the Zamzam Party and the new Muslim Brotherhood Association are accepted by state institutions, as processes have been initiated to facilitate their licensing. On the other hand, the RPP's initial profile, which is under construction, indicates a more critical opposition to official policies. These divisions are the following:

1. Zamzam, the National Congress Party

At the end of 2016, the establishment of the National Congress Party was formally approved. It became an official political party and participated in the parliamentary elections of the same year (2016). Without rosters or slogans, candidates belonging to the party won on the basis of their individual capacity, each relying on their respective social base. Despite the fact that the party later announced the victory of five of its candidates in the elections, they did not form a bloc within the parliament, nor did they adhere to one unified platform or common positions. This created fundamental doubts about the strength of the relationship of the newly elected members of parliament to the Zamzam Party and the organizational and intellectual strength of the party itself.

In order to understand the circumstances of Zamzam's founding and formation, three factors must be taken into account.

The first factor is the experiences of Dr. Rahil Gharaibeh and Dr. Nabil Kofahi. They were the primary leaders of the Zamzam initiative, and each has had a long history of experience in the Brotherhood. They both engaged early through student and youth activities, then later through their involvement in the planning department in the early 1990s, then with the centrist movement in the mid-1990s, and later during the heated period of organizational polarization within the Brotherhood, which began when the leader of Hamas was expelled from the group and escalated beginning in 2002 until it developed into a full-scale crisis in 2007.

In 2007, Gharaibeh and Kofahi had similar profiles, even within the moderate wing. Both suffered the bitterness of failure in parliamentary elections and, in Kofahi's case, even in municipal elections. They felt that they were targeted by the state and the media, despite their moderate stances as compared with the Hawks. The two also participated in the development of the "issue of nationalism" in the Brotherhood's internal debates and were accused by the Hawks of working with the state security apparatus or the Jordanian Regional Council.

At an internal conference for the Brotherhood, Nabil Kofahi presented a vision for political reform entitled "National Identity and Citizenship," in which he addressed the importance of approaching the nationalism issue in the Brotherhood's discourse. This was not accepted by the other movement. As Salem al-Falahat points out in his book, the papers of that conference disappeared—they were not published nor were the records maintained. In his document, Kofahi called for a reconsideration of the Brotherhood's position on the issue of nationalism and internal moderation, specifically the decision to break ties between the East and West Bank. This decision was rejected by the Brotherhood, but Kofahi proposed a stance of nonabsolutism, neither rejecting nor accepting the decision entirely, noting that it had its advantages and disadvantages.

Gharaibeh and Kofahi participated together in the inauguration of the Constitutional Monarchy Initiative in 2009–10, which was renounced by the hard-line faction. Behind this initiative, the leaders of the moderate wing felt that there was collusion between state institutions and the hard-line faction to exclude domestic national interest from the priorities and concerns of the Brotherhood and to categorize the Brotherhood as being more representative of the Jordanian-Palestinian identity than it was of the universal national identity. Both Gharaibeh and Kofahi reacted by adopting a new discourse based on the concept of constitutional monarchy with an emphasis on the concept of national identity.

There is a notable political aspiration that binds Gharaibeh and Kofahi, as well as a collaboration in the development of their intellectual and organizational experiences. But, more importantly, they are both characterized by an intellectual and personal dynamism. They are not afraid to revise and develop their ideas or shift to new ones, even if they clash with the prevailing ideology and convictions that govern most of the Brotherhood's social norms. Neither Gharaibeh nor Kofahi had much influence on these norms, perhaps for social and organizational reasons, although Kofahi had a clear presence in Irbid and was the mayor of Irbid at an earlier stage. This made them consider leaving the organization and focusing on broader horizons. This move constituted their exit from the vicious circle in which they were orbiting in the shadow of the Brotherhood's internal differences.

This brings us to the second factor—the organizational crisis. As was mentioned previously, the organization reached an unprecedented stage in 2007. There were numerous attempts to solve the crisis, none of which bore serious results. Polarization also reached unprecedented levels and eventually the moderate trend, namely, Gharaibeh and Kofahi, felt that they did not have the support of the organizational majority. They also felt that what they suggested about the issue of nationalism was not yet incorporated in the culture of the majority. There was also rising internal pressure on them by the other faction. Over time, all of this pushed them to think about launching another project. Eventually, they announced the results and ideas that they had developed about political reform and internal affairs. Initially, these ideas were difficult to market in the Brotherhood within the climate of polarization, so they turned their attention to other horizons outside of the Brotherhood.

The third factor is related to the events of the Arab Spring and the Muslim Brotherhood's experience in the Egyptian government. Kofahi mentioned this clearly in his speech at the meeting for the declaration of the Zamzam initiative, confirming that they were convinced of the need for participation and national cooperation in the current stage in order to avoid the ideological and political differences that engulfed the Egyptian revolution. His speech also emphasized the return of the military to power and brought the Arab democratic dream to a swift end.

Zamzam also noted the Brotherhood's mistake in trying to manage the transitional period in Egypt on their own, which led to the army's intervention and turned everything on its head. Zamzam's leaders concluded with the need to think about national priorities rather than partisan or organizational ones, to find common ground for all, and the necessity of a framework that goes beyond the political to the developmental, economic, and social dimensions. Dr. Gharaibeh explains his conclusions, which were poured into the concept of the new project (Zamzam), saying:

> We are witnessing a dangerous transition and we need the highest possible degree of wisdom and collective intelligence in order to learn from what is happening in surrounding countries. The transition requires consensus on the road map of the future as well as a clear agreement as to the form of the state and the rules of the political game prior to embarking on the process of party-based competition and before going to the polls.[30]

As for the importance of nationalist identity in the discourse of the new initiative, Gharaibeh said: "The Jordanian identity and the Jordanian state are settled beyond the level of dispute. This country, with its incontrovertible identity, is not merely a political arena, nor does it belong to any party. Jordanians bear the responsibility to protect their land and they have the capacity to build their state."[31]

The previous paragraph clearly points to the conclusions reached by Gharaibeh, Kofahi, and the Zamzam, as was summarized by Alaa al-Faroukh (who was later a member of the party's consultative body later and formerly a member of the Muslim Brotherhood), who said:

> Zamzam represents an alternative to the status quo, such as parties who are in the pocket of the authorities or movements with links abroad, which includes most of the political movements in Jordan. These parties view Jordan as a political arena, not as a homeland, a state, or a set of institutions, a society, and an identity. Therefore, we emphasize these concepts of Jordan as a state, institutions, and society, in response to the rhetoric of the "functional entity" that was associated with the state, and even in the minds of many politicians, including a segment of the Muslim Brotherhood.[32]

Dozens of Muslim Brotherhood leaders and young people participated in the establishment of the new initiative, but some of them later withdrew and joined the emerging Rescue and Partnership Party. The main ideas and conclusions they reached include:

1. A focus on national identity and emphasis on the concept of state, citizenship, and national identity
2. The importance and necessity of national cooperation and the search for common ground with others
3. Moving past the era of ideology and thinking in the language of economic and development programs based on collaboration, not exclusion
4. Transcending the concepts of political Islam and thinking outside of that structure. Islam, according to this proposal "is not a warehouse of ready-made, practical solutions. Islam stimulates the mind to think, create, and to keep up with the times, to follow the realm of wisdom, and the capture the human experience." Therefore, the obsession with identity that ruled the

Brotherhood's ideological discourse, was clearly no longer dominant among Zamzam's members.

5. The members of Zamzam (formerly from the Muslim Brotherhood) have gone beyond the assertions of the Islamic state and the application of *shari'a*. It is not referenced in their literature at all nor in their speeches. Rather, Dr. Nabil Kofahi defines the initiative's political project as one that

> aims to establish a modern civil state on the basis of citizenship, freedom, justice, equal opportunity, respect for human dignity, national cooperation, to preserve and social stability and growth, to develop political life on the basis of programmatic competition to achieve broad sociopolitical collaboration toward the principle of peaceful transfer of power and parliamentary governments and to fight financial, administrative, and social corruption.[33]

6. As evidence of overcoming the assertions of political Islam and the mindset that governs these assertions, Alaa al-Faroukh points out that they—the members of Zamzam who previously belonged to the Muslim Brotherhood—are not talking about an Islamic state in the known ideological sense. They speak clearly about a democratic, pluralistic, civil state where there is an exchange of power. The party does not care if a person prays, is religious, or wears the *hijab*. For them, Islam has shifted to become a general referential framework. That is, Islam serves as a system of values jointly with other universal human values, such as justice, dignity, freedom, honesty, faith, integrity, and others.

2. The New Muslim Brotherhood's Association

Along with dozens of Muslim Brotherhood members, including well-known leaders such as Dr. Rahil Gharaibeh, Dr. Nabil Kofahi, Dr. Jamil Deshisat, and Dr. Sharaf al-Qudah, among others, former inspector general of the Muslim Brotherhood, Abdul Majid Thunibat, applied for a new license for the Muslim Brotherhood in February 2015. He obtained the license from the Ministry of Political Development and the Ministry of Social Development in March. The background of this new step goes back to two issues. The first issue is related to the dynamics and interactions of the crisis within the Muslim Brotherhood. As mentioned earlier, the new group that founded the Association is from the Doves, which in turn split into two factions—those who supported this step and those who did not—and worked instead to contain problems and offer one last chance for internal reconciliation. It is clear that there was a feeling of hopelessness among those who initiated the founding of the new Association. With the intransigence of the hard-line faction, its attempt to overtake the leadership, and the clear division of the group's base between the two factions, they did not believe in the possibility of real, deep-rooted solutions to the internal crisis.

The second issue lies in the evolution of the relationship with the state. Thunibat, the founder of the new Association, confirmed that he received notification from the king of the need to correct the legal status of the Brotherhood to enable Jordan to confront regional and foreign pressure from the Arab allies after Egypt and some Gulf states banned the Muslim Brotherhood and declared it a terrorist organization. Because there is an ambiguity in the legal status of the Muslim Brotherhood in Jordan—according to state entities—and historically, whenever there was a crisis between the state and the Brotherhood there were indications from the state that it might dissolve the Muslim Brotherhood and exploit the ambiguity of the Brotherhood's legal status.[34]

The new Association attracted a broad slice of the moderate wing of the Muslim Brotherhood. The Association formed a following and branches in the provinces and invited people to join them in Irbid, Karak, Ajloun, Jerash, the Jordan Valley, Mafraq, and Ramtha. The Association obtained a fatwa to acquire real estate and property of the original Muslim Brotherhood, which they did. A committee was formed by the new Association to monitor and limit the property of the Muslim Brotherhood. In this way, the new Association snatched the legal license, real estate, and property from under the feet of the former Muslim Brotherhood.[35]

Of course, the greatest organizational component of the new Association are Jordanians of eastern Jordanian origin. In the January 2016 elections, Abdul Majid Thunibat was elected inspector general of the Association along with an executive office consisting of nine people and a Shura Council of forty-five members, forty of whom were directly elected by the General Assembly and five appointed by the Shura Council itself.

It is also worth noting that the new Association had a significant following in the northern provinces and in the provinces where the majority of eastern Jordanians reside, such as Ramtha, Irbid, Ajloun, Jerash, Mafraq, Karak, Aqaba, and Koura. These are the people who were active in trying to reform the crisis within the original Muslim Brotherhood. They are also the ones who held an important internal conference in 2014 in an effort to reform the Muslim Brotherhood. On the other hand, others in the province of Irbid, and particularly in the city of Irbid, have maintained their loyalty and total commitment to the Muslim Brotherhood. There is a clear demographic factor in the divisions among the Muslim Brotherhood in the city of Irbid between Jordanians of a Jordanian descent and those of a Palestinian origin.[36]

The deputy inspector general is Dr. Muhammad Sharaf al-Qudah, who was formerly a member of the Hawkish faction of the Muslim Brotherhood. Members of the executive office include Raed al-Shayb (who became the officer of the political bureau), Dr. Jamil Dheisat (a prominent member of the Zamzam Party), and Dr. Fathi al-Ta'mneh. There is also the current representative in the House of Representatives, Ibrahim Abu al-Ezz (from Aqaba), and Khalil Askar, who was a prominent leader in the Muslim Brotherhood.[37]

Although the new Association has maintained its basic statute of undertaking political action in addition to its religious preaching and educational work, there is a new trend of avoiding direct party-based or political action, in keeping with the principle of separating religious preaching (*da'wah*) from the politics in general. There were some indications that the Association believed Zamzam to be its closest

96   *Islamism and Revolution Across the Middle East*

representative in political action, especially given the overlap in membership between the two organizations.

In terms of ideas, it is notable that the issue of nationalism has taken a clearer and more explicit position within the new Association. The Association confirms its commitment to the Muslim Brotherhood's school of thought, in terms of both its philosophy and its approach. However, it is organizationally independent, as it has not declared itself as a branch of the parent organization in Egypt. Its basic statute also stipulates the Association's commitment to the Jordanian legal and national framework, saying

> "The Brotherhood" is an Islamic entity working within an Islamic national framework that carries out a National Reform Project aimed at protecting Jordan, preserving its security, stability, and its regime, laying the foundations of democracy, establishing a civil state, relying on a peaceful approach, adopting moderate thought based on tolerance and cooperation, participating in political action, building strong relationships with state institutions in the absence of suspicion and betrayal, preserving the prestige of the state, conserving its security and stability and national unity, adopting the process of gradual transition to democracy, and using rational, optimistic rhetoric based on openness and peace, and achieving the aims that represent the true spirit of Islam.[38]

It seems clear from the previous text that the Association makes a decisive break with the state of hesitation and confusion that the original Brotherhood displayed in dealing with key concepts, which itself formed part of the internal crisis in the former Muslim Brotherhood. The new Association emphasizes that the "National Reform Project" operates within an Islamic national framework and that it works for the protection of Jordan, democracy, and the civil state within a peaceful approach based on values of tolerance and cooperation.

The new approach is based upon bringing an end to the "underground organization." Thus, in its basic statute, the Association announced its commitment to principles of openness. The new leadership confirmed the end of the era of "secret organizing and public preaching," which was a fixed principle of the work of the original Muslim Brotherhood, and its replacement with public preaching and public organizing. Even in Hassan al-Banna's instructions and his main ideas, there was an emphasis on the concept of "organizational secrecy."[39]

3. *The Rescue and Partnership Party*

The Rescue and Partnership Party (RPP) was officially approved at the end of 2017. The party is aligned with Zamzam in that its founders are from the moderate wing, led by Salem al-Falahat, along with dozens of leaders and youth from the Muslim Brotherhood and the Islamic Action Front who submitted their resignations from the IAF. At the time of writing, the Muslim Brotherhood had not decided to remove members of the new party from its ranks. Despite having a common background with Zamzam leadership and members—being of the youth centrist

7. Islamists in Jordan

wing in the mid-1990s, then the moderate wing since 2002—the difference is that members of the RPP languished in their attempts to resolve the internal conflict within the Muslim Brotherhood. Their attempts at internal reform were ongoing, even after the establishment of the new Muslim Brotherhood Association and the announcement of the Zamzam initiative. They tried to maintain internal and organizational order in the face of those developments. Salem al-Falahat, one of the most prominent founders of the RPP, was a member of several committees for the Brotherhood's reconciliation, along with Dr. Abdel Hamid al-Qudah, Khaled Hassanein, Ahmad al-Kafwain, and Hassan Thunibat, who are all prominent leaders of the party. The most significant of these committees was the Committee of Elders, followed by the committee named after the party itself "Rescue and Partnership," which was established at the end of 2015. When the committee reached a blockage in the reconciliation process, its members issued a statement threatening to resign from the IAF and to withdraw from all leadership positions in the Muslim Brotherhood. Eventually, when the Rescue and Partnership group reached the conclusion that further attempts to resolve the internal crisis would be futile and that the other trend of leadership was dominating, some of its leaders decided to initiate the process of establishing a new party while remaining in the Muslim Brotherhood as long as the Brotherhood refrained from expelling them.[40] Among the most prominent founders of the party from the moderate wing are Salem al-Falahat, Abdel Hamid al-Qudah, Ahmad al-Kafawin, Hassan Thunibat, Khaled Hassanein, and Mohammed Rajoub. Among the younger generation is a former youth officer of the Islamic Action Front, Ghaith al-Qudah, as well as Dr. Mohammed Abdul Hamid Al-Qudah, Dr. Mohammed Hassan Thunibat, and Sa'id Al-Azm.

Under the leadership of al-Falahat, the group began to search for partners outside of the Brotherhood. The RPP banded together with another group, including well-known Islamic scholar Dr. Muhammad al-Hammouri, who was of a nationalist orientation and played an active role in the drafting of the basic statute and the establishment of the new party. His works in Islamic thought very much clash with the classic literature of the Muslim Brotherhood and the IAF, but they are aligned on the concepts of civil state, citizenship, democracy, pluralism, and nationalist-Islamic identity in general.[41] A close reading of the reports of the RPP founders, who were previously leaders of the Muslim Brotherhood, will reveal clear difference in the party's discourse. Perhaps the best example of this is Salem al-Falahat, one of the party's visionaries. In a press interview, he presents a summary of the circumstances and reasoning behind the new party, the conclusions they reached, and the ideas that they came to adopt. He said,

Arab, Islamist, liberal, nationalist, and leftist experiences over nearly 70 years— which is the age of the major Arab parties—after all of these long years, these parties finally rose to power and established a state. The nationalists were able to establish a state, as were the leftists and the Islamists. But all of these states, which emerged from ideological parties, remained on the chopping block. It wasn't long before they were overthrown, destroyed, or marginalized.[42]

Nationalism has become ideologized although it is not ideological in its essence. It has even been likened to a religion, a communist ideology, and the political interpretation of Islamic ideology. When parties decide to make definitive judgments without room for *ijtihad*, the space left for human development is limited. On the other hand, the intensity of nationalist politics isolates the vast majority from this work, be it Islamic or nationalist or otherwise. Nationalists do not constitute the majority of society, nor do political Islamists, leftists, and the like.

Where did this awareness come from? First, it flowed from the Brotherhood's internal crisis and the controversy about the "issue of nationalism" that dominated the organization. For this reason, we see that the focus in the statute of both parties is on the "strengthening of the state" and its institutions. Second, it came as a result of the Arab Spring and the collapse of the states, the military coup in Egypt which overthrew the "Brotherhood's rule," and their learning from what happened. Third, it came from the developments in Islamist political experiments, such as in the Turkish case. There is the Turkish Justice and Development Party (AKP), for example, which recognizes Dr. Rahil Gharaibeh and Dr. Nabil Kofahi as its inspiration. There is also the Tunisian and Moroccan experiments in government participation, which were successful compared to the mistakes made by the Brotherhood in Egypt.[43]

Conclusion

This chapter discussed the political debates within the Brotherhood in Jordan and their impact on internal alignments in an effort to outline the evolution of the Brotherhood's political discourse and its organizational-intellectual structure in recent decades. The transformations, themes, and most prominent figures have been outlined earlier. We have observed how the Brotherhood's internal intellectual debates can be understood through three main themes: their attitude toward democracy in the 1980s, the issue of nationalism in the 2000s, and later the separation of Islamic preaching from political action. These broad headings include several small intellectual minutiae, but the general framework of intellectual evolution is evident—a comparison of these headings with the traditional discourse of Islamic preaching that characterized the Brotherhood's rhetoric in the 1980s. This explains the Brotherhood's gradual trend toward political institutionalization, which is the current subject of debates on the separation of Islamic preaching from politics. This politicization came at a cost to the Brotherhood's intellectual constituents. The price of these debates and the historical emergence of the two factions, the Doves and the Hawks, was the gradual (and sometimes confrontational) withdrawal of the moderate wing from the Brotherhood's ranks. In the 1990s, they formed the Centrist Party, then the Zamzam initiative emerged in 2013. Then, the Association of the Muslim Brotherhood was licensed in 2015, and the RPP was established in 2017. In this way, the movement that usually called for reform and buffered against crisis with the state disappeared from the Brotherhood. However, the hard-line movement has adopted positions of reconciliation with the state more than the moderate wing during the period of the Arab Spring.

Demographically, Jordanians of eastern Jordanian origins dominated both leadership and overall membership in the moderate movement that broke off from the Brotherhood and the IAF. This reinforced the preexisting notion among the political forces that the Brotherhood represented Jordanians of Palestinian origin, which further highlighted the issue of nationalism and the political role of the Brotherhood in the ensuing debates. These factors and stages of the Brotherhood's internal intellectual debates make up the general intellectual framework for understanding the reasons that led to the rise of post-political Islamist parties that branched out from the Muslim Brotherhood after 2010. We can also see a clear trend toward politicization. From the 1950s until the late 1980s, the Brotherhood implemented a religious discourse linked to political positions. They campaigned for elections (in 1989, 1993, 2003, and 2007) under the slogan "Islam is the solution." Despite declaring acceptance of democracy, the Brotherhood's rhetoric remained linked to the theme of implementation of *shari'a* in vague general political language. But in the meantime, the Brotherhood's ideas and debates moved toward a more politicized discourse over time. In this context, a comparison of certain historical stages may help to demarcate these transformations. First is a comparison of the conditions required by the Brotherhood in order to show confidence in the government of Mudar Badran (1990)—which focused on issues closer to "traditional Islamic ideology" (alcohol, *shari'a* law, the establishment of a school of Islamic law)—with the reasons given by the Brotherhood to boycott the 1997 elections—which cantered on democracy and public freedoms. Later, the vision of the Islamic Movement for Reform in 2005 explicitly declared the group's acceptance of democracy. Compare this with the demands of the reformist Brotherhood during the Arab Spring phase (of a purely domestic reformist political nature), and finally with their entry into the 2016 parliamentary elections through the National Alliance for Reform without the slogan "Islam is the solution," and with a greater focus on political issues and reform. Although the group has traditionally been split into two streams, the first known as the Hawkish-extremist trend and the second known as the Dovish-moderate trend, this binary is highly reductionist and blurs many details. There are generations that constituted these organizational divisions.

The second generation of the group, *circa* the 1970s and 1980s, was divided into the first two groups. The first was closer to Qutb, and the other was more pragmatic. The third generation, which rose in the mid-1990s and was represented by the centrist movement, also split into two streams: one called the Internal Reformist movement and the other that was closer to Hamas. The second-generation Doves teamed up with the third-generation reformists, forming the moderate wing. Meanwhile, the second-generation Hawks allied themselves with the third-generation Hamas sympathizers to form the hard-liners wing. Since 2002, the internal crisis between the two wings has clearly escalated, and youth from the third and fourth generations have joined one of the two former wings. The terms "moderate" and "hard-line" or "extremist" are not entirely accurate and do not fully reflect the changes that took place in the Brotherhood, nor the exchanges of positions between the two sides. After 2007, the moderate wing took a confrontational stance toward the regime and the Brotherhood's discourse reached an unprecedented stage, even within the discourse of the Hawks. This is a major paradox. The two leaders from the Doves, Rahil Gharaibeh and Nabil Kofahi, were the ones calling for a constitutional monarchy and the hard-line wing was forced to distance itself from them. Salem al-Falahat was one of the leading figures in the popular movement calling for reform in 2011, including the movements with highly ambitious demands.

But the leaders of the constitutional monarchy initiative, Rahil Gharaibeh and Nabil Kofahi, then went back to declare the Zamzam initiative and later the officially accepted Zamzam Party, calling for reconciliation with the state. Meanwhile, the hard-line movement, which refused to yield to reformist demands, worked to complete a draft of a basic statute for the Brotherhood and the party, including many developments which were previously considered by the hard-liners as treason or concession, such as the complete separation from the Global Muslim Brotherhood, the separation of Islamic preaching from politics, and the focus on internal reform (see Figure 1). This shows that evolution of positions within the Brotherhood's crisis and the political and intellectual stances were shifting and developed in a disorganized way between hard-liners and moderates in that the two factions during that period alternated between a confrontational discourse and one of de-escalation.

Chapter 8

TRANSFORMATIONS OF THE ISLAMIC CONSTITUTIONAL MOVEMENT IN KUWAIT

Mubarak Aljeri

After the eruption of the Arab Spring, the rise of Islamism in Tunisia, Egypt, and Morocco became an important topic of research. Studies dealt with the phenomenon of the growing influence of political Islamist movements through an analysis of their sociological, political, and intellectual dimensions. However, these transformations were not limited to these three countries alone. Rather, the phenomenon spread to other Arab countries and impacted their respective parties as well as political and social movements.

This chapter explicates the transformations of the Islamic Constitutional Movement (al-haraka al-dusturiyya al-islamiyya) or "Hadas" in Kuwait. It argues that the events of the Arab Spring prompted Hadas to make changes into its political strategy and discourse in order to remain relevant and influential in the Kuwaiti society.

The Emergence of the Islamic Constitutional Movement

The Islamic Constitutional Movement (Hadas) was established in Kuwait on March 30, 1991, upon the declaration of its separation from the Muslim Brotherhood (MB). This came after the country's liberation on February 26, 1991.[1] The primary reason for this separation goes back to the Brotherhood's rejection of foreign intervention in the Gulf region. The Movement's official declaration, however, is preceded by a history of political and movement-based activity that cannot be overlooked. Since the early 1950s, the Kuwaiti state legally acknowledged the Brotherhood but under a different name—The Association of Islamic Guidance.[2] Three decades after its founding, in the 1980s, the Movement underwent an important development that consisted of a shift toward the political field when the leadership of the MB in Kuwait emphasized the need for political participation in the Kuwaiti parliament in order to support its preaching work. That decision resulted in internal differences among members of the movement, especially within the current that rejected political participation, which saw it as a deviation from the organization's preaching-based approach.[3] From the beginning of the 1990s until today, Hadas has maintained an influential parliamentary representation, albeit not a fixed one. The Movement's political power was the result of historical, political, and social components that became resources that allowed the Movement to strengthen its political position among other political currents until it became the movement most organized and capable of mobilizing.

Beginning in November 2011, Kuwait witnessed a phase that coincided with the Arab Spring and continued until July 2014. This period was foreshadowed by a set of political sit-ins in which Hadas participated along with a number of political and youth forces. This resulted in the dissolution of the 2009 parliament, the dismissal of former prime minister Nasser Mohammed al-Sabah at the end of November 2011, and the election of a new parliament in February 2012, in which the opposition won a majority of seats (35 out of 50). The results, however, were overturned by a Constitutional Court ruling in June 2012.

In the same context, Hadas moved from political participation to political boycott along with the rest of the movements and other sociopolitical elements who opposed the law enacted by the emir in October 2012. The law called for changing the voting system such that each voter would have one vote instead of four while retaining the five voting districts. The boycott transformed into a social movement that contributed to the organization of eight popular protest rallies known as "Dignity of the Homeland," which continued until July 2014.[4]

It should be pointed out that Hadas boycotted the February 2012 parliamentary elections and the July 2013 elections, but withdrew from the political boycott at its conference held in April 2016 because it considered political participation necessary in order to confront local and regional challenges and the reform deadlock.[5] The Movement participated in the November 2016 elections and managed to win four seats in the parliament. It is worth noting that despite the unique political situation in Kuwait, which regulates the activity of political currents, the political changes and transformations resulting from the Arab revolutionary movement influenced the scope of the protest movements' aspirations and the discourse of oppositional political movements. It should also be noted that Hadas is one of the most substantial elements of the Kuwaiti political movement and is one of the currents that is intellectually akin to the Islamist parties that ruled in Tunisia, Egypt, and Morocco. Owing to this ideological similarity, this study will examine how the experience of Islamists and the outcomes of those experiences impacted the movement.

This chapter revolves around the following questions: to what extent did the Arab revolutions and the rule of Islamists impact the Hadas' ideas and its political trajectory? What are the most significant political transformations that the Movement experienced as a result of the downfall of the MB in Egypt after July 3, 2014? What is the role of the unique character of Kuwait's sociopolitical field in controlling the extent of Hadas' interaction with the Arab revolutions?

In order to survey the most important developments of the Movement in the Arab revolutionary period, the study relied on two analytical tools: critical discourse analysis and semi-structured interviews. Eleven people were interviewed, including six members of Hadas and five political and academic figures, in order

8. Transformations of the Islamic Constitutional Movement in Kuwait 103

to identify the most important transformations of Hadas in Kuwait since the beginning of the Arab Spring.

A Brief Overview of the Political System in Kuwait

The political system in Kuwait combines hereditary rule with the characteristics of a constitutional emirate. This hybrid system plays a role in shaping the nature of activity in the political field. The nature of this political system was determined and documented in the constitution of Kuwait on November 11, 1962.[6] The activities of political currents may not exceed the framework set forth by the constitution. They do not compete for power or endeavor to change the system. Competition between political elements and the ruling family revolves around the subject of political reform, which forms the basis of the discourse of many political currents, including Hadas. It can be said that the role of political currents in Kuwait and their discourse can only be understood in the context of the system outlined above and what it follows in terms of the choices and opportunities that face each individual political movement.[7]

The Kuwaiti parliament can be considered among the most important elements of the country's political activity. Since its foundation and until today, it has formed the central focus of political interaction, along with other actors such as unions and student movements. Despite the long-standing history of political action in Kuwait—which dates back to the end of the 1930s after the establishment of the first political association, the National Bloc, which influenced the ideas of the Iraqi National Reform Movement[8]—the Kuwaiti constitution forbids the public declaration of political parties. Therefore, this study is not rooted in political party theory because the elements that constitute the concept of a political party[9] do not apply in the case of the State of Kuwait.

Islamist political movements in Kuwait, especially Sunni ones, are distinct from Islamist currents in the other Arab countries in that those in Kuwait have not been prohibited from engaging in the sociopolitical field since its establishment and until today. They did not face an existential crisis that lasted throughout the stages of its formation, or even its birth. On the contrary, movements in Kuwait have existed free of dilemma or crisis. The political obstacles they face are limited and do not prevent political participation in the parliament and entering to form a government. In addition, some of these movements have gained influence in the Kuwaiti economy and have a strong impact on culture and education.[10] Carine Lahoud says, "The uniqueness of political Islam in Kuwait lies in the mobilizing structures on which it depends and the strategies it uses to acquire resources. Their public presence does not pose a threat to their existence; on the contrary, it facilitates direct access to state resources."[11]

The ruling authority in Kuwait was not opposed to dealing with Islamist political movements. In contrast, the state was one of the most significant reasons for their strength and continued presence in the political arena.[12] The leaders of these movements, in particular, those of the Hadas, have good relations and meet regularly with the political leadership, led by the emir. Even in the most difficult domestic circumstances, there has been no fissure in relations between the figureheads of these movements and the ruling elite. The nature of these relations sometimes interferes with the way crises are managed, particularly those that occur between political currents and political leadership.

The history of stable relations between the ruling family and the Islamist political movements has contributed to shaping the uniqueness of the situation that characterizes this relationship. It can be said that the network of political currents and their interactions is based mainly on the social component, which often affects and determines political leanings, both on the level of political currents or citizens. Therefore, the social component is one of the most important elements of political culture in the State of Kuwait.

Hadas' Position on the Arab Spring

At the beginning of the Arab revolutions, Hadas' position was ambiguous. This position can be understood through a review of the statements of the leaders and cadres of the Movement at various levels, some of whom were supportive of the revolutions and others who were more conservative. However, after the arrival of the Tunisian Ennahda Party and the Egyptian Freedom and Justice Party, the Movement's position became clearer. This led to the expansion of its political aspirations toward the need for constitutional amendments, especially those related to the public declaration of political parties and elected government.[13]

Thus, the period in which the Arab revolutions coincided with the political movement in Kuwait resulted in a new discourse full of enthusiastic terms, especially when compared to prerevolutionary rhetoric. This is because the Islamic ties and perspectives that unite Hadas with the Islamist parties that came to power in Tunisia, Egypt, and Morocco increased the impact of the Arab revolutions on the Movement. Additionally, the experience of the Islamists led the Movement to conduct a deep, comprehensive revision aimed at developing its political culture. This included a review of democracy in all of its forms and the concept of political parties. Before these revisions, the knowledge of members of the Movement, especially in the realm of politics, was modest.[14]

The experience of the Islamists has caused an increase in the use of terms such as democracy and political freedoms in the Movement's political rhetoric. This was reflected in its interaction with the political movement and protest rallies in Kuwait from the end of 2011 until mid-2014.[15] Hadas' participation in the movement on the ground and in political sit-ins was not something new inspired by the Arab revolutions. In fact, Hadas played a historical role in the movement on the ground, along with the political currents and youth movements[16] before the outbreak of the revolutions. One of the most significant aspects of Hadas' involvement was in its participation, albeit belated, in the "We Want Five" or "Five for Kuwait" March in 2006, which was aimed at achieving electoral reforms and reducing the number of electoral districts from twenty-five to five.[17]

8. Transformations of the Islamic Constitutional Movement in Kuwait   105

In light of this, it can be said that the Movement constituted a significant presence in the history of political activity at the sit-ins and demonstrations that coincided with the Arab revolutions. Hadas' presence grew until the movement became situated at the heart of political activity, especially that of the "Dignity of the Homeland" movement, which destabilized Hadas' relationship with the Kuwaiti regime.[18]

The Arab revolutions served as a catalyst for the visions of the former political movement, especially with regard to the need for a broad reform movement, including the full spectrum of Kuwaiti political currents. This new vision seeks to develop political life. Ali al-Sanad noted that the Movement translated these visions to a political movement by demanding constitutional amendments, such as the declaration of political parties and the right of Kuwaiti citizens to elect their government. These demands became part of the Movement's discourse, as well as that of other opposition movements.[19]

Since its founding, Hadas' political behavior has witnessed a change that manifested in the specialization and dedication of one of its branches to political action. According to Nathan J. Brown, the Movement's shift into the field of political activity enabled it to exert pressure in order to achieve a high degree of political freedom and, in turn, present itself as an opposition group.[20]

It appears that specializing in politics has provided the Movement with greater leeway to interact with political issues under a new language, vision, and discourse that are subject to change according to the scale of political issues. This is particularly evident in the Movement's handling of the Arab revolutions and their transformations, whereby the issue of political reform shifted from a moral- and value-based framework to a political one.[21]

The concern of the Movement's cadres and leaders with the transformation of the local and broader Arab political scene (in the period between 2011 and 2014) led to an increased interest in political discourse rather than religious discourse. This political nature is what distinguishes Hadas' discourse from that of other Sunni political Islamist streams. The experience of the Islamists has led the Movement to functional specialization, to reexamine the integration between the political and the religious, and ultimately separate them, as did the Moroccan Justice and Development Party.[22] Mubarak al-Duwailah, leader of Hadas and a former member of the Kuwaiti parliament, said that

> the movement developed after the separation between the political and the religious. Previously, the movement was suffering from contradictions between the political arm (Hadas) and the religious preaching (da'wah) arm (The Social Reform Society) due to advocates' sensitivity and concern for their status and the relationship with the regime, which allows them to do Islamic preaching work. The Movement, on the other hand, has purely political objectives with regard to the parliamentary elections, so the separation served to remove this obstacle in its development.[23]

At the end of 2011, protest movements, such as "Irhal" or "Leave," and the political sit-ins in which a number of political currents and youth forces took part, succeeded in exerting the political pressure that culminated in the dissolution of the 2009 National Assembly and the removal of the former prime minister Nasser al-Mohammad al-Sabah. The effect of the Arab Spring revolutions on these protest movements is that they "merely breathed new life into the movements (the 'Dignity of the Homeland' march) that allowed them to introduce new demands and protest groups and facilitate their spread to areas that had not yet been mobilized."[24] These movements—including the cadres of Hadas—were able to organize themselves on the ground using social media, especially through Twitter, Instagram, and YouTube as new resources for mobilization or new feeders for the protests. This mobilization had a clear impact on the mood of the majority of voters, which led to the election of thirty-five representatives of the political opposition to the February 2012 parliament. They were later renamed the "majority bloc," which consisted of nineteen independent members, five members from Hadas, five members from the Popular Constitutional Movement, three members from the National Constituent Bloc, and three members from the Salafi Bloc. Hadas' representation increased in comparison to its presence in the 2009 parliament, in which only two members, Jamaan al-Harbash and Falah al-Sawag, were elected.[25] Hadas realized that its political power was not situated in the alliance with the Kuwaiti government but was rooted in the parliament. This realization increased its interaction with the issues on the ground and the political demands of the people, which, in turn, led to the Movement's shift away from movements loyal to the government of Nasser al-Mohammad al-Sabah toward opposition movements in the 2009 parliament.[26] Within the Movement were two currents, the first of which was the "Doves," who believed that their participation in Nasser al-Muhammad's government (the 2006 and 2008 parliaments) would contribute to support reform and development issues. The other current was the "Hawks," who opposed this alliance based on the conviction that reform should be carried out through the operationalizing of regulatory and legislative roles rather than through an alliance with the Kuwaiti government. It should be noted that Hadas' rise and fall in the parliament is not necessarily linked to the rise of Islamism, whether in Egypt, Tunisia, or Morocco, but the rise of Islamism was an influential factor in the direction of the Movement.

After the Constitutional Court dissolved the February 2012 parliament,[27] which coincided with the MB's arrival to power in Egypt, Hadas boycotted the parliamentary elections based on the five-constituency system and the one-vote law. Here we can see the impact of the rise of Islamism on the Movement's discourse and its interaction with the political movement under the "Dignity of the Homeland" initiative. Ali al-Zamie', the former leader of the MB in Kuwait and former minister of Awqaf and planning and development, stressed that Hadas' integration in the democratic process increased significantly during its interaction with the political movement in Kuwait after the Arab Spring revolutions. Prior to the revolutions, the Movement experienced a period of intellectual and political revision, but the revolutionary factor put pressure on the Movement to appeal to the political values of those demanding change.[28]

The concurrence of the political boycott in Kuwait with the period of Islamic rule, specifically in Egypt, boosted Hadas' commitment to the idea of an elected government and political parties, as can be seen in its political discourse. At this stage, the opposition coalition was formed in March 2013, consisting of a number of political currents (including Hadas), civil society organizations, and a variety of political activists. This coalition produced a roadmap called the "Political Reform Project" focused on achieving a full parliamentary system by separating the presidential and parliamentary systems. This would entail a number of parliamentary and judicial reforms.[29] The Movement used this project as an opportunity to strengthen itself, in particular by observing and following up on popular demands put forward by the political movement. Ali al-Kandari says that the political element of the discourse of the Islamist currents in Kuwait has increased alongside the evolution of the country's political trajectory. Hadas is at the forefront of these currents because of its long-standing political presence, its organized structure, and the student movement that ultimately feeds the Movement. The interaction of these components with local and regional events contributed to the production of a completely new discourse, especially when compared to the Movement's rhetoric prior to the Arab revolutions.[30]

What was different about the Movement's political discourse during the period of the Arab revolutions is that it broke the silence on the issue that became known among protest movements and opposition forces as "elected government." On the intellectual level, the movement was still unable to produce new ideas along the lines of the Tunisian Ennahda Movement and the Moroccan Justice and Development Party. In other words, the Arab revolutions and the political movement in Kuwait revealed the political flexibility of Hadas and its ability to renew and change its political discourse, but not its intellectual discourse. Ghanim al-Najjar, a professor of political science at Kuwait University, confirms this, saying that the nature of political action in Kuwait does not support this type of intellectual production because political party action is unconstitutional and Hadas' preoccupation with the political realm distances it from the intellectual one. This is what explains the rise and prevalence of political actors over intellectuals within the Movement.[31] Owing to this dearth of intellectual production, the Movement still feeds on the classic MB ideology and literature—despite the organizational separation— although there are some ideas within the Movement, particularly those related to partisanship and political pluralism, that go beyond the classic literature of the Brotherhood and indeed are rejected by the MB founder Hassan al-Banna.

There is a controversial relationship between thought and organization, which can be understood on the basis of reports given by some of the Movement's leaders and cadres via interviews. However, despite the separation of the Movement from the MB in the early 1990s and its organic independence, the ideas of the MB continue to interfere in the direction of the political organization. This intellectual relationship is impossible to break owing to the absence of alternative thought and the weak intellectual production of the Movement. Ali al-Zamie' says that the Hadas is going through a period similar to what nationalist and leftist movements experienced following the Six-Day War in 1967 and the collapse of the Soviet Union, respectively. The problem with these movements is that they subsist on the tradition of these ideas and at the same time deny any affiliation with them.[32]

The movement did not progress intellectually, despite the fact that it had opportunities that were not available to other Islamist political movements (in particular, the MB in Egypt and other Arab countries), especially in terms of its freedom to participate in the political field since the 1980s. Nevertheless, the Movement was able to grow in the political sphere because of its cumulative political experience.[33]

Hadas' Relationship with the Kuwaiti Regime

Hadas did not specifically adopt the demands of the Arab Spring, which toppled the ruling regimes in Tunisia and Egypt. In fact, it stressed on more than one occasion that its intention in interacting with these revolutions was for the purpose of political reform and rectification of the country's method of political administration, and not to overthrow the government. Protest movements and sit-ins are not strange to Kuwaiti sociopolitical history, but because "Dignity of the Homeland" in particular coincided with the events of the Arab Spring, the demands some of the political currents involved in this movement swelled. Hadas, however, despite the concurrence and influence of the Arab revolutionary movement, did not deviate from the distinct character of the Kuwaiti society and political system. Mubarak al-Duwailah believes that the tribal nature of the society in Kuwait and the Arabian Gulf has made the idea of regime change impossible and unwelcome, and Hadas is a part of this landscape that governs all political currents in Kuwait.[34] The social consideration, namely, ancestral and kinship-based values and alliances, shaped Hadas' interaction with the protest movements.[35]

In addition, the ruling authority in Kuwait maintains economic power through the rentier economy. The state has a primary responsibility for sources of oil and its financial dividends, salaries of state employees, donations, financial aid, etc. The management of wealth is in the state's political interest because it gives the state the ability to influence other political forces.[36] In other words, the state's political power is rooted in its control of the state's economy. The economy underpins politics in Kuwait, and there is a direct correlation between economy and politics in the state. Thus, the more economically powerful a political movement is, the more political influence it has. It should be noted that, for any given movement, political influence in the decision-making process is not necessarily related to the extent of popular support. This equation can be illustrated by the comparison between the power of the opposition political movements and the youth organizations that led the popular movement and the power of the ruling authority. The opposition was able to succeed in gathering and mobilizing the Kuwaiti people to varying degrees during the period of activity (from October 2012 to June 2014). The ruling authority confronted these protests with multiple sources of power (political, media, economic, social), which indicates the unequal balance of power in Kuwait. Emphasizing this point, Ghanim al-Najjar highlights the unique political character of Kuwait, noting that 90 percent of the sources of power are state-owned. The state manages access to these sources of power across political movements, society,

8. Transformations of the Islamic Constitutional Movement in Kuwait   109

and the media.[37] Thus, Hadas' interaction with any issue, whether local or regional, is dictated by this political and social environment. This can be seen in the changes of the Movement's political discourse, as was explained earlier. Ali al-Kandari says that during the Arab revolutions and the period of political mobilization in Kuwait, Hadas did not deviate from the status quo, and despite the amplification of its political discourse, the Movement made sure to take the country's unique political and social character into consideration.[38]

In the period of political boycotts and popular movements and in light of the democratic transformations in the Arab Spring countries, especially after the rise of Islamism, Hadas believed that the strategy of protesting outside the parliament would put pressure on the ruling authority to answer popular demands (including elected government, the amendment of the electoral system, and the declaration of political parties). However, after the Constitutional Court upheld the one-vote law in June 2013,[39] the boycott lost part of its popular support. A number of boycotters participated in the July 27, 2013 parliamentary election as both candidates and voters (this was the final parliament boycotted by Hadas) despite the fact that the opposition's majority bloc (of the dissolved February 2012 parliament) announced prior to the ruling that it would boycott the one-vote law in the event that it was upheld. After the ruling of the Constitutional Court, the bloc issued a statement (with the participation of twenty-eight members including representatives of Hadas) confirming its adherence to the boycott decision. The press arm of Hadas, "Mugtama," published the text of this statement.[40] Twenty days prior to the 2013 parliamentary elections, the majority bloc held a symposium entitled "al-Muqata' Awjab" (literally: "The Duty to Boycott") in which a number of former parliamentarians, including Jamaan al-Harbash and Falah al-Sawag of Hadas, participated. At this symposium, al-Harbash said, "People are sacrificing their lives in defense of the will of the people, so won't we offer the boycott as an extension of our will? Under laws of *fitna*, injustice, and autocracy, there will be no interpellation nor exposure of corruption."[41] Al-Sawag said, "The constitution denies the one-vote law; we respect our constitution and will preserve it."[42]

This intensification of Hadas' discourse was the result of the shock of the new phase. On the local side, the one-vote law reshaped the balance structure within the Kuwaiti parliament. On the regional level, the counterrevolutions backed by some Gulf states sparked the Movement's concern about being pushed out. After four years of boycott and revision, it became clear to the Movement that continuing with this choice would mean losing its state resources, which would affect its social and political power and could lead to a scenario similar to what occurred in Egypt but in a way consistent with the unique character of Kuwait. Kuwaiti writer and journalist Daham al-Qahtani noted that the Movement was willing to adapt to the political reality and owing to this flexibility was able to survive in a turbulent regional atmosphere. It also benefited from the ruling authority's calm approach in dealing with this climate, which helped the Movement carry on and succeed.[43]

The Movement's ability to adapt to the unique character of the political system, social structure, and the nature of the state economy was one of the main reasons for its continued presence. Thus, the Kuwaiti academic and former political

110 *Islamism and Revolution Across the Middle East*

scientist at Kuwait University, Abdullah Al-Nafisi, believes that there are a number of factors that may help the Islamist political movements in the State of Kuwait to survive and maintain their existence. The first is to stop simply reproducing what was previously dictated. The second factor is to generate their own political ideology relevant to the scenario. And the third factor is to work to bridge the relationship with the ruling regime in Kuwait.[44]

Transformations of the Islamic Constitutional Movement

The concurrence of the July 3, 2013 coup in Egypt with the rise of radical Islamist groups and organizations (such as ISIS) helped some Arab regimes that supported the counterrevolutions to portray their struggle with moderate Islamist movements as a "war on terror." This, without a doubt, led to the decline and fragility of these movements. One of the most important repercussions of the regional counterrevolutions and the setback of the Arab revolutions, which occurred in more than one country, was the shift in the concept of revolution among a wide segment of the Gulf population from a meaning of reform and political renewal to one of social and economic justice.

In this context, Hadas found itself in an unstable environment at a very critical stage in the face of counterrevolutions whose main objective was to exclude MB groups from political participation[45] and to classify them as terrorist organizations, as happened in Egypt, Saudi Arabia, and the UAE in late 2013 and early 2014.[46] The Movement's pioneering historical experience in the political field as compared to MB groups in the other Gulf states and its status as one of the most prominent political components in Kuwait put it at the forefront of counterrevolutionary objectives. In this context, it should be noted that the plight of the MB in Egypt coincided with the Movement's boycott of the Kuwaiti parliament and its participation in the protest movements against the one-vote law.

Under these circumstances, Hadas realized that its ability to mobilize politically was weak compared to the power of the ruling authority. This was especially true after the protests movement lost its power and influence after the Kuwaiti government's decision in June 2014 to withdraw citizenship from some political and media activists and to arrest a number of activists who played an influential role in the political movement. The regional anti-MB sentiment posed a threat to the influence held by the political movement and Hadas in particular. This threat, as noted by Carine Lahoud, "lied in the fact that the Kuwaiti government joined the Saudi/UAE axis, which posed a direct threat to the Movement's existence. Thus, the need to return to a more practical strategy based on cooperation rather than confrontation began to make its way into the political and religious elite."[47]

These transformations and the forces of the counterrevolution prompted Hadas to reevaluate its strategy of political boycotts and support of the protest movements. The Movement ultimately concluded that there was a need to shift its strategy to one of de-escalation and to participate in the upcoming parliamentary elections.[48] The Movement held a number of reasons for this transition from the stage of political boycotts to parliamentary participation. The first reason was the fact that its absence from parliamentary representation meant losing its most important source of strength, and that, in turn, would weaken its political position. The second was the inability of the Movement to confront the Kuwaiti regime and to continue political mobilization, in particular, since the regime was affected by the regional dynamic, especially in the Gulf, in the wake of the counterrevolutions. The third was the Movement's weakened influence within the circles of power and the sensitivity of its relationship with the ruling family.[49]

Islamists' experience and transformations and the subsequent political and intellectual repercussions can be considered one of the main historical milestones that launched Hadas into a number of revisions which led to:

1. **Dealing with the "deep state"** through understanding its historical, political, and social dimensions when it became clear to the Movement that its interaction with regional transformations and their resulting consequences should not go beyond the nature of the political system in Kuwait, which made the political reality a fundamental and regulating criterion in its management of politics. Abdulrahman Abdul Ghafour, a leading member of Hadas, said that the choice to reconstruct its stance on the limitations of the political reality and the problems therein should take the place of unbalanced political conflict. He added that "using the Movement's fragile sources of power to confront forces of the deep state in a critical transition phase will inevitably lead to failure."[50] According to the use of the term among some members of Hadas,[51] their definition of "deep state" resembles that of Patrick H. O'Neil,[52] who points to the components of this concept, such as guardianship, as one of its manifestations of the deep state's distrust in the ability of the government, state, or society to protect the homeland. Thus, actors within the deep state justify their actions taken against the government, society, and the state on the grounds that they are necessary to defend the homeland and the national identity in the face of "traitors." The amorphous nature of the deep state is accompanied by the belief that its members are "the beating heart of the nation."[53]

2. **Separating the religious from the political** came as the result of a series of reasons, the first of them being the Movement's electoral decline in the 2009 parliamentary elections, as well as its monitoring of the experiences of other Islamist parties, in particular, the Justice and Development Party of Morocco.[54] The separation was announced in 2014 at the offices of the Social Reform Society before a number of leaders of the Society and Hadas.[55] Attention should be drawn to an important issue—the fact that this decision was not documented in an official statement, but through internal dialogues. Ali al-Kandari notes that "the failure to implement the decision to separate political activity from preaching is the result of the absence of a law that regulates the work of political movements in general in the State of Kuwait in the first place and the history of overlap between the two activities, which exceeded six decades, remains an influential factor in complete separation."[56]

It seems that the young generation in the movement is more inclined to break ties between preaching (*da'wah*) and politics, given their conviction that a lack of separation would lead the interference of *da'wah* priorities and propositions in political goals and trajectories. The separation between the political process and *da'wah* has become an organizational necessity because Islamist political movements can no longer integrate the two tracks precisely because of the introduction of the idea separating *da'wah* into the circle of political debates, which has ultimately affected the size of the community and popular support for Islamist movements.[57] In addition, a lack of separation between the two branches would pose a threat to *da'wah* work, considering that it is one of the most important sources of support for the political arm, and thus would be subject to investigation and prosecution. However, despite the conviction that overlap in the roles of the politician and the religious advocate is not feasible, the decision to separate *da'wah* from politics remains unclear and incomplete. This development will not appear on a mere theoretical basis; there is an urgent need to implement the separation and translate it on the ground. This will only occur if the Movement rejects the politicization of its *da'wah* work and the exploitation of its religious domain (including mosques, sermons, charity) for political interests. Talal al-Khader, an academic close to Hadas says,

> there is still a religious influence on the political work of the Movement and the separation between them has not been realized. Perhaps what happened in the last parliamentary elections (November 2016) is the best evidence of that. Membership in the Movement (the political arm) is not open to all and is subject to standards and conditions in which leaders of religious preaching (*da'wah*) work sometimes interfere.[58]

3. Transformations in political strategy and prioritization. Although the idea of an elected government, which was one of the most fundamental premises of political reform, gained the highest possible level of support during the "Dignity of the Nation" movement, it is no longer a priority. Ali al-Sanad says that if the Movement wants to strengthen its political position, it must focus more on the parliament than on participating in forming a government. He adds, "Even if we assume the declaration of political parties and elected government are realized, the Movement, despite its strength and readiness for this stage, should not run for office so as not to take on preexisting problems in the government."[59]

4. Change in political position was the result of constraints that made the Movement more pragmatic in its dealings with the ruling authority, as it became clear that continuing to confront the counterrevolution would lead to its eventual elimination. Osama al-Shaheen, a member of the Kuwaiti parliament and Hadas, said that "after the protest movements were attributed to the administration and management of Hadas, it was careful not to situate itself at the forefront of any political or parliamentary movement and not to lead any sit-ins or political confrontations. The relentless war against Islamist political movements has solidified the Movement's stance on this matter."[60]

Future Challenges

At the beginning of the era of political action, on November 16, 2011, a number of demonstrators and some members of the parliament from various political currents and groups of political activists gathered at the Al-Erada Square opposite the Kuwaiti parliament building in response to a corruption scandal involving millions of dinars in wire transfers. This was the main driver behind the popular protest that led to the dismissal of the former prime minister Nasser al-Muhammad al-Sabah, as mentioned earlier. At the end of this sit-in organized by the "Nahj" movement, the Kuwaiti political history experienced an important event that has had a sharp impact on the future of the political opposition: the break-in of a number of parliamentarians and some demonstrators, which was later known as the "Parliamentary Break-In" and known by others as the "The Storming of Parliament." It was not planned but occurred because police forces forbade those gathered at the sit-in at Al-Erada to return to their cars because they believed that the demonstrators would plant themselves in front of the house of the former prime minister Nasser al-Muhammad al-Sabah, which is located at the end of the same street as the parliament building, about three kilometers to the north.[61]

On July 8, 2018, the Kuwaiti Court of Cassation issued a ruling that sentenced two current members of the Kuwaiti Parliament, Jamaan al-Harbash (a member of Hadas) and Waleed Al-Tabatabaie (an independent Islamist), and former parliamentarians, most notably Muslim al-Barak Secretary General of the Popular Action Movement, to prison in terms that ranged from two to three-and-a-half years. The sentence came in response to the storming of National Assembly in November 2011.[62] The majority of those who were sentenced are currently outside Kuwait, which raises three possible scenarios:

1. The emir of Kuwait could grant them special clemency. In this case, former and current members would not be able to run for election to the Kuwaiti parliament for a period of five years once the pardon is granted. This could lead to internal divisions within some political currents and the formation of new political movements. This scenario may affect the future of Hadas by causing it to lose social power, particularly among the tribes that form the base of MP Jamaan al-Harbash's support in the second electoral district.
2. General or universal pardon, which can only be issued by law. Similar to an acquittal, a universal pardon would completely eliminate the crime, unlike the special clemency granted by the emir. Under this type of amnesty, the majority of political currents who boycotted the one-vote law would participate in the upcoming parliamentary elections.
3. In the absence of any kind of amnesty, the sentenced parliamentarians could remain outside of Kuwait. This might solidify the impetus for trends to form an opposition movement abroad, which would increase the congestion and complexity of the domestic political situation.

The aforementioned transformations experienced by Hadas, especially in its relationship with the regime, will determine its position on the "Parliamentary Break-In" issue. This will undoubtedly raise internal challenges related to the Movement's future and its political scale. This can be understood in the framework of the influential nature of hereditary rule on Islamist political movements in the State of Kuwait.

Conclusion

Hadas has faced several critical issues arising from the transformations of Islamism in the Arab Spring countries, both on political and social levels, which are still underway. However, the choice of adhering to the status quo rather than overstepping the bounds of the political and economic system and the social reality in the State of Kuwait played an instrumental role in reducing the number of risks that could affect its political range. As explained previously, the reasons for the Movement's access to resources of power lies within its harmonious relationship with the ruling regime. These resources were frozen for a period of time during the Arab Spring revolutions when the Movement transformed into a protest movement acting outside of the parliament.

Politically, the Movement's handling of changes in regional circumstances and their impact on local affairs evolved, as did its handling of the regime's behavior toward the protest movements. It can be said that political realism played an important role in the Movement's ability to protect itself from the counterrevolutionary wave, especially after its decision to participate in the parliament and refrain from leading protest movements. On the intellectual level, the Arab revolutions and the experience of the Islamists, whether during their rise or decline, did not contribute any new or significant development. This goes back to the Movement's sole preoccupation with the political realm and the weakness of the role of the intellectual compared to the role of the politician or the sheikh/Islamic advocate. There remains an intellectual dependence on the MB despite the uniqueness of the Movement's political activity and its organizational independence. This is due to the dominance of old ways of thinking over attempts at intellectual renewal and intergenerational differences, especially between the conservative-leaning generation that is less amenable to change (the generation of pioneers and founders) and the younger generation that seeks to develop the Movement's thinking and push it toward its own intellectual productivity. Hadas has evolved politically but is intellectually hesitant, and this, in itself, poses internal problems that have resulted in individual defections over the last ten years.

The revolutions of the Arab Spring did not only topple the regimes of Ben Ali and Mubarak. They also raised the question of change, renewal, and reform through different intellectual methods and visions among the majority of the political players in the Arab countries, especially among Islamist movements. This is one conclusion that was reached through interviews with some members of Hadas. Despite differences in interviewees' personal opinions, their responses

8. *Transformations of the Islamic Constitutional Movement in Kuwait*

raise new ways of thinking about the controversial relationship between the Islamist movement and the secular question and their positions on the civil state and democracy. But this intellectual revolution remains limited to the minds of individuals and does not reflect the official thinking of the movement.

Islamist political movements are no longer simply religious groups or preaching movements active only in the religious field. In fact, they have begun to have a significant presence in the political field, which has made them the focus of scholarly research. It is for this reason that this study aims to shed light on one aspect of Hadas' interaction with the political issue at the local and regional levels, and to explore the effects of this on the Movement's way of thinking. This discussion serves to answer the research questions initially posed by this study, which relate to how the Movement reacted to the revolutionary factor and its transformations, the factors and reasons that governed the way it dealt with the Islamist experience in the Arab Spring countries, and the revolutionary ramifications on the ideological and political splits within the Movement.

This raises important questions, and we invite interested researchers to answer them. These questions are: What are the reasons for the lack of unique, alternative thinking among the majority of Islamist political movements in the Arab Mashreq? How come these movements have the ability to achieve organizational independence without ideological independence? What is the impact of the nature of hereditary rule on these movements, especially in terms of their political behavior and thought?

Chapter 9

ISLAMISM, AUTOCRACY, AND REVOLUTION

THE MORAL BANKRUPTCY OF ERADICATIONISM

Abdelwahab El-Affendi

In an earlier comment on aspects of the 2011 Egyptian revolution, I recorded my reaction to what I described then as one of the "most gripping and revealing episodes" of that revolution. The reference was to "a surreal scene in which a disoriented leader of the Egyptian Muslim Brotherhood (Ikhwan) was trying to explain to Al Jazeera news channel why he happened to be talking to the newscaster from a borrowed mobile phone outside a prison in the middle of the desert." It was intriguing how that individual (a certain Mohammed Morsi) was so keen to stress that he and his colleagues did not break out of jail. In fact, he was practically offering to hand himself back to the police, on live television! However, he could not find anyone to talk to: the whole setup of the prison had disappeared.[1]

My judgment at the time was that the Brotherhood leadership had not yet grasped the reality of the revolution: the fact that the police state that had terrorized the group for over half a century had completely collapsed during the hours between late on the night of Thursday, January 27, when the group was rounded up, and the morning of Sunday, January 30, when Morsi made that bizarre phone call. Unaware of this, the dazed leaders were still gripped by the terror of any accusation of defiance against the reigning Mukhabarat.

This long and bitter experience with repression was no doubt vividly present in the minds of the stranded prisoners in front of the now-deserted jail in the middle of nowhere. Many have endured long jail terms and suffered torture. For decades, they have learned to play the game according to the rules the Mukhabarat has laid down: you do not challenge the regime openly, and you must endure the measured amounts of repression meted out to you stoically, and the regime would not go for the kill. When Essam El-Erian was woken up by his wife at 2 a.m. to be informed that the police had come for him, he recalled that this was the fifth time he had to receive such a visit since the big sweep of 1981, with the last being in January 2010. He had, in addition, been arrested twice at more civil hours, one in broad daylight in front of the Lawyers' Union headquarters in 2005 and another at dusk in 2009.

Fast forward two years almost to the day, and the whole episode appears in a new light, since this "jailbreak" was one of the main accusations used against Morsi, who later became Egypt's first democratically elected president, before being deposed in a coup in July 2013, in his trial on January 28, 2014. (Again, this is deliberately symbolic, since January 28, 2011 was the famous Day of Rage, which marked the first major turning point in the revolution.) During the trial, in which Morsi was one of 131 defendants (and in which he was sentenced to death), the prosecution alleged that the jailbreak was masterminded by a joint task force from Hamas and Hezbollah.[2] Apparently, the two militias discovered the detention location of Ikhwan leaders (who only found out about this themselves late on Saturday evening and had no way of communicating it to anyone). They were then able, within a few hours, to organize a joint military operation that managed to storm the jail, release all prisoners, and leave safely, undetected by the Egyptian authorities.

This fiction apart, the incident and its aftermath indicate the lengths to which the entrenched Mukhabarat state could go to maintain its grip on power. It also shows the extent to which the terror of Mukhabarat had influenced the way its victims reacted. In my initial comments on the Morsi incident, I have highlighted the latter point, judging the leaders to be too frightened of the brutal security apparatus to see things straight. However, it looks that this judgment may need to be reexamined in the light of the current vindictiveness of the resurgent Mukhabarat state.

Revisiting a "Jailbreak"

The details of the background story are now well known: the Ikhwan leaders were rounded up before dawn on what was dubbed the "the Friday of Rage" and sent to a state security detention center in a Western Cairo suburb. On Saturday, after a protest by the prisoners, they were driven ostensibly to be interviewed by state prosecutors. Instead, however, they were sent to Wadi al-Natroun prison on the edge of the desert, halfway between Cairo and Alexandria. That same night, a prison riot broke out. The Ikhwan detainees were not part of it, since they had been consigned to a separate part of the prison and were locked up in their cells at the time. After things quietened down in the morning, Ikhwan detainees were the only prisoners left, as the guards disappeared and all prisoners were able to escape. Some of the remaining prisoners dropped a mobile phone through the cell window, which the detainees used to summon local help. Volunteers, who included some of the other prisoners, helped break the cell doors and free them. Hence that strange phone conversation.[3]

The apparent internalized terror of the ubiquitous police state, displayed by these "accidental escapees," even as it was visibly disintegrating, is an incontrovertible fact of Egyptian political life. In fact, some authors regard it as a decisive factor in the "moderation" and increasing pragmatism of the Brotherhood.[4] It is of course understandable that the imprisoned leaders were unable to contemplate the eventuality of what was probably the most dramatic transformation any country in the world has witnessed in a space of forty-eight hours. Since the early 1970s, when the strict ban on the Brotherhood was gradually relaxed (but never formally lifted), the Brotherhood has virtually become the "other" of the Egyptian state. The Mukhabarat never trusted it, but it was highly dependent on it. This was first due to the deep crisis of identity experienced by the Mukhabarat state, which had to endure many shifts during and after the Nasserist era. Ikhwan was *the* enemy during the Nasserist period, but the Mukhabarat believed it had completely vanquished it. Following the formal ban on the movement in 1954 and the execution of six of its leaders the following year, the movement was deemed to have become history. Another crackdown in the mid-1960s prevented a very clumsy attempt at a revival.

No less significantly, the state has stolen Ikhwan's thunder and its clothes. The Nasserist regime was more anti-colonialist than Ikhwan, and its Arabism and anti-Zionism left the movement's pan-Islamism in pale shadows. Ikhwan prisoners even begged in 1956 to be permitted to fight in the Suez War. During that time, Nasserism viewed the conservative monarchies of the Arab region, and the residual Arab liberalism allied to them, as the main threat, especially since these forces enjoyed Western support, which Ikhwan did not. All this became history when the Mukhabarat was transformed in the few years following the crushing defeat in the June 1967 war with Israel. Arabism held its head in shame, and the conservative monarchies and the conservative forces in Egyptian and other Arab societies witnessed a resurgence. This had nothing to do with Ikhwan who were completely (physically and intellectually) out of the scene. However, formidable societal forces were at work, completely independent of formal Islamism. First, the emergence of Saudi Arabia as a resurgent conservative power, soon to be flush with oil cash from the early 1970s, radically changed the balance of political and intellectual power. Nasserism was on the defensive, while the radical Arab nationalists were at each other's throats in Iraq, Syria, and the Yemens, and sobering up in Algeria. The Saudis used Ikhwan and Islamism as foreign policy tools in the "Arab Cold War." This meant giving refuge to fugitives from the radical regimes, allowing them to publish and disseminate their work. Additionally, the Saudis helped republish many of the classical Islamic works, and these were widely available throughout the Arab world. Even in Egypt itself, the classical works were also being published by the state and sold at subsidized prices, in order to compete with the works of Islamists. The official religious establishment was also doing its bit.

In addition, powerful intellectual trends were beginning to have their impact around the Arab region. While Ikhwan was practically eliminated in Egypt from the mid-1950s, branches elsewhere remained active, including in Syria, Iraq, Sudan, and some Gulf countries like Kuwait. In addition, prominent independent intellectuals, such as Malek Bennabi in Algeria, Muhammad Baqir al-Sadr in Iraq, Sheikh Mohammed al-Ghazali in Egypt, began to produce widely influential Islamic texts. Coupled with this, popular clerics such as Sheikh Muhammad Mutawlli Sha'araoui in Egypt, used television to influence large audiences all over the Arab region, often with government encouragement. Television was also used by "born-again" Muslims, such as the Egyptian physician Mustafa Mahmoud, a former atheist who became a hugely influential proponent of a "modernist" Islamic worldview popular with the youth and secular audiences. To this was added an influential section of former left-wing intellectuals who began to promote a liberal

Islamist line. This included the journalist Muhammad Jalal Kishk, who wrote devastating and widely read indictments of the dominant secular nationalist trends against the background of the June 1967 defeat. Others included the former judge Tarek Elbechri, the lawyer Muhammad Said Al Awwa, and the literary critic Abdelwahab El-Messiri. The combined result was what Asef Bayat described as Egypt's "passive revolution," or Islamization without the state.[5]

Egypt also witnessed a powerful student protest movement from 1968, as the youth expressed their disillusionment with the regime, its rhetoric, and its disastrous performance. While the protests were largely secular in orientation, the student scene became the site of the widest "Islamist" revival in most of the Arab region from the late 1960s. One outcome of this was the emergence from the late 1960s of radical Islamist movements (such as Gama'a Islamiyya and Islamic Jihad). These were not splinter groups of Ikhwan, as the official narrative, supported by many analysts, has it, but the product of its eclipse. In particular, revulsion against the brutal tactics used to eradicate Ikhwan was directly responsible for the rise of violent extremist Islamist groups from the late 1960s. These groups accused Ikhwan of being too soft on a regime that had transgressed all boundaries of decency, arguing that violent confrontation was the only way to respond.[6]

Ironically, the success of the Egyptian regime in practically eradicating Ikhwan opened the door for developments that later came to be called the "Islamic revival," spearheaded mainly by student groups, but propped up by the many influences outlined earlier. These included the eclipse of rival trends, such as pan-Arabism, left-wing radicalism, and liberalism, in addition to the shift of the balance on the intellectual scene in favor of a virtual Islamic hegemony. The Mukhabarat had to contend with this radically shifting scene, at a time when it was itself facing internal turmoil. The June defeat led to recriminations, purges, and significant loss of morale and public standing for the Mukhabarat state, forcing it to adapt and tolerate open popular discontent. Before the crisis was over, the death of Nasser led to a power struggle ending in the triumph of Anwar Sadat and the elimination of the bulk of the stalwarts of the Mukhabarat state. As a result, the Mukhabarat was tasked with going to war against the very personnel and the ethos that gave it its distinct character. The problem was complicated when Sadat turned his back on Nasserist ideology and its brand of socialism, espousing a capitalist pro-Western approach. This culminated in the 1978 peace treaty with Israel, and a decisive turn against pan-Arabism. He also permitted Ikhwan to operate openly, but with constraints, and espoused an "Islamist" line, amending the constitution twice, first to make Islamic shari'a a source of legislation, and then *the* source of legislation.

In a supreme irony, Islamism began to shape the Mukhabarat state, first as a social reality, then as an ally, and finally as an enemy of choice. As Sadat began to assert his authority against the stalwart of the Nasserist regime, the enemy was redefined as the left and pan-Arabism, including the radical regimes in Iraq, Algeria, Libya, Syria, and South Yemen. After the Camp David accords with Israel, the PLO also joined this lineup. Islamists were tolerated and helped to uproot the left from universities and professional associations. Later, as radical violent Islamists began to challenge the regime, Ikhwan specifically were co-opted to

9. Islamism, Autocracy, and Revolution

counter their influence. However, Ikhwan were not that keen to cooperate after the Camp David accords, leading to a new crackdown. However, when Sadat was assassinated in 1981 by radical Islamists, his successor, Hosni Mubarak, took a softer line, even permitting Ikhwan to contest elections in 1984, albeit under the banner of an existing party. However, when it became clear that Ikhwan could win elections, the Mukhabarat again changed tactics and began to depict them as *the* enemy. Mubarak persistently informed his Western allies, whenever they pressed him on democracy and human rights, that democracy would certainly bring Islamists to power.[7]

It is also ironic that all the dictators in Arab countries affected by the popular uprisings (Bin Ali, Mubarak, Assad, Gaddafi, Salih) issued the same warning: "Islamists will take over if we go." These pre- and post-revolutionary claims were gratuitous propaganda for Islamists, portraying them as the most formidable popular force on the one side, and showing them as the only worthy enemy of despots on the other. This had the reverse influence on popular sentiments. It is clear in elections in Egypt, Tunisia, and Libya that the voters rewarded politicians who had been vocal in opposing the regimes, while punishing not only those close to the old regimes but also those who were not as vocal in opposition.

Islamists and the Revolution

This brings us back to the dual question of the role of the Islamists in the revolutions, and the impact of the revolutions on Islamists. The general wisdom as expressed in the bulk of treatment of the issue was that Islamists were not part of the revolution, at least not an important part. But then they became "free riders" who benefited from revolutions led by others. These claims are inaccurate for a number of reasons. First, the revolutions would not have occurred, let alone succeeded, without support from Islamists. Most important, without the effort Islamists in many countries (Yemen, Jordan, Palestine, Tunisia, Morocco, etc.) to build political coalitions, revolutions wouldn't have achieved their goals and toppled the despotic regimes. In Egypt, this was exemplified in the role Islamists played in building and sustaining the umbrella organization *Kefaya* from 2004. This effort was replicated in April 2010 in the setting up of the Egyptian Association for Change (EAC), headed by the former International Atomic Energy Agency chief and Noble Peace Prize laureate Mohamed ElBaradei. They did this jointly with other groups, such as the April 6 Youth Movement. In both cases, Ikhwan activists were as inconspicuous as possible but formed the backbone of the agitation, nevertheless.

The rounding up of the Ikhwan leadership before the Friday of Rage was a recognition by the government that Ikhwan support was crucial for the success of the protests. It also came one day after the leadership rejected a second warning not to take part in the ongoing protests. Three days before the January 25 protests were due to start, the Mukhabarat summoned Ikhwan leaders in the provinces, and warned them against taking part. This came shortly after the Ikhwan leadership, inspired by the Tunisian precedent, issued a statement incorporating ten demands the regime must address to avert a revolution.[8] These included lifting the state of emergency, holding new parliamentary elections, releasing all political prisoners, combating corruption, and reforming the political system. In the meantime, Ikhwan offered conditional support for the planned protests, even though one of its leaders, Al-Erian, was quoted by the *New York Times* on January 22 as hinting at nonparticipation.[9] In more explicit statements he gave to the Egyptian daily *Al-Dustur* on January 19, however, Al-Erian made it clear that the movement would not officially take part in the protests, but Ikhwan members were free to join.[10] He hinted at a "Tunisian scenario," adding that "conditions in Egypt were much worse." The movement warned the government of an impending revolution if reforms were not instituted, reproducing a remark by the movement's founder, Hassan al-Banna, which warned of "a revolution which would not be of our making, but one we could not prevent."[11] On the following day, the group issued a communiqué deploring what it called the regime's "threats and intimidation" to dissuade it from backing the protests, adding that the movement can but be "in the midst of the people," cooperating "in all activities that will bring the hour of freedom closer."

It is true that the Islamists appeared overcautious in their approach to politics, precisely because of the aforementioned cycle of repression.[12] This has meant that movements played a paradoxical role, being the most powerful and effective political opposition actor, but the least willing to initiate concrete action and take responsibility. However, caution is sometimes useful and desirable. During the January 2011 protests (and subsequent ones in Libya, Yemen, and Syria), Islamists managed to conduct themselves in an optimum manner: they participated effectively but kept their presence discreet enough so as not to alarm or overwhelm other partners nor provide credibility for the regimes' attempts to label this as "Islamist revolutions."

The Egyptian Islamist Scene

While the convergence of political developments and intellectual trends facilitated the consensus that made the Arab revolutions possible, the post-revolutionary competitive pressures undermined the solidarity against dictatorship. Again, Ikhwan appeared to be standing apart and seen as a threat by others, precisely because they appeared to be the most powerful and best organized. The first rift occurred over the constitution. Ikhwan backed the Military Council's plan of partial amendments to the constitution, to be endorsed in a referendum in March 2011. All other political forces wanted a totally new constitution. The fact that the referendum was held and endorsed the Ikhwan-Military Council option made the other groups even more wary. They demanded a postponement of the parliamentary elections, scheduled for September 2011, for fear that Ikhwan and other Islamists would win a majority. This became a serious cause for tensions.

Attempts to reassure rivals by announcing a new party, the Freedom and Justice Party, with a Christian as vice-president and avowed commitment to democracy

9. Islamism, Autocracy, and Revolution 123

did not satisfy the skeptics. The alarm of Ikhwan's rivals is justified in a sense. For if this movement could be described as "the most successful social and political movements in modern Arab history," in spite of having "lacked formal legal existence for six decades,"[13] then what can it do now that it is free for the first time?

The central problem stems from Ikhwan offering only assurances not to seek exclusive power, but not assurances about what to do in power. The pledge not to support a theocracy or a religious state, calling instead for a "civic state" (*dawla madaniyya*) with an "Islamic basis" (*marji'iyya Islamiyya*), remained difficult to pin down. However, in putting self-limits on its role in terms of shying away from assuming full political responsibility, the movement makes a public admission that its assumption of power would be disastrous for Egypt. Instead of offering credible and practical policies, it only sought to merely try to mitigate the impact of its admittedly problematic policies. The situation was exacerbated by the fact that the main competition to Ikhwan came from the even more conservative Salafis, who did not favor more accommodation with the secular-liberal opposition. The Salafis boast hundreds of thousands of supporters, but they do not have a unified leadership nor distinct organizations and programs. Rather, they congregate around prominent individuals or local centers, and coordinate their activities loosely.[14] The more radical Salafis caused more alarm as local groups engaged in their own battles: conflicts with the Coptic church (the most serious incident occurred in the popular Cairo suburb of Imbaba on May 8, causing eight deaths and over 100 injuries) or mounted attacks on Sufi shrines.

Still, Ikhwan had the primary responsibility of overcoming these difficulties. As "the largest, most popular, and most effective opposition group in Egypt,"[15] the movement's role became crucial for leading (or obstructing) the democracy drive.[16] Ideally, it should have tried to transform itself along the lines of similar movements in Turkey, Malaysia, Indonesia, Morocco, or even Tunisia. They worked to overhaul their programs to enable them to realistically undertake governing responsibilities.

Ironically, when Ikhwan's General Guide explained their (initial) decision not to field a presidential candidate, his justification was that they did not want to repeat the Hamas experience and put Egypt under international sanctions because of a premature installation of an Islamist government. However, the movement changed its mind and fielded a candidate who won unexpectedly. But that was not the problem as much as the way the new president conducted himself in office. He managed to alienate former allies and seemed to confirm Ikhwan's critics' worst fears about the group's authoritarian tendencies.

Sleepwalking into Disaster?

The Egyptian revolution (and to a lesser extent, its Tunisian precedent) succeeded in large part because of a combination of Islamist pragmatism and disillusionment among the secular opposition with the regimes that claimed to be their protectors. Islam, and the political forces associated with agitation for its public role, did not

124   *Islamism and Revolution Across the Middle East*

disappear from the public arena because of this consensus. Only their role was transformed. The more radical and conservative Islamist forces were conspicuous by their absence during the protests, while the mainstream Islamists merged seamlessly into the broader democratic revolutionary trend. This was seen by some as a confirmation that Egypt (and the Arab world) was finally witnessing a "post-Islamist turn," similar to that experienced in Iran in the late 1990s, "where pious sensibilities are able to incorporate a democratic ethos."

> The growth of such "post-Islamism" out of the anomalies of Islamist politics represents an attempted fusion of elements hitherto often seen as mutually exclusive: religiosity and rights, faith and freedom, Islam and liberty. The daring logic is to turn the underlying principles of Islamism on their head by emphasising rights instead of duties, plurality in place of a singular authoritative voice, ambiguity instead of certainty, historicity rather than fixed scripture, and the future instead of the past.[17]

For the "post-Islamist generation," which launched the revolution, "the great revolutionary movements of the 1970s and 1980s are history—something that mattered to their parents but not to them. This new generation is not interested in ideology."[18] This may be an overstatement of the case. While the term "post-Islamist" is useful in trying to capture a condition that cannot be adequately covered by other terms such as "secular" or "Islamic liberal," its application has been plagued with confusion and contradictions. The significance of what happened in Egypt, and to some extent in Iran, Turkey, and elsewhere, is that the phenomenon in question did not coincide with a decline in religiosity; quite the reverse, in fact. The countries in question have become much *more* Islamic in countless ways. However, as Roy himself noted, "the paradox" of this process of extensive and intensive Islamization is that "the very success of the Islamic revival has largely de-politicized Islam."[19] In this regard, it is not exactly the case that the revolutionaries of Arab squares have taken secularism as a given; they have, rather, taken Islam as a given.

> It is not that Islam has receded in importance, it is simply that it has become one of the realities to deal with, without being either the solution or the cause of all the ills of the Arab world. In other words, it has been de-problematized.[20]

I had earlier suggested the term "trans-Islamic" to refer to the Arab revolutions to avoid the confusions and to register the fact that they have moved beyond the Islamist problem. One has to just observe Tahrir Square to note how almost everybody joined the prayers, while those who did not (mostly Christians) felt no awkwardness about it. For protesters from Tunisia through Egypt, and later Libya, Yemen, Bahrain, and Syria, the big protests were organized on Fridays, with mosques as starting points. Islam was everywhere and nowhere. It was no longer an issue. Democracy, and how it could be achieved and sustained, became the main concern.

However, while specific Islamist themes are not a bone of contention, this does not mean that new lines of polarization around threatened identities could not

9. Islamism, Autocracy, and Revolution

be drawn. They have now, and the charge is that Islamists are using the popular mandate they have received to change the rules of the game and rig them in favor of Islamist hegemony. The disintegration of the Arab Spring coalition brought Islamism back to the center of political life.

Post-Post-Islamism

Islamism was brought to the center of things before the Arab Spring, as we have seen, because of internal cultural and sociopolitical dynamics. In one of his few perceptive comments, Bernard Lewis noted in his famous article "The Return of Islam" that the salience of Islam in Middle Eastern political life was linked to the entry of the masses into politics. As colonialism was replaced by national governments, and as more locals became involved in politics, Islamic themes gained prominence.[21] One important point highlighted in Lewis's article, though not articulated directly, was that the involvement of the masses in politics was due to incitements, such as Bourguiba's attempt to abolish fasting in Ramadan in the early 1960s and the Syrian regime's blatant attack on Islam in the spring of 1967.

Emerging secular Arab regimes made Islam a central state concern, cracking down on Islamist or conservative groups, and meddling in the affairs of local religious establishments. During the Arab Cold War, Islam also became an issue, since the conservatives used religion as a tool in their fight against secularists, forcing the latter to make an extra effort to prove their religious credentials. At a later stage, with the Islamic revival and the ascendancy of Islamist trends, most regimes reacted violently against certain groups, tried to play the religious card, or did both. This made Islam a central issue, even when the aim was banishing it. For example, when regimes try to ban women headscarves, they inevitably politicize an issue that would normally pertain to private life. Similarly, when regimes constantly broadcast anti-Islamist propaganda, they make difficult to remove the issue from the agenda. This is especially the case when the argument is that "Islamist" groups are not "really Islamic." This promotes endless conversations about what is really Islamic and what is not, a conversation in which the regimes and their supporters are at a disadvantage. When the same regimes are known to be corrupt, brutal, uncaring, and incompetent, the continuous barrage of attacks on Islamists becomes virtual praise.

However, the post-Arab Spring period, a new dimension entered the game. During the earlier period, the leading secular actors in the postcolonial era were heroes of national liberation (Ataturk, the Algerian FLN, Bourguiba, Yemeni Socialist party), or champions of reconstruction and anti-imperialism (Nasser, Gaddafi, Assad, Saddam). They promoted rival ideologies of Arabism, socialism, or liberalism; advocated national programs of rebuilding and development; had grand schemes for change; etc. However, the emerging coalition of the pan-Arab counterrevolution has no agenda other than defeating Islamism and blocking any path to democratization. The two goals are interlinked: those fearing democracy, such as Saudi Arabia and its allies, fear that Islamists are the only force that can

126   *Islamism and Revolution Across the Middle East*

challenge absolutism; those fearing Islamism, as in Egypt, warn that democracy would open the way to Islamist triumph. Those fearing both, as in Syria, have an easier argument to make. However, none has a positive agenda of national liberation, liberalism, social justice. The brutal methods they adopt, the silencing of free debate, and with it the shameless promotion of lies, is the epitome of moral bankruptcy. Here, we have patrimonial regimes with the narrowest of bases, with no redeeming factors.

The Egyptian regime exemplifies this model, becoming an epitome of what the UNDP's 2004 Arab Human Development Report dubbed the "black hole state." It started by a claim that it wanted to end the hijacking of the Egyptian state by Islamists, and promising to restore democracy. It went on to crack down not only on the Islamists but also moved on to punish and destroy many of the political forces that supported its anti-Islamist crackdown. They then proceeded to close down the public space, taking total control of the media and silencing voices even on the social media. Then it began attacking civil society groups and charities, including health and educational charities. Now even minor dissent from the military or civilian forces is not tolerated.

It is not clear how such a morally bankrupt agenda can replace and vanquish Islamism, or for that matter, any other ideology or approach. It does not offer a viable alternative, and its propaganda incessantly promotes Islamism as its ethically challenged media keeps blaming all good deeds on Islamists. Even Obama and Hilary Clinton were dubbed Ikhwanis by that media because they were not as enthusiastic as they were expected about the acts of the new regime. As mentioned earlier, this turns the label "Islamist" paradoxically into a badge of honor.

The fact that the regimes are also deeply corrupt, with economic and social policies working to the disadvantage of the impoverished majority, while generously rewarding those manning the brutal state repression apparatus (the military, security, police, judiciary, prison guards, etc.), is also likely to generate popular anger. The crackdown on the health charities and schools formerly run by Ikhwan sympathizers has already generated popular anger, as beneficiaries of those services are beginning to complain.[22] Thus anti-Islamism becomes a virtual war on existing Muslim communities, a form of internal colonization, where the nation is not trusted to rule itself and has to remain under some form of "guardianship." In this sense, the regimes align themselves with foreign interests hostile to the people and their aspirations, as can be seen in the way in which the regimes leading the counterrevolution tend to be more sympathetic toward, and trusting of, the current extreme right-wing regime in Israel. The media in those countries now openly voice contempt and hatred for the Palestinians, as they express admiration for Israel. Even during the colonial era, nothing like this happened.

The Identities of Insecurity

Initially, the apparent explanation for this identity shift and hostility toward democracy and Arab-Muslim values could be explained in terms of an intense sense of insecurity that gripped sections of the political spectrum (liberal, secular, left wing) following the shock of witnessing the overwhelming support Islamist groups enjoyed in the post-Arab Spring contests. In despair, the otherwise fragmented opposition began to unite and enlist the support of remnants of the "ancient regime" to undermine the new democratic order. Thus, the judiciary began to play a proactive role in the contests to shape the new political order, dissolving elected parliaments, other elected assemblies, and bodies. It later became the repressive arm of the new dictatorships, sometimes more so than the security forces.

Islamists also felt a deep insecurity, as rumors of plots to overthrow the elected government through concerted judicial moves began to circulate, and later proved true. One consequence was the most serious political polarization to date. The secular-Islamist rift was paralleled (or reinforced) by other divides: sectarian, ethnic, regional, national, etc. The language of all sides attained a shrill tone of mutual demonization, creating an atmosphere of virtual civil war. The polarization in Tunisia was less sharp, but still palpable. Here, the defining moment was the murder of Chokri Belaid, a leading figure in the opposition in February 2013. The shock led to the fall of the Islamist-led government and raised tensions to a dangerous level. The Islamist-secularist polarization operates along multiple dividing lines, some self-reinforcing and others mitigating. Islamism was originally constructed around narratives of insecurity (around threats to Islamic identity, threats of foreign domination, threats to the moral fabric of society, etc.). Unlike their secular rivals, however, Islamist groups were simultaneously tight-knit intimate groups and mass organizations. In this regard, they were impacted not only by perceptions of the threats mentioned earlier but also by threats to the organizations themselves. This sense of threat took a new dimension in the light of bitter and prolonged experiences with brutal persecution. But there are other dimensions to the identity alignments. As some analysts have noted, a class dimension is present as well, with the more "conservative" Islamists (including the Muslim Brotherhood) aligned with the classes benefiting from the new oil wealth, while the more radical groups representing the poorer and marginalized classes.[23] Regional identities also played a part (for example, Upper Egypt versus the more affluent cities to the north).

Sectarianism also plays a part. Islamist groups, both Sunni and Shia, tend to pursue religious "purity," which entails hostility to all forms of heterodoxy, and consequently the exclusion of groups associated with it. Again, this ties in with ethnicity and nationalism. It is thus often difficult to disentangle claims associated with varieties of radical Islamism and of identities such as Pashtun, Arab, Persian, and Najdi. Thus, many Saudi Salafis would see defending Najdi identity and Salafi radicalism as interchangeable, and so it is with Taliban and Pashtun identity or Sudanese Islamists and "Arab" Sudanese identity.[24] At another level, since Islamism is focused on the insecurity generated by foreign influences, their hostility to outsiders can transfer to local non-Muslims and secular groups, which in turn can lead to some form of "sectarian" confrontation. In this regard, it is extremely interesting (and revealing) how the intensifying sectarian confrontations in

Syria, Bahrain, and now Iraq has influenced the political debate and shaped its parameters, and not only among the Islamists. For example, two prominent Syrian intellectuals, Sadik Al Azm and his compatriot and (former) close friend, the poet Adonis, have sharply different views on the Syrian revolution. It was an interesting coincidence that an English translation of Al Azm's 1968 *Self-Criticism After the Defeat* came out in 2011, just as the Arab revolutions erupted.[25] At that time, he was still friends with Adonis and recalled how the two experienced the 1967 war and its aftershocks.[26] Both men called for a radical overhaul of Arab culture, which they held responsible for the defeat and backwardness. A clean break was needed with the past. For Al Azm, the model to be followed was Russia after the defeat in the war with Japan in 1905: a revolution that would sweep the slate clean and start history anew. For Adonis, the need was for a comprehensive overhaul of the Arab culture, which has not happened, as all revolutions and reform initiatives have only scratched the surface. As a consequence, the fragile new cultural contributions are threatened by being absorbed into the old system. As things stand, Arab intellectuals, including "progressive" intellectuals, are governed by "tribal" loyalty to party, sect, or similar groups, and lack independence and the capacity to innovate. Most are also co-opted by the state or are silenced by fear. So only a radical break with this situation would bring the desired change.[27] When the Syrian revolution erupted, however, Al Azm and Adonis parted ways, with the former backing the revolution and the latter opposing it. Some of Adonis's more sober critics argue that his stance was not surprising, given that he had become (in spite of his critiques of the conformism of Arab intellectuals) "fully integrated into the Arab cultural establishment," writing his columns in Saudi-owned media without uttering a word of criticism of the Gulf monarchies. Instead, he has taken to rehashing "stale Orientalist notions about 'the Arab mind' and reduces the complex problems and challenges facing the Arab world to the need for a reinterpretation of religion." As a result, he "sadly sounds like a fusion of Bernard Lewis and Irshad Manji."[28]

Facing the Arab revolutions, Adonis concentrated on invoking the fear of a takeover of "moderate Islam" and reiterated that he would never take part in protests that started in mosques. He also failed to condemn the brutality of the Syrian regime or salute the courage of its unarmed victims, instead stalking the fears of the Islamist alternative. No prodding from his friends would convince him to make a clear and principled stance, and in fact, his interventions tended to be worse than silence. Not only did they reproduce "the obligatory Orientalist canard about the Arabo-Islamic fusion of religion and politics, and claims like: 'Politically, Arabs have never known democracy in their modern history, nor in their ancient history,'" but, in fact, also his rhetoric "dovetails with the regime's propaganda as it tries to delegitimize the protests and demonize the protesters."[29]

There was another twist to this interesting debate. Adonis, who happened to come from a Shiite background, was accused of committing another of his list of cardinal sins: acting in a "sectarian" and "tribalist" way, rather than the progressive intellectual he claims to be. However, these accusations occasioned a counterattack from Adonis sympathizers. In particular, Al Azm, who hails from the Syrian Sunni

9. Islamism, Autocracy, and Revolution 129

"aristocracy," became a target. Again, these exchanges uncovered another angle to this convoluted debate, since one of the attackers, As'ad AbuKhalil of California State University, Stanislaus, happens to be a disciple of Said and says that the latter had never forgiven Al Azm for his "treacherous" attacks on him. AbuKhalil launched a bitter diatribe against Al Azm, starting from branding his critiques of the Arab culture "crass orientalism" and accusing him of silence in the face of the Syrian regime's excesses in the past, trading on his critiques of Said to get in the good books of the American establishment. He also branded Al Azm's insinuation of sectarian motives to Adonis as in itself sectarian, since it was clear that the so-called revolutions in the Arab world were being supported by the autocratic regimes in the Gulf.[30]

We note here how accusations of sectarianism and "Orientalism" are traded by both sides in this debate. Issues touched upon area in relation to petrodollars and the media also figure here, as does the ubiquitous threat of Islamism. However, the central issue remains the increasingly intense polarization along self-reinforcing identity lines. In the Syrian case, the sectarian dimension remains the primary dividing line, backed up by narratives of anti-imperialism and anti-fundamentalism. In these narratives, the untold suffering of the Syrian people and the multiple atrocities visited on them are brushed out of the story. To observe how these self-contained narrative communities evolve around these identity fault lines, one has to follow the comments on the web page of AbuKhalil's article, most of which are laudatory, with additional vitriolic attacks on Al Azm and his "treachery," but no mention at all (let alone a condemnation) of the atrocities being committed in Syria! Interestingly, one comment chastised AbuKhalil for mentioning the Holocaust: "Why do you have to pester us with the Holocaust in every article?" this individual protested. "It is not our fault," he fumed, "and in any case the Jews were complicit in it." So it is not only current atrocities in Syria that are a nuisance to this particular audience. For these impervious "sectarian" (in a generic sense of the term) communities, those on the other side do not exist as human beings: their voices are not heard and do not deserve to be, their suffering does not register, no cost is too high to achieve their annihilation, and complete subjugation is desirable. For we are not dealing with human beings here, but with evil terrorists or deluded agents of imperialism and its local "petrodollar" agents.

It is ironic that, even internationally, these atrocities do not seem to register. Millions of Syrians have been driven from their homes, and over half a million killed. Hundreds of thousands more are missing, or languishing in jails, suffering grievous torture. However, the international community does not seem to bother. Similarly, in Egypt, tens of thousands (may over a hundred thousand) Ikhwan affiliates and sympathizers and their families are in jail or in exile, with over 2,000 killed or tortured to death. However, when there is an international outcry, it is usually over the death of an Italian student, or the arrest of a couple of famous human rights activists. "Sectarianism" has been internationalized. It is naïve to believe that this would not have serious political consequences for the countries concerned, or the world. Organizations like ISIS and Al-Qaeda do not come from nowhere.

Conclusion

The "miracle of Tahrir Square" as the transformation of a whole people into a self-governing entity has been achieved only at the price of some groups deciding to become quasi-invisible. Particularistic identities and divisive loyalties (sectarian, ethnic, religious, political, etc.) had to take backstage as a condition for this unilateral "declaration of independence" by the people, constituting itself as a *demos* and defining its identity in terms of being Egyptian (Tunisian, etc.) and being free. In this process, Islamist groups and other marginalized entities were able to emerge from claustrophobic isolation and become part of a broader movement.[31] However, where divisive identity prematurely emerged on the scene and tried to assert specific demands before an agreed democratic framework of action could be put in place, the habitual fracturing of democratic coalitions could be observed. Worse still, where these identities refused to go away (as was the case in Syria and Bahrain), the *demos* failed to materialize. Instead, a civil war with the objective of mutual annihilation erupted and continues to rage.

Elsewhere, we have characterized this as an "autoimmune condition," where the "body politics" is at war with itself, turning its defensive mechanisms against the body itself, rather than toward alien bodies attacking it. In the sharply polarized "sectarian" debates, integral parts of the political community (often the majority) are *made* invisible, written out of the narrative, in preparation for actual annihilation. This is, needless to say, a far cry from choosing to be invisible by choice, through blending in. A number of strategies are needed to remedy such situations. At one level, the exclusivist rhetoric of demonization and annihilation, together with the attendant lowering of the threshold of tolerance to brutality and atrocities, must be condemned and rejected unequivocally. On the other hand, the insecurities of those who feel threatened by the apparently unstoppable Islamist ascendancy, or fear sectarian exclusion or oppression, need to be addressed. Islamists have a bigger responsibility toward producing a discourse and programs that would disarm anti-democratic actors who want to use the "Islamist menace" to stop democratization, even removing it as an option. It might sound strange to demand from the victims of current brutal oppression to be the ones giving assurances to those who have been committing atrocities against them for decades. But as the case of South Africa shows, sometimes the burden falls on the victims to save their tormentors from themselves. One of the ironies of the current situation is the unbreakable link made, by the resurgent autocratic regimes no less, between Islamism and democracy. Regardless of the hesitancy of Islamists toward committing to democracy, the proponents of the counterrevolution treat the two as one interlinked threat. Islamists challenge autocrats and thus pave the way for democratization, while democracy is most likely to empower Islamists. It is now imperative for Islamists to take this link seriously and commit unequivocally to democracy. There are many lessons that could be learned from history, mainly about what not to do. In 1952, Ikhwan alienated other groups by accepting the status of the only political group exempted from the dissolution of political parties decreed by the military regime. When they overplayed their cards, causing the

9. Islamism, Autocracy, and Revolution

regime to turn against them, they did not find many sympathizers. During the early phases of the revolutions, most Arab political actors, including Islamists, managed to hit the right formula for concerted and well-coordinated *peaceful* political action. Since then, that magical formula has been lost, and we are back to antagonistic politics of the worst kind. It is time to go back to Tahrir Square, as it was in January–February 2011.

No less important is the lesson about the futility of attempted genocide, or in this case, politicide. Arab (and Turkish, Iranian, and Soviet) regimes have spent decades trying to banish Islam from politics (and in the Soviet case, from life as a whole). These efforts did not banish Islam or weaken Islamic forces. Quite the reverse, in fact. By exposing the brutal regimes as politically and morally bankrupt, they have become a living advertisement for the virtues of Islamism. In the current phase, the character of the anti-Islamist, anti-democracy coalition makes it manifestly unable to offer an alternative, moving the region toward anomie and a gaping moral and political vacuum. When you have regimes that constantly lie, murder, torture, and disappear citizens, do not permit freedom of speech and association, have no political credibility and do not even seek it, what argument do you have against ISIS and other rogue groups? More importantly, how long can states survive before collapsing into failure and chaos?

It is not without significance to recall that the choice of January 25 (National Police Day) as the day to launch the protests was a reminder that this day commemorated the 1952 defiant stance by the police against British forces in the Suez Canal town of Ismailiyah. That was not the whole story, however. The following day witnessed the Great Cairo Fire, when the whole of the capital erupted into violent riots. Many buildings and establishments associated with Western interests, or the lifestyle of the westernized elite, were torched. These included cinemas, nightclubs, and posh hotels. The riots brought the army onto the streets and made it easy for Nasser and his Free Officers to organize their July coup. But the events remain a salutary lesson about what could go wrong with popular anger. It was not just the wanton self-destructiveness and the uncontrolled rage that could be a cause for concern, but the ease with which the prospect of chaos could be exploited by those who want to impose yet more tyranny.

NOTES

Chapter 1

1 Olivier Roy, "There Will Be No Islamist Revolution," *Journal of Democracy*, 24, no. 1 (2013): 14.
2 See, for example, Ziad Munson, "Islamic Mobilization: Social Movement Theory and the Egyptian Muslim Brotherhood," *Sociological Quarterly*, 42, no. 4 (2001): 487–510; Carrie Rosefsky Wickham, *Mobilizing Islam: Religion, Activism, and Political Change in Egypt* (New York: Columbia University Press, 2002); Quintan Wiktorowicz, ed., *Islamic Activism: A Social Movement Theory Approach* (Bloomington: Indiana University Press, 2004).
3 See, for example, Mohammad M. Hafez, *Why Muslims Rebel: Repression and Resistance in the Islamic World* (Boulder: Lynne Rienner, 2003); Jillian Schwedler, *Faith in Moderation: Islamist Parties in Jordan* (Cambridge: Cambridge University Press, 2006).

Chapter 2

1 Carrie Rosefsky Wickham, *Mobilizing Islam: Religion, Activism and Political Change in Egypt* (New York: Columbia University Press, 2005), p. 208.
2 In January 2004, Mohamed Mahdi Akef was chosen to be the Brotherhood's seventh General Guide (*al-Murshidal-A'm*). Akef was a veteran Brotherhood leader who was arrested and imprisoned for twenty years under Nasser. After being the Brotherhood's General Guide, Akef issued a political reform initiative in March 2004, which was considered the Brotherhood's first comprehensive political platform since its return to politics in 1970. For more, see, "Mubadrat Jam'at al-Ikhwan al-Muslimīn al-Iṣl'ḥ fī Maṣr," *Al Jazeera Arabic* (The Initiative of the Muslim Brotherhood in Egypt), March 4, 2004, http://www.aljazeera.net/specialfiles/pages/a7d9e130-0f09-4b77-bbb0-ee07dd61afd3
3 For example, see, Khalil al-Anani, *The Muslim Brotherhood: A Gerontocracy Fighting against Time?* (Cario: Shorouk Bookstore, 2007).
4 For example, see, Samer Shehata and Joshua Stacher, "The Brotherhood Goes to Parliament," *Middle East Report,* no. 240 (Fall 2006): 32.
5 Nathan Brown, "When Victory Becomes an Option: Egypt's Muslim Brotherhood Confronts Success," *The Carnegie Papers* (January 2012): 4.
6 The Brotherhood ran in elections under the umbrella of the Democratic Alliance, which included, in addition to the FJP, other new and small parties such as Ghad Al-Thawra Party, Labor Party, Al-Islahwal-Nahda Party, Al-Hadara Party, Al-Islah Party, Al-Geel Party, Misr Al-Arabi Al-Ishtiraki Party, Al-Ahrar Party, and Al-Horiyyawal-Tanmiya Party. For more, see, "Egypt's Brotherhood Wins 47% of Parliament Seats," *Egypt Independent,* January 21, 2012, http://www.egyptindependent.com/news/egypts-brotherhood-wins-47-parliament-seats

7 For a detailed account on the Brotherhood's 2007 platform, see, for example, Abdel Monem Said Aly, "Understanding the Muslim Brothers in Egypt," *Middle East Brief,* no. 23 (December 2007).

8 It is worth mentioning that the FJP was banned by a court ruling on August 10, 2014.

9 Yasmine Saleh, "Muslim Brotherhood Says It Won't Force Islamic Law on Egypt," *Reuters,* May 30, 2011, http://blogs.reuters.com/faithworld/2011/05/30/muslim -brotherhood-says-it-wont-force-islamic-law-on-egypt/

10 "Muslim Brotherhood: 'We Are Not Seeking Power,'" *CNN,* February 10, 2011, http:// www.cnn.com/2011/WORLD/africa/02/09/egypt.muslim.brotherhood/

11 Brown, "When Victory Becomes an Option," 3.

12 Kristen Chick, "In Major Reversal, Muslim Brotherhood Will Vie for Egypt's Presidency," *Christian Science Monitor,* April 1, 2012, http://www.csmonitor.com/ World/Middle-East/2012/0401/In-major-reversal-Muslim-Brotherhood-will-vie-for -Egypt-s-presidency

13 Noha El-Hennawy, "Brotherhood Contests over 50 Percent of Parliamentary Seats," *Egypt Independent,* October 25, 2011, http://www.egyptindependent.com//news/ brotherhood-contests-over-50-percent-parliamentary-seats

14 David F. Gordon and Hani Sabra, "The Muslim Brotherhood's Dangerous Missteps," *Reuters,* April 11, 2012, http://blogs.reuters.com/great-debate/2012/04/11/the-muslim -brotherhood%E2%80%99s-dangerous-missteps/

15 Tom Perry, "As the Government-in-Waiting, Egypt's Muslim Brotherhood Finds Its Voice," *Reuters,* February 28, 2012, http://blogs.reuters.com/faithworld/2012/02/28/as -the-government-in-waiting-egypts-muslim-brotherhood-finds-its-voice/

16 Hasan al-Banna, "The Tract of the Fifth Annual Meeting," in *Majmou't Rass'l al-Imam Hasan al-Banna* (A Collection of Hasan al-Banna Tracts) (Cairo: Dar Al-Da'wa for Printing, Publishing and Distributing, 2002).

17 al-Anani, *The Muslim Brotherhood,* 65.

18 al-Banna, "The Tract of the Fifth Annual Meeting," 65.

19 Interview by the author with Salah Ghorab, a middle-level leader in the Brotherhood, December 24, 2010, Cairo, Egypt.

20 Abigail Hauslohner, "Has Egypt's Muslim Brotherhood Staged a Coup against the Military?," *Time,* August 12, 2012, http://world.time.com/2012/08/12/has-egypts -muslim-brotherhood-staged-a-coup-against-the-military/

21 Nathan Brown, "Egypt's Constitution Conundrum: The Good, the Bad, and the Unruly in Cairo," *Foreign Affairs,* December 9, 2012, http://www.foreignaffairs.com/ articles/138495/nathan-j-brown/egypts-constitution-conundrum

22 Aya Batrawy, "Egypt's President Praises Police Despite Criticism," *Associated Press,* March 15, 2013, http://bigstory.ap.org/article/egypts-president-praises-police-despite -criticism

23 In 1996, a group of the middle generation of the Brotherhood, spearheaded by Madi and Sultan, rejected the rigid and ambiguous ideology of the Brotherhood and called for internal change. They called for establishing a political party for the Brotherhood; however, the movement's leadership aborted their attempt, which led them to leave the movement and establish the "al-Wasat Party." For more on the al-Wasat Party, see, for example, Carrie Rosefsky Wickham, "The Path to Moderation: Strategy and Learning in the Formation of Egypt's Wasat Party," *Comparative Politics Journal,* 36, no. 2 (January 2004): 205–28; al-Anani, *The Muslim Brotherhood.*

Notes   135

24 For more details on different factions and generations within the Brotherhood, see, for example, Khalil al-Anani, "al-Ikhwan al-Muslimīn fi Maṣr yukasaroon al-muhẓūrāt wa al-shuyūkh la yaktarathūna," *Al-Hayat*, November 23, 2007.

25 Ezzat left Egypt after the July 3 coup and it is believed that he, along with Mahmoud Hussien, the secretary general of the Brotherhood, and Mahmoud Ghozlan, the Brotherhood's former spokesperson, are playing an important role in leading the Brotherhood from exile.

26 El-Shater was arrested two days after the July 3 coup and has been accused of killing nine people and injuring many others outside the Brotherhood's headquarters in Cairo in March 2013, as well as joining a militant group and inciting violence and espionage in tandem with Hamas.

27 The Shura Council has 108 members and is responsible for selecting the 16 members of the Guidance Bureau and the General Guide.

28 Noha El-Hennawy, "Political Freedom, Competition Drives Rifts between Muslim Brotherhood Factions," *Egypt Independent*, March 24, 2011, http://www .egyptindependent.com//news/political-freedom-competition-drives-rifts-between -muslim-brotherhood-factions-0

29 "In Egypt, Youth Wing Breaks from Muslim Brotherhood," *The New York Times*, June 22, 2011, http://www.nytimes.com/2011/06/23/world/middleeast/23egypt.html

30 For example, see, Edmund Blair, Paul Taylor, and Tom Perry, "How the Muslim Brotherhood Lost Egypt," *Reuters*, July 25, 2013, http://www.reuters.com/ article/2013/07/25/us-egypt-mistakes-specialreport-idUSBRE96O07H20130725

31 Another account reveals the details of the voting environment and how it was conducted. According to Gehad al-Haddad, a young leader and spokesperson for the Brotherhood, the Guidance Bureau was against the presidential nomination. Al-Haddad stresses that the young Brotherhood members lobbied for the decision and had put pressure on the Shura Council members in order to vote for nominating al-Shater. He states, "We literally lobbied. We put up a chart of the Shura council members and decided which ones to pressure to change their vote." For more, see, Edmund Blair, Paul Taylor, and Tom Perry, "How the Muslim Brotherhood Lost Egypt," *Reuters*, July 25, 2013, http://www.reuters.com/article/2013/07/25/us-egypt -mistakes-specialreport-idUSBRE96O07H20130725

32 Interview by the author with Ahmed Shehata, April 5, 2012, Zagazig, Egypt.

33 Marc Lynch, "The Muslim Brotherhood's Presidential Gambit," *Foreign Policy*, April 1, 2012, http://www.foreignpolicy.com/posts/2012/04/01/the_muslim_brotherhoods _presidential_gambit

34 Fahmy Howeidy, "Waq ū fi al-fakh," *Shorouk Newspaper*, April 1, 2012, http://www.shorouknews.com/columns/view.aspx?cdate=01042012&id=2c3ddfd1 -beb9-4e7e-9d23-f800997fa7d7

35 Interview by the author with Mohamed Mustafa, head of one of the Brotherhood's local offices (*shu'ba*), March 25, 2012, Zagazig, Egypt.

36 During Morsi's tenure, his political opponents floated the notion of "brotherhoodization" of the state (*akhwant ad-dawlya*), an idea that was amplified by the anti-Brotherhood media in order to intensify public suspicions toward the Brotherhood.

37 On July 8, 2013, around fifty-one Brotherhood supporters were killed and hundreds more were injured in front of the Republican Guards' club. For more, see, Patrick Kingsley, "Killing in Cairo: The Full Story of the Republican Guards' Club Shootings,"

The Guardian, July 18, 2013, http://www.theguardian.com/world/interactive/2013/jul /18/cairo-republican-guard-shooting-full-story

38 On August 14, 2013, Egypt's security forces, backed by the military, gunned down more than 800 protesters of the Brotherhood's members and supporters who were in a sit-in at Rab'a al-Adawiyya and al-Nahda Squares. According to Human Rights Watch, these massacres were "the most serious incident of mass unlawful killings in modern Egyptian history."

For more, see, "According to Plan: The Rab'a Massacre and Mass Killing of Protesters in Egypt," *Human Rights Watch*, August 12, 2014, http://www.hrw.org/sites /default/files/reports/egypt0814web_0.pdf

39 There are no generally agreed upon figures for the number of political prisoners in Egypt since the July coup, but different sources place the number to be somewhere between 16,000 and 41,000; most of these come from Morsi supporters. For instance, unnamed government officials told the Associated Press in March 2014 that security forces detained at least 16,000 people, including approximately 3,000 top- or mid-level members of the Muslim Brotherhood. For more, see, Hamza Hendawi, "Egypt crackdown Brings Most Arrests in Decades," *Associated Press*, March 16, 2014, http:// bigstory.ap.org/article/egypt-crackdown-brings-most-arrests-decades. However, according to WikiThawra, an initiative run by the Egyptian Center for Economic and Social Rights, this number is closer to 41,000 people.

For more, see, "ḥuṣr al-maqabūḍ 'lihum wa al-mulāḥaqīn qaḍayatan khilāl al-ʿhida al-sīsī," *WikiThawra*, January 9, 2014, http://wikithawra.wordpress.com/2014 /01/09/sisi-mansour-detainees/

40 Louisa Loveluck, "Egypt Court Bans Muslim Brotherhood, Eliminating Its Critical Social Services," *The Christian Science Monitor*, September 23, 2013, http://www .csmonitor.com/World/Middle-East/2013/0923/Egypt-court-bans-Muslim -Brotherhood-eliminating-its-critical-social-services-video

41 "Egypt to Take Over Banned Muslim Brotherhood Assets," *BBC*, October 3, 2013, http://www.bbc.com/news/world-middle-east-24391796

42 Erin Cunningham, "Egypt's Military-Backed Government Declares the Muslim Brotherhood a Terrorist Organization," *The Washington Post*, December 25, 2013, http://www.washingtonpost.com/world/middle_east/egypts-military-backed -government-declares-muslim-brotherhood-a-terrorist-organization/2013/12/25 /7cf075ca-6da0-11e3-aecc-85cb037b7236_story.html

43 Many of the Brotherhood's senior officials and members fled to Qatar after the coup. However, some of these figures had to leave Doha after intensive pressure from other Gulf countries, particularly the United Arab Emirates (UAE) and Saudi Arabia. For example, see, Ian Black, "Qatar-Gulf Deal Forces Expulsion of Muslim Brotherhood Leaders," *The Guardian*, September 16, 2014, http://www.theguardian .com/world/2014/sep/16/qatar-orders-expulsion-exiled-egyptian-muslim -brotherhood-leaders

44 Stéphane Lacroix, "Saudi Arabia's Muslim Brotherhood Predicament," *The Washington Post*, March 20, 2014, http://www.washingtonpost.com/blogs/monkey -cage/wp/2014/03/20/saudi-arabias muslim-brotherhood-predicament/

45 Michael Peel, Camilla Hall, and Heba Saleh, "Saudi Arabia and UAE Prop Up Egypt Regime with Offer of $8bn," *The Financial Times*, July 10, 2013, http://www.ft.com/ intl/cms/s/0/7e066bdc-e8a2-11e2-8e9e-00144feabdc0.html#axzz3EuE4te5U

46 Andrew Critchlow, "Saudi and UAE Ready $20bn Boost for Egypt's El-Sisi," *The Telegraph*, June 1, 2014, http://www.telegraph.co.uk/finance/newsbysector/

banksandfinance/10868522/Saudi-and-UAE-ready-20bn-boost-for-Egypts-El-Sisi
.html

47 Fayed, 2016, https://www.brookings.edu/wp-content/uploads/2016/07/Ammar-Fayed
-RPI-Response-English-FINAL.pdf.

48 According to several human right reports, extrajudicial killing and forced
disappearance have become a common practice by Egyptian security forces,
particularly against Islamists. Also, mass death sentences against the Brotherhood's
leaders and members has become a norm in Egypt. For human rights abuses, see, for
example, https://www.hrw.org/news/2014/06/09/egypt-new-leader-faces-rights-crisis
and for extrajudicial killings in Egypt, see, https://www.washingtonpost.com/
world/middle_east/since-trumps-mideast-visit-extrajudicial-killings-have-spiked-in
-egypt/2017/08/30/62bf48c0-8200-11e7-9e7a-20fa8d7a0db6_story.html?utm_term=
.8ba842b703a2 and http://www.bbc.com/news/av/world-middle-east-35610351/
human-rights-groups-warn-of-extrajudicial-killings-in-egypt. Also, according to
the Brotherhood's official English website, Egypt's security forces extrajudicially
killed 135 members of the movement between January and June 2017, http://www
.ikhwanweb.com/article.php?id=32757

49 On August 14, 2013, Egypt's security forces, backed by the military, killed more than
800 protesters of the Muslim Brotherhood's members and supporters who were in
a sit-in at the Rabi'a al- 'Adawiyya and Nahda Squares. According to Human Rights
Watch, these massacres were "the most serious incident of mass unlawful killings in
modern Egyptian history." For more, see Human Rights Watch, "According to Plan:
The Rab'a Massacre and Mass Killing of Protesters in Egypt" (August 2014), www.hrw
.org/sites/default/ les/reports/egypt0814web_0.pdf

50 *Washington Post*, July 12, 2013. https://www.washingtonpost.com/world/mohamed
-morsis-supporters-muslim-brotherhood-protest-across-egypt/2013/07/12/96cb887c
-eb19-11e2-a301-ea5a8116d211_story.html

51 The National Alliance to Support Legitimacy was established a few days before the
coup by eleven Islamist parties and aimed to endorse President Mohamed Morsi and
counterbalance the calls for the June 30 protests. Among these parties in the alliance
were the Brotherhood's Freedom and Justice Party (FJP), Al-Wasat Party, Al-Gamaa
Al-Islamiyya's Construction and Development Party, and the Salafi Al-Watan Party.
However, many of these parties have withdrawn from the alliance owing to its failure
in achieving its objectives, http://english.ahram.org.eg/NewsContent/1/64/75145/
Egypt/Politics-/-Islamist-parties-launch-Legitimacy-Support-allian.aspx

52 For a detailed account on the anti-coup protests in Egypt, see Neil Ketchley, *Egypt
in a Time of Revolution: Contentious Politics and the Arab Spring* (Cambridge:
Cambridge University Press, 2017).

53 Ketchley, *Egypt in a Time of Revolution*, 142.

54 Schams Elwazer, "Egypt Court Bans Brotherhood Activities," *CNN*, September 23,
2013, http://edition.cnn.com/2013/09/23/world/africa/egypt-muslim-brotherhood/
index.html

55 Interview by the author with Abdurrahman Youssef, an Egyptian journalist who
covered the Brotherhood and other Islamist movements in Egypt until 2015, April 24,
2014, Washington, DC.

56 Al-Masry Al-Youm, September 30, 2013. https://today.almasryalyoum.com/article2
.aspx?ArticleID=398521&IssueID=3004

57 Al-Masry Al-Youm, November 27, 2013. https://today.almasryalyoum.com/article2
.aspx?ArticleID=404737&IssueID=3062

Notes

58 Ironically, the designation of the Muslim Brotherhood as a terrorist organization was political and not by a court ruling. The designation decision was issued by Hazem El-Beblawy's government and was declared by the Deputy Prime Minister Hossam Essa. To watch Essa's video, see https://www.youtube.com/watch?v=R -F5MSD2LUM and "Egypt Designates Muslim Brotherhood Terrorist Organization," *Reuters,* December 25, 2013, https://www.reuters.com/article/us-egypt-explosion -brotherhood-idUSBRE9BO08H20131225

59 Interview by the author with Mustafa, November 25, 2017.

Chapter 3

1 Shadi Hamid, *Temptations of Power: Islamists and Illiberal Democracy in a New Middle East* (Oxford: University Press, 2014).

2 Jillian M. Schwedler, "Can Islamists Become Moderates? Rethinking the Inclusion-Moderation Hypothesis," *World Politics: A Quarterly Journal of International Relationsi,* 63, no. 2 (2011): 348.

3 Khalil al-Anani, "Islamist Parties Post-Arab Spring," *Mediterranean Politics.* 17, no. 3 (2012): 468.

4 Frédéric Volpi, and Ewan Stein, "Islamism and the State after the Arab Uprisings: Between People Power and State Power," *Democratization,* 22, no. 2 (2015): 276–93.

5 Tarek Chamkhi, "Neo-Islamism after the Arab Spring: Case Study of the Tunisian Ennahda Party," (Masters by Research thesis), Murdoch University, 2015.

6 Ibid.

7 Mohammed Ayoob, *The Many Faces of Political Islam: Religion and Politics in the Muslim World* (Ann Arbor: University of Michigan Press, 2010), 2.

8 Robin Wright, *The Islamists Are Coming: Who They Really Are* (Washington, DC: Woodrow Wilson Centre Press, 2011, 2012), 9.

9 Rachid Ghannouchi, *Public Liberties in the Islamic State* (Tunis: Almojtahed Publishing House, 2011).

10 Olivier Roy, *The New Islamists. Foreign Policy*, April 16, 2012, http://www .foreignpolicy.com/articles/2012/04/16/the_new_islamists

11 Asef Bayat, *Post-Islamism: The Many Faces of Political Islam* (Oxford: Oxford University Press, 2013).

12 Ennahda, 2016, http://congres10.ennahdha.tn/ar

13 Chamkhi, "Neo-Islamism after the Arab Spring."

14 Hamid, *Temptations of Power*; Hamid, 2017, https://www.amazon.com/Rethinking -Political-Islam-Shadi-Hamid/dp/0190649208

15 Al-Anani, "Islamist Parties Post-Arab Spring," 467.

16 https://data.worldbank.org/indicator/NY.GDP.MKTP.CD?locations=ZQ

17 Hamid, *Temptations of Power,* 6.

18 https://www.aljazeera.com/features/2011/10/27/who-are-tunisias-political-parties

19 https://carnegieendowment.org/2014/04/30/can-secular-parties-lead-new tunisia -pub-55438

20 ICG, 2013, https://d2071andvip0wj.cloudfront.net/tunisia-violence-and-the-salafi -challenge.pdf

21 Alaya Allani, "The Islamists in Tunisia between Confrontation and Participation: 1980-2008," *The Journal of North African Studies* 14, no. 2 (2009): 257–72.

Notes

22 Anne Wolf, *Can Secular Parties Lead the New Tunisia?*, 2014, http://m.ceip.org/2014/04/30/can-secular-parties-lead-new-tunisia/h9mn&lang=en

23 ICG, 2013.

24 Michele Penner Angrist, "Understanding the Success of Mass Civic Protest in Tunisia," *The Middle East Journal*, 67, no. 4 (2013): 547–64.

25 Angrist, "Understanding the Success of Mass Civic Protest in Tunisia," 547–64.

26 Francesco Cavatorta, and Fabio Merone, "Moderation through Exclusion? The Journey of the Tunisian Ennahda from Fundamentalist to Conservative Party," *Democratization*, 20, no. 5 (2013): 857–75.

27 Ibid, 857

28 Ibid.

29 Hamid, *Temptations of Power*, 8.

30 Cavatorta and Merone, 862.

31 Angrist, "Understanding the Success of Mass Civic Protest in Tunisia," 562.

32 Cavatorta and Merone, 863.

33 Burhanettin Duran, "The Fall of Ikhwan and the Future of Ennahda," 2013, http://setav.org/en/the-fall-of-ikhwanand-the-future-of-ennahda/opinion/12130; Feldman, "Tunisia's Government Falls, Arab Democracy Is Born," 2013, http://www.bloombergview.com/articles/2013-09-30/tunisia-s-government-falls-arab-democracy-is-born

34 Wolf, *Can Secular Parties Lead the New Tunisia?* 7.

35 Ibid.

36 Rachid Channuchi, *Secularism and the Relation of Religion to the State from the Perspective of Al-Nahdha Movement* (Tunis, Tunisia: Centre for the Study of Islam and Democracy, 2012).

37 Cavatorta and Merone, "Moderation through Exclusion? The Journey of the Tunisian Ennahda from Fundamentalist to Conservative Party."

38 Ibid., 874.

39 Ibid.

40 Ibid.

41 Ibid.

42 https://www.youtube.com/watch?v=IVZVP0uLOLQ

43 https://www.youtube.com/watch?v=FOP3uDQdnnU

44 John Voll, Peter Mandaville, Steven Kull, and Alexis Arieff, "Political Islam in the Arab Awakening: Who Are the Major Players?" *Middle East Policy*, 19, no. 2 (2012): 10–35.

45 Cavatorta and Merone, "Moderation through Exclusion? The Journey of the Tunisian Ennahda from Fundamentalist to Conservative Party," 862.

46 Olivier Roy, "There Will Be No Islamist Revolution." *Journal of Democracy*, 24, no. 1 (2013): 14–19; Hamid, *Temptations of Power*.

Chapter 4

1 Anouar Boukhars, "Morocco's Islamists: Bucking the Trend?," *FRIDE*, June 2014, 6.

2 Mohammed Masbah, "Rise and Endurance: Moderate Islamists and Electoral Politics in the Aftermath of the 'Moroccan Spring,'" in Hendrik Kraetzschmar and Paola

140   *Notes*

Rivetti, *Islamists and the Politics of the Arab Uprisings: Governance, Pluralisation and Contention* (Edinburgh: Edinburgh University Press, 2018).

3 "Morocco's Stability in the Wake of the Arab Spring," Combating Terrorism Center at West Point, May 23, 2013, https://ctc.usma.edu/moroccos-stability-in-the-wake-of -the-arab-spring/.

4 Nathan J. Brown, *When Victory Is Not an Option: Islamist Movements in Arab Politics* (Ithaca, NY: Cornell University Press, 2012).

5 Francesco Cavatorta and Fabio Merone, "Moderation through Exclusion? The Journey of the Tunisian *Ennahda* from Fundamentalist to Conservative Party," *Democratization,* 20, no. 5 (August 2013): 857–75, https://doi.org/10.1080/13510347 .2013.801255.

6 Marina Ottaway Hamzawy Amr, "Islamists in Politics: The Dynamics of Participation," *Carnegie Endowment for International Peace,* 2008, http:// carnegieendowment.org/2008/12/11/islamists-in-politics-dynamics-of-participation -pub-22540.

7 Hendrik Kraetzschmar and Paola Rivetti, *Islamists and the Politics of the Arab Uprisings: Governance, Pluralisation and Contention*; Quinn Mecham and Julie Chernov Hwang, *Islamist Parties and Political Normalization in the Muslim World* (Philadelphia: University of Pennsylvania Press, 2014), http://www.upenn.edu/ pennpress/book/15245.html.

8 "Adaptation Strategies of Islamist Movements," POMEPS Studies (The Project on Middle East Political Science [POMEPS], April 2017), https://pomeps.org/2017/04/27 /adaptation-strategies-of-islamist-movements/.

9 Khalil al-Anani, "Understanding Repression-Adaptation Nexus in Islamist Movements" *in,* "Adaptation Strategies of Islamist Movements," POMEPS Studies (The Project on Middle East Political Science [POMEPS], April 2017).

10 Khalil al-Anani, *Inside the Muslim Brotherhood: Religion, Identity, and Politics* (New York, NY: Oxford University Press, 2016).

11 Avi Spiegel, "Succeeding by Surviving: Examining the Durability of Political Islam in Morocco," *The Brookings Institution,* August 2015, 16.

12 Matt Buehler, "Safety-Valve Elections and the Arab Spring: The Weakening (and Resurgence) of Morocco's Islamist Opposition Party," *Terrorism and Political Violence* 25, no. 1 (January 2013): 137–56, https://doi.org/10.1080/09546553.2013.733274.

13 Mohamed Masbah: au Maroc, "Benkirane and the King are Interdependent," *JeuneAfrique.com* (blog), June 5, 2015, http://www.jeuneafrique.com/233835/ politique/mohamed-masbah-au-maroc-benkirane-et-le-roi-sont-interd-pendants/. [in French]

14 Intissar Fakir, "Morocco's Islamist Party: Redefining Politics Under Pressure," Carnegie Endowment for International Peace, https://carnegieendowment.org/2017 /12/28/morocco-s-islamist-party-redefining-politics-under-pressure-pub-75121, accessed April 22, 2018.

15 Quinn Mecham, "A Government of the Opposition: How Moroccan Islamists' Dual Role Contributes to their Electoral Success," *in* "Adaptation Strategies of Islamist Movements."

16 "His Royal Majesty's Speech to the Nation on the Draft of the New Constitution," Maroc.ma, March 26, 2013, http://www.maroc.ma/ar/%D8%A7%D9%84%D8%AE %D8%B7%D8%A7%D8%A8-%D8%A7%D9%84%D8%B3%D8%A7%D9%85%D9 %8A-%D8%A7%D9%84%D8%B0%D9%8A-%D9%88%D8%AC%D9%87%D9%87- %D8%AC%D9%84%D8%A7%D9%84%D8%A9-%D8%A7%D9%84%D9%85%D9

%84%D9%83-%D8%A5%D9%84%D9%89-%D8%A7%D9%84%D8%A3%D9%85
%D8%A9-%D8%AD%D9%88%D9%84-%D9%85%D8%B4%D8%B1%D9%88%D8
%B9-%D8%A7%D9%84%D8%AF%D8%B3%D8%AA%D9%88%D8%B1-%D8%A7
%D9%84%D8%AC%D8%AF%D9%8A%D8%AF/%D8%AE%D8%B7%D8%A7%D8
%A8%D8%A7%D8%AA-%D9%85%D9%84%D9%83%D9%8A%D8%A9. [in Arabic]

17 The Moroccan Constitution, Chapters 41–59, The Official Journal, no. 5964, July 30, 2011. [in Arabic]

18 The Moroccan Constitution, Chapter 47, The Official Journal, no. 5964, July 30, 2011. [in Arabic]

19 Mohammed Masbah, "Palace Edges Ahead in Morocco's Constitutional Power Struggle," *Chatham House*, March 24, 2017, https://www.chathamhouse.org//node /28707.

20 Mustafa al-Khalfi, Representative of Morocco, "We Chose Reform Under Stability," AlJazeera.net, September 12, 2014. [in Arabic]

21 Driss Maghraoui and Saloua Zerhouni, "Searching for Political Normalization: The Party of Justice and Development in Morocco," in *Islamist Parties and Political Normalization in the Muslim World* (Philadelphia: University of Pennsylvania Press, 2014), 112–33, http://www.jstor.org/stable/j.ctt6wr8hs.8.

22 Bruce Maddy-Weitzman and Daniel Zisenwine, *Contemporary Morocco State, Politics and Society under Mohammed VI*, Routledge Studies in Middle Eastern Politics (London and New York: Routledge, 2017).

23 Mohamed Kareem Bokhsas, "Hidden Information in the Relations Between the Palace and Islamic Leaders," Jaridat al-Ayam, edition 7971, March 15, 2018. [in Arabic]

24 Al-Aoual website, *Two Hours with Benkirane... Facts That Reveal HIS Relationship with the King and His Surroundings for the First Time*, 2016, https://www.youtube.com /watch?v=BN1bquwV2zA. [in Arabic]

25 "Oukfir and the Left Criticize Minister Yatim for 'Love of Being a Minister,'" https:// www.hespress.com/orbites/361169.html, accessed on May 3, 2018. [in Arabic]

26 Author's interview with Abdellah Baha, Rabat, Summer 2011.

27 Abdel Latif Hida, "Background: After Benkirane's Dismissal, the PJD has No Choice but the Opposition," *Akhbar Alyom*, March 16, 2017, http://www.alyaoum24.com /847001.html?fbrefresh=2. [in Arabic]

28 Author's interview with a member of the secretariat of the Justice and Development Party, Meknes, August 2018.

29 Tarek Benhada, "Al-Ramid: There May Be Unknown Reasons for Morocco's Decision to Dismiss Benkirane," *Hespress*, March 18, 2017, https://www.hespress.com/politique /343267.html. [in Arabic]

30 Mohamed Marouf, "Morocco: Benkirane's Second Government, 38 Ministers including 5 Women and 16 New Members," *Al-Quds Al-Araby*, October 11, 2013, http://www.alquds.co.uk/?p=92463. [in Arabic]

31 "Boanu: Ministry of the Interior Accedes to Control in Unconstitutional Electronic Recording," *Al-'Amq al-Maghrebi*, July 13, 2016, https://al3omk.com/105255.html. [in Arabic]

32 Abdelilah Benkirane, The King Warned of Electoral Fraud and Said to Him «I will not let you go», *AlYom*, October 5, 2016, http://www.alyaoum24.com/730863.html ?fbrefresh=7. [in Arabic]

33 Lakome2, "Benkirane and the King's 'Bootlickers,'" 2016, https://www.youtube.com/ watch?v=WlkSy6ps5rU. [in Arabic]

34 Al-Aoual website, "Two Hours with Benkirane... Facts that Reveal His Relationship with the King and His Surroundings for the First Time," 2016, https://www.youtube .com/watch?v=BN1bquwV2zA. [in Arabic]

35 Al-Aoual website, "This Is How Benkirane's Conversation with AlAoual Made the King Angry with Him," AlAoual (blog), July 29, 2016, http://alaoual.com/politique /30283.html. [in Arabic]

36 "Morocco: Mohammed VI Unhappy with Abdelilah Benkirane," *JeuneAfrique .com*, July 20, 2016, http://www.jeuneafrique.com/mag/342177/politique/maroc -mohammed-vi-mecontent-a-lencontre-dabdelilah-benkirane/. [in French]

37 "Maroc."

38 "The Royal Chamber: The Recent Statement by Mr. Nabil Benabdallah Is Nothing but a Means of Political Deception in an Election Period That Requires Refraining from Making Unfounded Statements," Maroc.ma, September 14, 2016, http://www .maroc.ma/ar/%D8%A7%D9%84%D8%AF%D9%8A%D9%88%D8%A7%D9%86- %D8%A7%D9%84%D9%85%D9%84%D9%83%D9%8A-%D8%A7%D9%84D8 %AA%D8%B5%D8%B1%D9%8A%D8%AD-%D8%A7%D9%84%D8%A3%D8%AE %D9%8A%D8%B1-%D9%84%D9%84%D8%B3%D9%8A%D8%AF-%D9%86%D8 %A8%D9%8A%D9%84-%D8%A8%D9%86%D8%B9%D8%A8%D8%AF-%D8%A7 %D9%84%D9%84%D9%87-%D9%84%D9%8A%D8%B3-%D8%A5%D9%84%D8 %A7-%D9%88%D8%B3%D9%8A%D9%84%D8%A9-%D9%84%D9%84%D8%AA %D8%B6%D9%84%D9%8A%D9%84-%D8%A7%D9%84%D8%B3%D9%8A%D8 %A7%D8%B3%D9%8A-%D9%81%D9%8A-%D9%81%D8%AA%D8%B1%D8%A9- %D8%A7%D9%86%D8%AA%D8%AE%D8%A7%D8%A8%D9%8A%D8%A9-0. [in Arabic]

39 Alayame24, "The Possible Resignation of Nabil Benabdallah from the Secretariat of Progress and Socialism!" October 8, 2016, http://www.alayam24.com/articles-29324 .html. [in Arabic]

40 "'Control' Missing from Benkirane's Speech... Message Received." *Hespress*, September 27, 2017, https://www.hespress.com/politique/322220.html. [in Arabic]

41 Obeid Abeed, "Why Did Al-Ramid Back Away from Seizing the Opportunity to Announce the Preliminary Results of the October 7 Election?" *Akhbar Al-Youm*, October 8, 2016, http://www.alyaoum24.com/734417.html?fbrefresh=7. [in Arabic]

42 Abdelilah Benkirane, "The Conversation Is Over," *Website of The Justice and Development Party*, January 8, 2017, http://pjd.ma/الكلام-انتهى-كيران-ابن/الاخبار. [in Arabic]

43 "Benkirane: I Was on the Verge of Giving My Resignation to the King," *AlJazeera.net*, March 26, 2017, http://www.aljazeera.net/home/Getpage/f6451603-4dff-4ca1-9c10 -122741d17432/157df8cb-3d02-4f3d-a836-c6c3dee31c34. [in Arabic]

44 Bokhsas, "Hidden Information in the Relations Between the Palace and Islamic Leaders."

45 Mohamed El Hachimi, "Democratization as a Learning Process: The Case of Morocco," *The Journal of North African Studies*, 20, no. 5 (October 20, 2015): 754–69, https://doi.org/10.1080/13629387.2015.1081463.

46 Eva Wegner, "The Inclusion of Islamist Movements into the Political Institutions: The Case of the Moroccan 'Party of Justice and Development'" (Thesis, 2006), http:// cadmus.eui.eu//handle/1814/5429.

47 Esen Kirdiş, "Between Movement and Party: Islamic Movements in Morocco and the Decision to Enter Party Politics," *Politics, Religion & Ideology*, 16, no. 1 (January 2, 2015): 65–86, https://doi.org/10.1080/21567689.2015.1012159.

48 Abdelali Hamidine, "From Preaching Group to Ruling Party: A Reading of the Experience of the Moroccan Justice and Development Party," *Arab Reform Initiative*, 2016, https://www.arab-reform.net/ar/node/980. [in Arabic]

49 Suveyda Karakaya and A. Kadir Yildirim, "Islamist Moderation in Perspective: Comparative Analysis of the Moderation of Islamist and Western Communist Parties," *Democratization*, 20, no. 7 (December 2013): 1322–49, https://doi.org/10.1080/13510347.2012.696612.

50 Vish Sakthivel, "Justice and Development Party," *Oxford Islamic Studies Online*, February 10, 2016, 5.

51 Abdelrahim AlSheikhy, "For Unification and Reform, the Relationship between Preaching and Politics One of Differentiation," June 11, 2016, http://www.alislah.ma/%D8%A3%D8%AE%D8%A8%D8%A7%D8%B1/%D9%85%D8%B3%D8%AA%D8%AC%D8%AF%D8%A7%D8%AA-%D8%A7%D9%84%D8%AD%D8%B1%D9%83%D8%A9/%D8%B4%D9%8A%D8%AE%D9%8A-%D9%84%D9%84%D9%85%D8%B3%D8%A7%D8%A1-%D8%A7%D9%84%D8%B9%D9%84%D8%A7%D9%82%D8%A9-%D8%A8%D9%8A%D9%86-%D8%A7%D9%84%D8%AF%D8%B9%D9%88%D9%8A-%D9%88%D8%A7%D9%84%D8%B3%D9%8A%D8%A7%D8%B3%D9%8A-%D8%B9%D9%86%D8%AF-%D8%A7%D9%84%D8%AA%D9%88%D8%AD%D9%8A%D8%AF-%D9%88%D8%A7%D9%84%D8%A5%D8%B5%D9%84%D8%A7%D8%AD-%D8%B9%D9%84%D8%A7%D9%82%D8%A9-%D8%AA%D9%85%D8%A7%D9%8A%D8%B2. [in Arabic]

52 Ahmed Mansour, "The Islamist Movement in Morocco," *Without Bounds* (Al Jazeera Channel), September 1, 2012, http://www.aljazeera.net/home/Getpage/0353e88a-286d-4266-82c6-6094179ea26d/d5cddf38-96dc-4a65-9425-8ab7a57e918a. [in Arabic]

53 The Moroccan Constitution, Chapter 7, The Official Journal, July 29, 2011. [in Arabic]

54 "Rabat June 30, 2003: The Text of His Majesty's speech to the nation on the occasion of the fourth anniversary of the ascension to the throne," http://www.habous.gov.ma/2012-01-26-16-08-52/8791-الرباط-30-يوليوز-2003-نص-خطاب-جلالة-الملك-إلى-الأمة-بمناسبة-الذكرى-الرابعة-لاعتلاء-العرش.html, accessed March 23, 2018. [in Arabic]

55 Saadeddine Othmani, *Religion and Politics: Distinction, Not Separation* (Arab Cultural Center, 2009). [in Arabic]

56 Ibid.

57 Saadeddine Othmani, Conversation with Saadeddine Othmani, Secretary General of the Moroccan Justice and Development Party, *Carnegie Endowment for International Peace*, August 28, 2008, http://carnegieendowment.org/sada/21686?lang=ar. [in Arabic]

58 Mohammed al-Kokhi, "Moroccan Islamists and the Failure to Transition Beyond the Islamist Movement," Al Jazeera Center for Studies, February 4, 2018, http://studies.aljazeera.net/ar/reports/2018/02/180201114201277.html. [in Arabic]

59 "Benkirane to 'al-Hurra': WE DO NOT BELONG to the Muslim Brotherhood and We Are Not a Religious Movement," Al Hurra Channel, https://www.alhurra.com/a/moroccan-prime-minister-benkiran-muslim-brotherhood-egypt-/255300.html, accessed March 26, 2018. [in Arabic]

60 Mohammed Masbah, "Morocco and Lessons Learned from Egypt," *Carnegie Endowment for International Peace*, August 28, 2013, http://carnegieendowment.org/sada/52781. [in Arabic]

61 "Sisi welComes Benkirane and the Upcoming Arab Summit in Morocco," *Ar.Le360. Ma,* March 29, 2015, http://ar.le360.ma/politique/40073. [in Arabic]

62 "Meeting between Sisi and Benkirane Causes a Stir Among Activists on Facebook," *Sasa Post,* March 31, 2015, http://www.sasapost.com/elsisi-and-binkiran/. [in Arabic]

63 Sanae El Mellouki, "The Infusion of Islam into Pluralistic Politics: The Need to Explore the Islamist Identity beyond Ideological Boundaries – The Case of the Moroccan Party of Justice and Development," *Discourse & Society,* 26, no. 6 (November 2015): 662–81, https://doi.org/10.1177/0957926515592778.

64 Mellouki, "The Infusion of Islam into Pluralistic Politics."

65 "Morocco Agrees to UN Decision to Protect Freedom of Religion and Faith," *Hespress,* https://www.hespress.com/societe/171201.html, accessed April 5, 2018. [in Arabic]

66 "Al-Ramid: International Authorities Do Not Exceed National Authorities," Website of the Justice and Development Party, January 14, 2018, http://www.pjd.ma/%D8%A7 %D9%84%D8%A7%D8%AE%D8%A8%D8%A7%D8%B1/%D8%A7%D9%84%D8 %B1%D9%85%D9%8A%D8%AF-%D8%A7%D9%84%D9%85%D8%B1%D8%AC %D8%B9%D9%8A%D8%A7%D8%AA-%D8%A7%D9%84%D8%AF%D9%88%D9 %84%D9%8A%D8%A9-%D9%84%D8%A7-%D8%AA%D8%B3%D9%85%D9%88- %D8%B9%D9%84%D9%89-%D8%A7%D9%84%D9%85%D8%B1%D8%AC%D8 %B9%D9%8A%D8%A7%D8%AA-%D8%A7%D9%84%D9%88%D8%B7%D9%86 %D9%8A%D8%A9. [in Arabic]

67 Faraj Ismail, "Benkirane to 'Arabiya.Net': If We Wanted to Fail, We Would Force Women to Wear the Head Coverings," *Arabiya.Net,* November 27, 2011, https://www .alarabiya.net/articles/2011/11/27/179365.html. [in Arabic]

68 Emanuela Dalmasso and Janine A. Clark, "State Actor-Social Movement Coalitions and Policy-Making Under Authoritarianism: The Moroccan Party of Justice and Development in the Urban Municipality of Kenitra," *Middle East Law and Governance,* 7, no. 2 (August 31, 2015): 185–211, https://doi.org/10.1163/18763375 -00702001.

69 Author's interview with leaders of the Justice and Development Party, January 2017.

70 Author's interview with leaders of the Justice and Development Party, Ramadan 2016.

71 Amr al-Jabari, "President of the Resigning Parliamentary Group of Moroccan Fundamentalist 'Justice and Development Party' Alludes to Outside Actors Behind His Resignation," *Al-Sharq al-Awsat,* October 27, 2003, 9099 edition, http://archive .aawsat.com/details.asp?issueno=8800&article=199907#.WuspnS-ZPVo. [in Arabic]

72 "Belkoura: My Dismissal from Meknes Was Political," Website of the Justice and Development Party, *Pjd.Ma,* November 21, 2013, http://www.pjd.ma/node/12501. [in Arabic]

73 "What Is Behind the Arrest of Elected Islamist Jama Al-Mu'tasim?" *Unity and Reform Movement,* January 13, 2011, http://www.alislah.ma/%D8%A3%D8%AE%D8%A8 %D8%A7%D8%B1/%D8%A3%D8%AE%D8%A8%D8%A7%D8%B1-%D9%88%D8 %B7%D9%86%D9%8A%D8%A9/17499. [in Arabic]

74 Bokhsas, "Hidden Information in the Relations Between the Palace and Islamic Leaders."

75 "Benkirane Is Called a 'Modernist' and Guarantees Individual Freedom in Morocco," *Agencia EFE,* October 2, 2016, https://www.efe.com/efe/espana/portada/benkiran-se -dice-modernista-y-garantiza-la-libertad-individual-en-marruecos/10010-305657. [in Spanish]

Notes   145

76   Michael Willis, "Morocco's Islamists and the Legislative Elections of 2002: The Strange Case of the Party That Did Not Want to Win," *Mediterranean Politics*, 9, no. 1 (March 1, 2004): 53–81, https://doi.org/10.1080/13629390410001679928.

77   "Risouni Pulls Back the Curtain on Session in which He Scolded the PJD Leaders," *TelQuel*, August 29, 2018, http://ar.telquel.ma/ال-فيها-وبّخ-جلسة-كواليس-يكشف-الريسوني/. [in Arabic]

78   Brown, *When Victory Is Not an Option.*

79   "Benkirane: Sitail's Time Left Is Short and She Has Connections with Undisclosed Parties," *Al3omk*, June 19, 2016, https://al3omk.com/109992.html. [in Arabic]

80   Abdelilah Benkirane, "Benkirane: The King Rules Morocco, My Powers Are Limited," May 13, 2015, http://www.aljazeera.net/home/Getpage/0353e88a-286d-4266-82c6-6094179ea26d/b10bf6bc-5926-4c76-bf59-25bde4f8a5d1. [in Arabic]

Chapter 5

1   Lisa Wedeen, *The Ambiguities of Domination: Politics, Rhetoric, and Symbols in Contemporary Syria.* Translated by Najib AlGhadban (Beirut: ElRayyes, 2010), 111–2. [in Arabic]

2   Raymond Hinnebusch, *The Formation of the Totalitarian State in Baathist Syria.* Translated by Hazem Nahar, submitted by Radwan Ziadeh (Beirut: ElRayyes, 2014), 237. [in Arabic]

3   Khader Zakkariah, "Traditional Party Opposition in Syria: Positions and Trends," in multiple authors, *Background of The Revolution: Studies on Syria* (Beirut, Doha: Arab Center for Research and Policy Studies, 2013), 257. [in Arabic]

4   Azmi Bishara, *Syria, A Painful Path Towards Freedom: An Attempt in Recent History* (Beirut, Doha: Arab Center for Research and Policy Studies, 2013), 44. [in Arabic]

5   For more information, see: Hamzah Almustafa, *The Public Domain of the Syrian Revolution: Characteristics, Trends, Mechanisms of Public Opinion* (Beirut, Doha: Arab Center for Research and Policy Studies, 2012), 14–5. [in Arabic]

6   "Did You Hear about the Brigades?" *YouTube*, January 4, 2012, https://goo.gl/zPMFQ5, accessed on April 3, 2017. [in Arabic]

7   Guido Steinberg, "Ahrar al-Sham: The 'Syrian Taliban,'" *German Institute for International and Security Affairs(SWP)*, May 27, 2016, 5–6, https://goo.gl/TvuxvR, accessed on April 10, 2017.

8   Personal interview with Iyad al-Sha'ar, adviser to the Political Bureau and former Deputy Military Commander, Turkey, February 25, 2017.

9   Ibid.

10   Policy Analysis Unit, "The Evolution of the American Stance on the Syrian Regime: From Calls for Reform to Negotiation," Arab Center for Research and Policy Studies, April 2, 2015, https://goo.gl/MnVzie, accessed on April 3, 2017. [in Arabic]

11   "Statement of the Declaration of the Islamist Movement Ahrar al-Sham," Youtube, January 31, 2013, https://goo.gl/iLN5Ep, accessed on April 2, 2017. [in Arabic]

12   https://studies.aljazeera.net/ar/files/2010/201172113136718105.html.

13   Personal interview with Ammar al-Ahmad, former fighter of "Ahrar al-Sham," Turkey, January 3, 2017.

14   Personal interview with one of the leadership of Ahrar al-Sham (who wished to remain anonymous), Turkey, February 26, 2017.

146 *Notes*

15 To view the full text of the charter, see: ___ "Project Nation: The Full Text of the Charter of the Islamic Front," Zaman Alwsl, November 23, 2013, https://goo.gl/JvJ5ww, accessed on April 10, 2017. [in Arabic]

16 Rateb Shabo, "Ahrar al-Sham: Between Jihadism and Brotherhood," Arab Center for Research and Policy Studies, April 15, 2016, 8, https://goo.gl/i95rpb, accessed on April 10, 2017. [in Arabic]

17 Personal interview with Abdul Rahman al-Kilani, Syrian activist and Director of *Ahrar al-Sham* (film), Safar Headquarters, Turkey, February 28, 2017.

18 "Meeting with Hisham al-Sheikh: Iran Rescued the Syrian Regime," *YouTube,* April 17, 2015, https://goo.gl/kZNEAN, accessed on April 3, 2017. [in Arabic]

19 Labib al-Nahhas, "The Deadly Consequences of Mislabeling Syria's Revolutionaries," *Washington Post*, July 10, 2015, https://goo.gl/hwWvvN, accessed May 3, 2016.

20 Labib al-nahhas, "I'm a Syrian and I Fight Isil Every Day. It Will Take More than Bombs from the West to Defeat This Menace," *The Telegraph*, July 21, 2015, https://goo.gl/ZBmHUc, accessed on April 3, 2016.

21 Personal interview with Burhan Ghalyoun, Syrian philosopher and former president of the Syrian National Council, Doha, December 25, 2016.

22 Abu Yehia AlHamoudi, "Leader of 'Ahrar al-Sham,'" *Al-Hayat*, September 14, 2015, https://goo.gl/fFccgh, accessed on April 2, 2017. [in Arabic]

23 "Ahrar al-Sham: Changes and Legal Transformations," *Al-Sharq Al-Awsat*, June 20, 2016, no. 13719. [in Arabic], and personal interview with Ahmad Mousa.

24 Personal interview with Mohammed Jalal.

25 Personal interview with Osama Abu Zaid.

26 Personal interview with Eyad al-Shaar.

27 Hamzah Almustafa, "Al-Nusra Front to Ahl al-Sham," *Siyasat Arabiya*, 5 (2013): 63–4. [in Arabic]

28 Ibid., 64.

29 Personal interview with Muhammad Birqdar, President of Jaysh al-Islam's Political Bureau, Turkey, February 23, 2017.

30 Policy Analysis Unit, "Jaysh al-Islam: The Search for a Role in Syria's Future," Arab Center for Research and Policy Studies, pp. 1–2, July 7, 2015, https://goo.gl/EdI8o6, accessed on April 9, 2017. [in Arabic]

31 Personal interview with Muhammad Birqdar.

32 "Jaysh al-Islam in Brief," Official Website of Jaysh al-Islam, https://goo.gl/mC8QaJ, accessed on April 9, 2016. [in Arabic]

33 Personal interview with Islam Alloush.

34 Skype interview with Ahmad Hussam (code name), one of Jaysh al-Islam's fighters, March 5, 2017.

35 "The Return of the Umayyad Glory to the Levant," *YouTube*, January 4, 2015, https://goo.gl/vZDZyL, accessed April 9, 2016. [in Arabic]

36 Personal interview with leaders of Jaysh al-Islam who wish to remain anonymous, Turkey, April 23, 2017.

37 Personal interview with Muhammad Birqdar.

38 Personal interview with Ahmad Abazayd.

39 Hamzah Almustafa, "Beyond Yarmouk Camp," *AlAraby*, April 21, 2015, https://goo.gl/eeC1uT, accessed on April 10, 2017. [in Arabic]

40 Personal interview with leaders of Jaysh al-Islam (names withheld), Turkey, February 27, 2017.

41 Ibid.

Notes

147

42 Policy Analysis Unit, "Jaysh al-Islam: The Search for a Role in Syria's Future," 11–2.

43 Phone interview with Riyad Hijab, April 10, 2017.

44 Phone interview with Haitham Rahma, April 13, 2017.

45 Aron Lund, "Struggling to Adapt: The Muslim Brotherhood in a New Syria," Carnegie Middle East Center, May 7, 2013, https://carnegie-mec.org/2013/05/07/ar-pub-51715, accessed on April 13, 2017. [in Arabic]

46 Personal interview with Abdel Rahman al-Hajj.

47 Lund, "Struggling to Adapt."

48 Phone interview with Haitham Rahma.

49 Ibid.

50 "The Civil Protection Authority, Which Is Close to the Muslim Brotherhood, Is Demanding Foreign Fighters to Leave," *AlQuds AlAraby*, January 10, 2014, http://www.alquds.co.uk/?p=178298, accessed on April 28, 2017. [in Arabic]

51 Phone interview with Ibrahim Abdel Jaber, a fighter in the central forces of the Sham Legion, April 28, 2017.

52 Personal research carried out by the author.

53 "Jaysh al-Fatah," AlJazeera.Net, April 30, 2015, https://goo.gl/pEkcKU, accessed April 28, 2016. [in Arabic]

54 Anas al-Kurdi, "Syria: 'The Sham Legion' Withdraws from 'Jaysh al-Fatah' to Support Aleppo," AlAraby, January 3, 2016, https://goo.gl/kFwT5Q, accessed on April 28, 2017. [in Arabic]

55 Will Todman, "Gulf States' Policies on Syria," *Center For Strategic and International Studies (CSIS)*, 4–5, https://csis-prod.s3.amazonaws.com/s3fs-public/publication/161019_Gulf_States _Policies_on_Syria.pdf, accessed October 18, 2016.

56 Personal interview with Osama Abu Zaid.

57 Skype interview with Mohamed Aldughaim.

58 Ahmad Abazayd, "Abu Khaled al-Suri: The First Generation Facing the Recent Deviation," Zaman Alwsl, April 26, 2014, https://goo.gl/rPCJ82, accessed on April 26, 2017. [in Arabic]

59 Yemeni Suleiman, "Institutional Structure of the Muslim Brotherhood: An Analytical Approach," Egyptian Institute for Studies, April 26, 2017, https://eipss-eg.org/%D8 %A7%D9%84%D8%A8%D9%86%D9%8A%D8%A9-%D8%A7%D9%84%D9%85 %D8%A4%D8%B3%D8%B3%D9%8A%D8%A9-%D9%84%D9%84%D8%A5%D8 %AE%D9%88%D8%A7%D9%86-%D8%A7%D9%84%D9%85%D8%B3%D9%84 %D9%85%D9%8A%D9%86-%D8%A7%D9%82%D8%AA%D8%B1%D8%A7%D8 %A8-%D8%AA%D8%AD%D9%84%D9%8A%D9%84%D9%8A/, accessed on February 4, 2014. [in Arabic]

60 Aron Lund, "Struggling to Adapt."

61 Personal interview with Ahmed Mousa.

62 Personal interview with Ahmad Abazayd.

63 Personal interview with Osama Abu Zaid.

64 "'Operation Euphrates Shield' . . . Objectives and Challenges," *Orient News*, August 27, 2016, https://goo.gl/4yNQGh, accessed on April 29, 2017. [in Arabic]

65 Amr Mashoh, "Syrian Brotherhood: Four Repositioning Strategies." https://www .aljazeera.net/opinions/2016/12/5/%D8%A5%D8%AE%D9%88%D8%A7%D9%86- %D8%B3%D9%88%D8%B1%D9%8A%D8%A7-%D8%A3%D8%B1%D8%A8%D8 %B9-%D8%A5%D8%B3%D8%AA%D8%B1%D8%A7%D8%AA%D9%8A%D8%AC

%D9%8A%D8%A7%D8%AA-%D9%84%D8%A5%D8%B9%D8%A7%D8%AF%D8%A9.

66 Policy Analysis Unit, "The Syrian Opposition and its Challenges in 2016," Arab Center for Research and Policy Studies, 13–4, June 15, 2016, https://goo.gl/c9k0OB, accessed on April 27, 2017. [in Arabic]

67 The movement even commissioned a team of lawyers to defend it before a local German court in the state of Stuttgart to abolish the ruling which classified it as a terrorist organization. Personal interview with Mohammed Jalal.

68 Charles R. Lister, *The Syrian Jihad: Al-Qaeda, the Islamic State and the Evolution of an Insurgence* (Oxford, USA: Oxford University Press, 2015), 260–9.

69 Personal interview with Ahmad Mousa.

70 Personal interview with Ahmad Abazayd.

71 Personal interview with Osama Abu Zaid.

72 Skype interview with Mohamed Aldughaim.

73 Personal interview with Ahmad Abazayd.

74 Personal interview with Mohammed Birqdar.

75 Personal interview with Islam Alloush.

76 Personal interview with Mohammed Jalal.

Chapter 6

1 Khalil Al-Anani, "Islamist Parties Post-Arab Spring," *Mediterranean Politics*, 17, no. 3 (2012): 466–72.

2 Lackner, 2018, https://www.amazon.com/Yemen-Crisis-Autocracy-Neo-Liberalism -Disintegration/dp/0863561934.

3 Ibid.

4 Al-Batati, 2015, https://www.aljazeera.com/news/2015/8/21/yemen-at-war-no-side-is -willing-to-capitulate.

5 Interview by the author with Mayssa Shuja al-Deen, a Yemeni academic political researcher and observer of the Islah party's activism, September 15, 2018, Yemen, via email.

6 Interview by the author with Nabil al-Bukiri, a Yemeni political researcher and observer of the party's politics August 7, 2018, via email.

7 April Longley Alley, "Yemen Changes Everything . . . and Nothing," *Journal of Democracy*, 24, no. 4 (2013): 74–85. Page 2.

8 Nabil al-Bukiri interview; interview by the author with Sami Noaman, a Yemeni writer and Journalist, July 18, 2018, Taiz city, Yemen.

9 Sami Noaman interview.

10 Mayssa Shuja al-Deen interview.

11 Ibid.

12 El Yaakoubi, Aziz: Yemen Islamist party suspends membership of Nobel laureate Karman. Yemen. *Reuters*, February 4, 2018. www.reuters.com/article/us-yemen security-islamist/yemen-islamist-party-suspends-membership-of-nobel-laureate -karman-idUSKBN1FO0DB, accessed August 2, 2018.

13 Interview by the author with Eyad Damaj, a political researcher, November 29, 2018. Sana'a, Yemen.

14 Interview by the author with Adnan al-Odaini, Islahi leader and deputy of the party's Media and Cultural Secretariat, August 26, 2018, via email.

Notes 149

15 Nabil al-Bukiri interview.
16 *Akhbar al-Youm Newspaper*, Mohammed Qahatan: Islah does not see Houthis as par equivalent, January 22, 2013. http://www.akhbaralyom-ye.net/news_details.php?sid= 63814, accessed June 2, 2018.
17 Outcomes of Yemen NDC 2013, see the full version of the statement, accessed July 12, 2018.
18 Beverley Milton-Edwards, *The Muslim Brotherhood: The Arab Spring and Its Future Face* (London: Routledge, 2015), 155.
19 https://pomeps.org/wp-content/uploads/2018/02/POMEPS_Studies_29_Yemen_Web -REV.pdf
20 Al Jazeera, "Yemen's Saleh Declares an Alliance with Houthis," *Al Jazeera*, May 11, 2015, http://www.aljazeera.com/news/2015/05/cloneofcloneofcloneofstrikes -yemensaada- Breach-150510143647004.html, accessed July 20, 2018.
21 Ikhwanweb. Islah Party Announces Decisive Storm Support. Khwanweb, April 4, 2015. http://www.ikhwanweb.com/article.php?id=32080, accessed November 2, 2018.
22 Interview by the author with Ali al-Garadi, Head of Media Secretariat of Islah party, Yemen, July 10, 2018, via email.
23 Interview by the author with a middle-ranked member of Islah party July 13, 2018, Taiz, Yemen, July 2018.
24 Ali al-Garadi interview.
25 "Politics, Governance, and Reconstruction in Yemen." Brookings. Project on Middle East Political Science. January 2017. Project on Middle East Political Science. https:// pomeps.org/2018/01/10/politics-governance-and-reconstruction-in-yemen/, accessed October 25, 2018, Page 8.
26 Ibid.
27 Adnan al-Odaini interview.
28 "USDS: United States Designates bin Laden Loyalist," February 24, 2004. https://www .treasury.gov/press-center/press-releases/Pages/js1190.aspx, accessed September 2, 2018.
29 Adnan al-Odaini interview.
30 Ibid.
31 Saeed Al-Batati, "Yemen's Islah Party Distances Itself from Brotherhood," Gulf News. January 9, 2018. https://gulfnews.com/world/gulf/yemen/yemens-islah -party-distances-itself-from-brotherhood-1.2154324, accessed November 29, 2018.
32 "Islah party Accuses Qatar of Supporting Houthis in Yemen," Taiz online. November 11, 2018. https://sahafahnet.net/news5983979.html, accessed November 27, 2018.
33 "Bloomberg - Are You a Robot? 2018," Bloomberg. Available at: https:// alsahwa-yemen. 2018. Leaders of Islah party meet UAE Crown Prince. November 15, 2018. http://www.alsahwa-yemen.net/en/p-25283, accessed November 29, 2018.

Chapter 7

1 Dr. Rahil Gharaibeh, "The Evolution of the Internal Scene of the Muslim Brotherhood in Jordan," Papers from the Center for Strategic Studies, University of Jordan, August 2017, 8–9. [in Arabic]
2 Although Abduallah Azzam and Ahmed Nofal along with Abu Fares and Hammam Saeed supported Qutb's ideas, Nofal and Azzam, according to Gharaibeh, did not

150 Notes

mind working under the existing political systems, and participated in the camps for sheikhs at an early age with the Fatah movement, while Saeed and Abu Fares remained skeptical and rejected the principle of working under the umbrella of political regimes, describing them as ignorant. Private conversation with Rahil Gharaibeh, December 29, 2017.

3   Ibid.

4   See: Salem al-Falahat, *The Islamist Movement in Jordan*, Dar Ammar, 1st edition, 1 (2016): 25–6. [in Arabic]

5   Ibid., 26–32.

6   Mohammed Abu Rumman and Hassan Abu Haniyeh, "The Islamic Solution in Jordan," Center for Strategic Studies, University of Jordan and the German Friedrich Ebert Foundation in Amman, 2nd edition, 2014, 86–90. [in Arabic]

7   Ibid., 90–1.

8   See: Ibid., 91–3.

9   Azayyida is considered one of the most important leaders of the Brotherhood during the 1980s and 1990s, especially during the period of democratic transition in 1989 and the founding of the Islamic Action Front. He was president of the Madaba municipality in the 1980s, and later a member of the House of Representatives. He died at a young age in 1992 due to an illness. Researchers view him as the inspiration for the new generation of leadership in the Muslim Brotherhood, such as Imad Abu Dayyah, Salem al-Falahat, and others. Private conversation with Salem al-Falahat, January 4, 2018.

10 Private conversation with Dr. Rahil Gharaibeh, mentioned above.

11 al-Falahat, *Islamist Movement in Jordan*, 23.

12 He separated from the movement in 2000 due to his participation in the government of Ali Abu al-Raghib. He was formerly one of the prominent leaders of the Muslim Brotherhood, reaching the position of Deputy Inspector General and previously serving as a member of the House of Representatives in Jordan; Representative of the Muslim Brotherhood.

13 He was among the prominent leadership figures of the Muslim Brotherhood and was well-known for his pragmatic opinions. He served as a member in the House of Representatives for consecutive terms and as a minister in the government of Mudar Badran, in which the Brotherhood participated in the 1990s. In 1997, he wrote a controversial oppositional paper on the Muslim Brotherhood project in Jordan. The paper called for realism and constituted the first acknowledgment that the Brotherhood's Islamic state project was not suitable for Jordan. He demanded that the Muslim Brotherhood commit to political realism without thinking about instituting a system of governance in Jordan and coexistence with the regime. However, he later left the Brotherhood after the decision to boycott elections in 1997. He participated in the 1997 parliamentary elections and won, which led to his separation from the Brotherhood. See: Abdullah Al-Akaily's paper, "The Experience of the Islamist Movement in Jordan," in Azzam al-Henaidi (ed.), *Islamists' Participation in Power* (London: Liberty Organization, 1994). [in Arabic]. Also see: Faisal al-Shabul, "Al-Akaily Attacks Sheikhs and Accused the Brotherhood of Stagnation. Islamic Perestroika, the Jordanian Way," *Al-Hayat*, February 10, 1997. [in Arabic]. Also see: Mashari Althaidi, "Conversations in Fundamentalism and Politics (2–5), The Muslim Brotherhood in Jordan . . . Between the Beaks of the Hawks and the Wings of the Doves," *Al-Sharq al-Awsat*, October 10, 2005. [in Arabic]

Notes   151

14   He was one of the prominent leaders of the Doves in the Muslim Brotherhood and one of the most prominent representatives of the movement. He was a university professor of *shari 'a* law and attacked the Brotherhood's decision to boycott parliamentary elections in 1997. He also wrote an article in the newspaper *al-Rai* entitled "Why did they boycott?" a criticism of the decision, which led to his separation from the Brotherhood and his appointment as a minister in Abdelsalam Majali's government in 1998, and later in Fayez al-Tarawneh's government.

15   For more about the separation of this group from the Muslim Brotherhood and the message that was sent to the inspector general of the Muslim Brotherhood in protest against 1997 boycott decision and the reasons for the formation of the Islamic Center Party, see: al-Falahat, *The Islamist Movement in Jordan*, 45–53.

16   See: Abu Rumman and Abu Haniyeh, "The Islamic Solution in Jordan," 91–3.

17   See Gharaibeh, "The Evolution of the Internal Scene of the Muslim Brotherhood in Jordan," 10–11.

18   Ibid., 93–5.

19   Ibid., 95–6.

20   See: The Islamic Movement's Vision for Reform, Amman, *The Muslim Brotherhood*, 2005. [in Arabic] Also: al-Falahat, *Islamist Movement in Jordan*, vol. 2, 137–236.

21   See: "Jordan Jails Two Islamists Who Attended Zarqawi's Funeral," AlJazeera.net, August 6, 2006. [in Arabic]

22   In his book *The Islamist Movement in Jordan*, former inspector general Salem al-Falahat presents important details about the meeting that the Brotherhood held for the press release between the government and the intelligence director on the hand, and Brotherhood leaders on the other. It outlines reactions to the statement, the reasoning behind holding a meeting of the Shura Council, and what that document— the press release—sparked in terms of heated debates and fervent discussions within the Brotherhood. See: al-Falahat, *Islamist Movement in Jordan*, 272–301.

23   See Gharaibeh, "The Evolution of the Internal Scene of the Muslim Brotherhood in Jordan," 15–16.

24   Backers of the initiative confirmed that they received the confidence of the Brotherhood's executive office, under the leadership of Hammam Saeed, while other sources, such as Zaki Bani Irsheid, denied that and stressed that the Brotherhood did not want to bear the burden of the repercussions of this unconventional discourse in its relationship to the state. See, for example, Mohammad al-Najjar, "Muslim Brotherhood in Jordan Discuss the Constitutional Monarchy," AlJazeera.net, December 6, 2010, http://www.aljazeera.net/news/reportsandinterviews/2010/12/6/ %d8%a5%d8%ae%d9%88%d8%a7%d9%86-%d8%a7%d9%84%d8%a3%d8%b1%d8 %af%d9%86-%d9%8a%d9%86%d8%a7%d9%82%d8%b4%d9%88%d9%86-%d8%a7 %d9%84%d9%85%d9%84%d9%83%d9%8a%d8%a9-%d8%a7%d9%84%d8%af%d8 %b3%d8%aa%d9%88%d8%b1%d9%8a%d8%a9. [in Arabic], See also: al-Falahat, *Islamist Movement in Jordan*.

25   The Muslim Brotherhood's stance regarding Jordanian disengagement from the West Bank remains vague. The resolution was enacted by the late King Hussein bin Talal and marked the end of the "Unification of the Two Banks" (1950). The Brotherhood's only official decision was one that followed Hussein's and consisted of a refusal to accept the disengagement. But after that, the subject disappeared entirely from the Brotherhood's discussions and literature until the moderate movement began to raise the need to acknowledge the decision to disengage (beginning in 2008, almost

152   *Notes*

two years after the decision was made). The hard-line movement maintains its reservations in this regard and has tried to avoid delving into the subject.

26   See: Kheir al-Din al-Jabari, "Jordan's Muslim Brotherhood: A Soft Solution for Organization and Community in the Most Difficult Stages," *Noon Post*, March 3, 2015, https://www.noonpost.org/content/5678. [in Arabic]

27   The two organizations of the Muslim Brotherhood in Jordan and Palestine together formed the so-called Organization of the Levant in 1978. Hamas remained part of the Muslim Brotherhood in Jordan, and the Palestinian section served as its regulatory organ. The foreign administrative offices of the Muslim Brotherhood in Jordan were mixed between elements of Hamas and the Muslim Brotherhood and were represented in the Brotherhood's Shura Council.

28   See al-Falahat, *Islamist Movement in Jordan*, vol. 1, 199, where Salem al-Falahat provides important historical documentation of the stages in the relationship between the Jordanian and Palestinian organizations, the rise of Hamas, and the associated organizational relationships. In addition, he provides information on the process of separation and the positions of various Brotherhood factions on that process.

29   See Mohammed Abu Rumman, The Crisis of the Muslim Brotherhood in Jordan . . . the end of the ongoing conflict and the beginning of political floating." https://studies .aljazeera.net/ar/reports/2016/06/160615121451366.html.

30   Gharaibeh, "The Evolution of the Internal Scene of the Muslim Brotherhood in Jordan," 18.

31   Ibid.

32   The concept of "functional entity" refers to the fact that Jordan was established by British colonialism to protect Israel and to separate it from the major Arab countries and to absorb Palestinian refugees as an alternative homeland.

33   Sultan Alhattab, "Zamzam: Expansion and Flow," *Al Rai Newspaper*, October 7, 2013, http://alrai.com/article/610803.html.

34   The Muslim Brotherhood received licensure from the state in 1964 as an association that belonged to the Muslim Brotherhood in Egypt. In 1953, it received a new license after the establishment of a statue by the new leadership of the Brotherhood. It was approved by the Jordanian government headed by Tawfid Abu al-Huda at that time. See: al-Falahat, *Islamist Movement in Jordan*, vol. 2, 344–5.

35   The legislative council of Yifti transferred the property of the (original) Muslim Brotherhood in Jordan to the "Licensed Association." The fatwa was rejected by the (original) Brotherhood and considered it political discrimination and therefore unlawful, Al-Sharq al-Awsat newspaper, May 29, 2015, [in Arabic]. See also: "The Brotherhood Declares Legal Battle," *Saraya News*, July 26, 2015, http://www .sarayanews.com/article/318822. [in Arabic] See also: "The Brotherhood 'Association' Forms Internal Committee to Pursue the Prosecution of the Existing 'Society,'" *Saraya News*, July 28, 2015, http://www.sarayanews.com/article/319010. [in Arabic]. See also: "Jordan: Muslim Brotherhood's Investments in the Names of 'Persons,' No Inheritance for Defectors and Property is Returned to Members of Charitable Organizations, not the Organization," *AlRai AlYoum*, March 9, 2015, http://www .raialyoum.com/?p=232876. [in Arabic]

36   Compare with: "Irbid is the Most Dangerous File for the Brotherhood, Details from Meeting #50, Warning of the Schism," *Shaab News*, May 8, 2014, http://shaabnews .com/news-37172.htm. [in Arabic]

37   See: "Thunibat Inspector General of the Muslim Brotherhood," *Al Rai Newspaper*, January 9, 2016. [in Arabic]

Notes

38 The Muslim Brotherhood Association in Jordan, the Political System, Amman, 2016. [In Arabic]

39 See: Faisal Malkawi and Salah al-Abaadi, "The Muslim Brotherhood Renews its Call 'Come to a Common Word,'" *Al Rai Newspaper*, April 13, 2017. [in Arabic]

40 Among them were other prominent leaders from the Brotherhood and the Islamic Action Front, especially from the second generation of the Brotherhood, such as Hamza Mansour, Abdel Latif Arabiyat (both of whom served as secretary general of the IAF), Jamil Abu Bakr, and Azzam al-Hinaidi, and others. However, these leaders abandoned the idea of forming a party for a variety of reasons. A number of these leaders stayed with a group of the new youth generation insisting on the idea, so they established the RPP with other political figures from outside of the Muslim Brotherhood.

41 The most prominent of his works in this field is the book *Freedoms Trapped Between the Tyranny of Government and the Exploitation of Religion*. [in Arabic]. See: Nasser Al-Majali, Discussions of Philosophers and Researchers in the Arab Thought Forum on: *Freedoms Trapped Between the Tyranny of Government and the Exploitation of Religion*, Eplah, July 31, 2017, http://elaph.com/Web/News/2017/7/1160452.html. [in Arabic]

42 Ibrahim Gharaibeh, An Interview with Salem Al-Falahat, *Amman Times*, September 11, 2007.

43 Mohammed Abu Rumman, "An Important Development, But . . ." *AlGhad Newspaper*, January 2, 2012. [in Arabic]

Chapter 8

1 A. AlKandari, *The Muslim Brotherhood in Kuwait, 1941-2000 A Social Movement within the Social Domain* (Exeter: University of Exeter, 2014), 203–4.

2 Falah al-Madirs, *The Muslim Brotherhood in Kuwait*, 2nd edition (Kuwait: Qurtas Publishing House, 1999), 13. [in Arabic]

3 Abdelghani Ammad, and Salah al-Jorshi, *Islamist Movements in the Arab World*, vol. 1 (Beirut: Centre for Arab Unity Studies, 2013), 519. [in Arabic]

4 See: Mubarak Aljeri, "Islamist Currents in Kuwait After the Arab Spring: Islamic Constitutional Movement as a Model," Doha: Al Jazeera Center for Studies, 2016, http://studies.aljazeera.net/ar/reports/2016/09/160922044927190.html, accessed February 28, 2018. [in Arabic]

5 Ibid.

6 See: The Constitution of Kuwait, www.kna/pdf/dostoor.pdf, accessed on March 2, 2018. [in Arabic]

7 Nathan Brown and Amr Hamzawy, *Between Religion and Politics: Islamists in Arab Parliaments*, 1st edition (Beirut: Arab Network for Research, 2011), 157. [in Arabic]

8 Carine Lahoud, *Islam and Politics in Kuwait*, 1st edition (Beirut: Centre for Arab Unity Studies, 2017), 18. [in Arabic]

9 Kamal Al-Menoufi, *The Origins of Comparative Political Systems*, 2nd edition (Kuwait: Al Rabeaian Publishing House, 2010), 196–202. [in Arabic]

10 Mubarak Aljeri, "The Struggles of Political Islam in Kuwait. Conference on the Prospects of Political Islam in a Troubled Region: Islamists and 'Post-Arab Spring' Challenges" (Amman: Friedrich Ebert Foundation, 2017), 129–35. [in Arabic]

11 Lahoud, *Islam and Politics in Kuwait*, 64.

12 Al-Madirs, *The Muslim Brotherhood in Kuwait*, 30.

13 Ali al-Kandari, professor of History at the University of Kuwait and member of the Islamic Constitutional Movement, interview with the author. Kuwait, January 26, 2018.

14 Osama al-Shaheen, member of the Kuwaiti Parliament and of the Islamic Constitutional Movement, interview with the author. Kuwait, January 25, 2018.

15 Abdel Rahman Abd al-Ghafour, political activist and member of the Islamic Constitutional Movement, interview with the author. Kuwait, January 22, 2018.

16 Brown, *Between Religion and Politics*, 156.

17 For more details on the March, see: Abu Salib, Faisal (January 2016). "Influential Factors in the Political Movement in Kuwaiti Society During the 2009–2014 Period: Field Studies," *Journal of Gulf and Arabian Peninsula Studies* (Kuwait), no. 160: 67–122. [in Arabic]

18 Ghanim al-Najjar, professor of Political Science at Kuwait University, interview with the author. Kuwait, February 1, 2018.

19 Ali al-Sanad, professor of Islamic Studies at PAAET Basic Education College with close ties with the Islamic Constitutional Movement, interview with the author. Kuwait, January 29, 2018.

20 Brown, *Between Religion and Politics*, 185.

21 Ali al-Kandari, interview with the author.

22 See: Aljeri, *Islamist Currents in Kuwait*.

23 Mubarak al-Duwailah, former member of the Kuwaiti Parliament and leader of the Islamic Constitutional Movement, interview with the author. Kuwait, January 16, 2018.

24 Lahoud, *Islam and Politics in Kuwait*, 221.

25 The success of both MP Jamaan al-Harbash in the second electoral district and MP Falah al-Sawag in the fifth district is primarily due to tribal support or power that far exceeded the Movement's own power. The former belongs to the Anza tribe and the latter to the al-Awazim tribe. Candidates' failure in the first, third, and fourth districts demonstrates voters' attitudes toward the Movement during this period.

26 Dahem al-Qahtani, Kuwaiti writer and journalist, interview with the author. Kuwait, March 9, 2018.

27 See: "Constitutional Court Deems 2012 Parliamentary Elections Invalid and Reinstates 2009 Parliament . . . the Solution Does Not Exist," *alRai*, http://www .alraimedia.com/Home/Details?Id=66d5326c-5af0-4180-928e-a3f28ddc1588, accessed on March 10, 2018. [in Arabic]

28 Ali al-Zamie', former minister of Awqaf and Planning and Development, interview with the author. Kuwait, February 4, 2018.

29 See: "The Opposition Coalition Presents Political Reform Project: Toward a Full Democratic Parliamentary System," http://www.alraimedia.com/Home/Details?Id =4b2bb417-a8cb-482a-92bc-38b351e92342, accessed on March 8, 2018. [in Arabic]

30 Ali al-Kandari, interview with the author.

31 Ghanim al-Najjar, interview with the author.

32 Ali al-Zamei', interview with the author.

33 Ahmed Althaidi, professor of Shari'a Law at Kuwait University, interview with the author. Kuwait, March 20, 2018.

34 Mubarak al-Duwailah, interview with the author.

Notes 155

35 Osama al-Shaheen, interview with the author.

36 Khaldoun al-Naqib, *Society and State in the Gulf and the Arabian Peninsula from a Different Perspective*, 2nd edition (Beirut: Centre for Arab Unity Studies, 1989), 122–3. [in Arabic]

37 Ghanim al-Najjar, interview with the author.

38 Ali al-Kandari, interview with the author.

39 See: "Statement of the Constitutional Court on the One-Vote Decree," June 17, 2013, www.kna.kw/clt-html5/news-details.com, accessed on March 18, 2018. [in Arabic]

40 See: "Majority Bloc Confirms Commitment to Boycott the Upcoming Parliamentary Elections," *Mugtama'*, no. 2059, June 29–July 5, 2013, p. 6. [in Arabic]

41 See: "'The Duty to Boycott' Symposium: Political Forces Demanding Approval of Constitutional Reforms," *Mugtama'*, no. 2061, July 13–19, 2018, p. 6. [in Arabic]

42 Ibid.

43 See: Aljeri, *Islamist Currents in Kuwait*.

44 Abdullah al-Nafisi, Kuwaiti scholar and political theorist, interview with the author. Kuwait, March 31, 2018.

45 See: Aljeri, *Islamist Currents in Kuwait*.

46 See: "The United Arab Emirates Classifies Muslim Brotherhood as Terrorist Group," https://ara.reuters.com/article/topNews/idARAKCN0IZ0PK20141115, accessed on March 10, 2018. [in Arabic]

47 Lahoud, *Islam and Politics in Kuwait*, 234.

48 See: "The Islamic Constitutional Movement, Statement on the Upcoming Parliamentary Elections," May 26, 2016, http://www.icmkw.org/portal/pages/topics /bian-alxhrk629-aldsturi629-al625slami629-bsh623n-alantxabat-albrlmani629 -almqbl629.php?p=20#.WqZn97lG3Aw, accessed on March 11, 2018. [in Arabic]

49 Lahoud, *Islam and Politics in Kuwait*, 233.

50 Abdel Rahman Abd al-Ghafour, interview with the author.

51 Based on interviews conduct by the author.

52 Hacene Masbah, "The Deep State: An Emergent Concept in Comparative Politics" (translated paper), *Siyasat Arabiya*, no. 30 (2018 January): 83–102. [in Arabic]

53 Ibid., 86.

54 Aljeri, *Islamist Currents in Kuwait*.

55 In an interview conducted by the author, a leading member of Hadas (who wished to remain anonymous) said that the executive officer of this announcement was the leader of the Social Reform Society Hisham al-Amoumi. He noted that after this announcement the Muslim Brotherhood of Kuwait joined the Social Reform Society.

56 Ali al-Kandari, interview with the author.

57 Khalil Al-Anani, "Arab Islamists Five Years After the 'Arab Spring': Questions of Project, Ideology, and Organization," *Siyasat Arabiya*, no. 18 (January 2016): 41–51.

58 Talal al-Khader, Kuwaiti scholar and Arab political theorist with close ties to the Islamic Constitutional Movement, phone interview with the author. Kuwait, April 1, 2018.

59 Ali al-Sanad, interview with the author.

60 Osama al-Shaheen, interview with the author.

61 Interview with the author, a former member of the Kuwaiti parliament who participated in the sit-in.

62 See: "Post-July 8 in Kuwait," https://www.alaraby.co.uk/amp//opinion/2018/7/29/ 1-الكويت-في-يوليو--8بعد-ما, accessed on September 10, 2018. [in Arabic]

Chapter 9

1 Abdelwahab El-Affendi, "A Trans-Islamic Revolution?" *Critical Muslim*, 1, no. 1 (2012): 1.

2 "Trial of ex-Egyptian President Morsi on Prison Escape Postponed," January 28, 2014. Available at: https://www.upi.com/Trial-of-ex-Egyptian-President-Morsi-on-prison -escape-postponed/28571390917539/, accessed October 3, 2018.

3 Essam El-Arian, "Yawmiyyat Thawrat 25 Yana'ir- 4" (Diaries of the 25 January Revolution), *Misress*, April 6, 2011. Available at: http://www.masress.com/almesryoon /53766.

4 Shadi Hamid, *Temptations of Power: Islamists and Illiberal Democracy in a New Middle East* (Oxford: Oxford University Press, 2014).

5 Asef Bayat, *Making Islam Democratic: Social Movements and the Post-Islamist Turn* (Stanford, CA: Stanford University Press, 2007), 136–86.

6 Gilles Kepel, *Muslim Extremism in Egypt: The Prophet and Pharaoh* (Berkeley: University of California Press, 2003), 26–35.

7 See for example the *Washington Post* interview with Mubarak: Youssef Michel Ibrahim, "Democracy Be Careful What You Wish For," *The Washington Post*, March 23, 2003, http://www.cfr.org/world/democracy-careful-you-wish/p5747, accessed May 1, 2011.

8 For an overview of Islamist changing role during the revolution see: Ibrahim El-Houdaiby, "Islamism Now: How the January 25 Revolution Changed Political Islam in Egypt," *The Cairo Review of Global Affairs*, 6 (Summer 2012): 130–49.

9 Michael Slackman, "In Mideast Activism, New Tilt Away from Ideology," *The New York Times*, January 22, 2011, at: http://www.nytimes.com/2011/01/23/world/ middleeast/23egypt.html?_r=1&partner=rss&emc=rss.

10 *Addustour*, January 19, 2011, at: http://www.dostor.org/politics/egypt/11/january/19 /35341.

11 Ibid.

12 Hamid, *Temptations of Power,* 113–16.

13 Amr Hamzawy and Nathan J. Brown, *The Egyptian Muslim Brotherhood: Islamist Participation in a Closing Political Environment*, Carnegie Papers, Number 19, March 2010 (Washington DC: Carnegie Middle East Center, 2010), 3.

14 Munib, *Dalil al-Harakat Al-Islamiyya* (Cairo: Madbouli Press, 2010), 121–40.

15 Carrie Rosefsky Wickham, "The Muslim Brotherhood after Mubarak," *Foreign Affairs Online*, February 3, 2011. Available at: http://www.foreignaffairs.com/articles/67348/ carrie-rosefsky-wickham/the-muslim-brotherhood-after-mubarak?page=show.

16 Abdelwahab El-Affendi, "The Islamism Debate Revisited: in Search of 'Islamist Democrats,'" in Michelle Pace (ed.), *Europe, the USA and Political Islam: Strategies for Engagement* (London: Palgrave, 2010), 125–38; See also Hamzawy and Brown, *The Egyptian Muslim Brotherhood.*

17 Asef Bayat, "Democracy and the Muslim World: The "Post-Islamist" Turn," *Open Democracy*, March 6, 2009, http://www.opendemocracy.net/article/democratising-the -muslim-world, Cf. Bayat, *Making Islam Democratic*, 10–15.

18 Olivier Roy, "Révolution Post-islamiste," *Le Monde*, February 14, 2011. Available at: http://www.lemonde.fr/idees/article/2011/02/12/revolution-post-islamiste_1478858 _3232.html.

19 Roy, "Révolution post-islamiste."

Notes

20 Samer Frangie, "The Arab Revolutions: An End to the Post-1967 Problematic," *Open Democracy*, March 17, 2011, at: http://www.opendemocracy.net/samer-frangie/arab-revolutions-end-to-post-1967-problematic.

21 Bernard Lewis, "The Return of Islam," *Commentary,* (January 1976): 39–49.

22 Hamid, *Temptations of Power.*

23 Salwa Ismail, "Confronting the Other: Identity, Culture, Politics, and Conservative Islamism in Egypt," *International Journal of Middle East Studies,* 30, no. 2 (1998): 199–225.

24 Abdelwahab El-Affendi, "The Islamic State without Islamists: : The Case of Sudan," A paper presented to the conference "Islamists and Democratic Governance: Experiments and Trend," organized by the Arab Centre for Research and Policy Studies, Doha, 6–8, October 2012.

25 Sadik J. al-'Azm, *Self-Criticism After the Defeat.* Translated by George Stergios (London: Saqi Books, 2011).

26 Adam Shatz, "Prophecy and Deliverance: Reading al-'Azm in An Age of Revolution," *Jadaliyya*, December 20, 2011, http://www.jadaliyya.com/pages/index/3674/prophecy-and-deliverance_reading-al-azm-in-an-age, accessed May 3, 2013.

27 Issa J. Boullata, "Review Essay. Adonis: Towards a New Arab Culture," *International Journal of Middle East Studies,* 20, no. 1 (1988): 109–12.

28 Sinan Antoon, "The Arab Spring and Adunis's Autumn," *Jadliyya*, July 11, 2011, at: http://www.jadaliyya.com/pages/index/2047/the-arab-spring-and-aduniss-autumn, accessed May 3, 2013.

29 Ibid.

30 As'ad AbuKhalil, "Sadik Jalal Al Azm: Naqd al-fikr al-Ta'ifi ba'd al-Hazima" (Sadik Jalal Al Azm: The Critique of Sectarian Thought after the Defeat), *Al-Akhbar*, April 27, 2013, http://www.al-akhbar.com/node/182102.

31 Abdelwahab El-Affendi, "Constituting Liberty, Healing the Nation: Revolutionary Identity Creation in the Arab World's Delayed 1989," *Third World Quarterly*, 32, no. 7 (2011): 1255–71.

SELECT BIBLIOGRAPHY

Books

al-Anani, Khalil. 2016. *Inside the Muslim Brotherhood: Religion, Identity, and Politics*. New York, NY: Oxford University Press.

Al-Awadi, Hesham. 2004. *In Pursuit of Legitimacy: the Muslim Brothers and Mubarak, 1982–2000*. London: I. B. Tauris.

Ashour, Omar. 2010. *The De-radicalization of Jihadists: Transforming Armed Islamist Movements*. London: Routledge.

Ashour, Omar. 2021. *HOW ISIS FIGHTS: Military Tactics in Iraq, Syria, Libya and Egypt*. Edinburgh: Edinburgh University Press.

Ayoob, Mohammed. 2010. *The Many Faces of Political Islam: Religion and Politics in the Muslim world*. Ann Arbor: University of Michigan Press.

Bayat, Asef. 2007. *Making Islam Democratic: Social Movements and the Post-Islamist Turn*. Stanford, CA: Stanford University Press.

Bayat, Asef. 2013. *Post-Islamism: The Many Faces of Political Islam*. Oxford: Oxford University Press.

Bjørgo, Tore. 2009. *Leaving Terrorism Behind: Individual and Collective Disengagement*. Milton Park: Routledge.

Brown, Nathan J. 2012. *When Victory Is Not an Option: Islamist Movements in Arab Politics*. Ithaca: Cornell University Press.

Clark, Janine A. 2010. *Islam, Charity, and Activism: Middle-Class Networks and Social Welfare in Egypt, Jordan, and Yemen*. Bloomington: Indiana University Press.

Fraihat, Ibrahim. 2016. *Unfinished Revolutions Yemen, Libya, and Tunisia after the Arab Spring*. New Haven: Yale University Press.

Hafez, Mohammed. 2003. *Why Muslims Rebel: Repression and Resistance in the Islamic world*. Boulder, CO: Lynne Rienner Publishers.

Hamid, Shadi. 2015. *Temptations of Power Islamists and Illiberal Democracy in a New Middle East*. Oxford: Oxford University Press.

Horgan, John. 2008. *Walking Away from Terrorism*. London: Routledge.

Kepel, Gilles. 2003. *Muslim Extremism in Egypt: The Prophet and Pharaoh*. Berkeley: University of California Press.

Kraetzschmar, Hendrik, and Paola Rivetti. 2018. *Islamists and the Politics of the Arab Uprisings: Governance, Pluralization and Contention*. Edinburgh: Edinburgh University Press.

Maddy-Weitzman, Bruce, and Daniel Zisenwine. 2017. *Contemporary Morocco: State, Politics and Society Under Mohammed VI*. London: Routledge Taylor & Francis Group.

Mecham, Quinn, and Julie Chernov-Hwang. 2014. *Islamist Parties and Political Normalization in the Muslim World*. University of Pennsylvania Press.

Roy, Olivier, and Amel Boubekeur. 2012. *Whatever Happened to the Islamists? Salafis, Heavy Metal Muslims and the Lure of Consumerist Islam*. New York, NY: Columbia University Press.

Schwedler, Jillian. 2007. *Faith in Moderation: Islamist Parties in Jordan and Yemen*. Cambridge: Cambridge University Press.

Wedeen, Lisa. 2015. *Ambiguities of Domination: Politics, Rhetoric, and Symbols in Contemporary Syria: With a New Preface*. Chicago: The University of Chicago Press.

Wickham, Carrie Rosefsky. 2005. *Mobilizing Islam: Religion, Activism and Political Change in Egypt*. New York: Columbia University Press.

Wickham, Carrie Rosefsky. 2013. *Muslim Brotherhood: Evolution of an Islamist Movement*. Princeton, NJ: Princeton University Press.

Wiktorowicz, Quintan. 2012. *Islamic Activism: A Social Movement Theory Approach*. Bloomington: Indiana University Press.

Articles

al-Anani, Khalil. 2012. "Islamist Parties Post-Arab Spring." *Mediterranean Politics*. 17 (3): 466–72.

al-Anani, Khalil. 2019. "Rethinking the Repression-Dissent Nexus: Assessing Egypt's Muslim Brotherhood's Response to Repression since the Coup of 2013." *Democratization*. 26 (8): 1329–41.

Allani, Alaya. 2009. "The Islamists in Tunisia between Confrontation and Participation: 1980–2008." *Journal of North African Studies*. 14 (2): 257–72.

Allani, Alaya. 2013. "The Post-revolution Tunisian Constituent Assembly: Controversy over Powers and Prerogatives." *Journal of North African Studies*. 18 (1): 131–40.

Alley, April Longley. 2013. "Yemen Changes Everything... And Nothing." *Journal of Democracy*. 24 (4): 74–85.

Angrist, Michele Penner. 2013. "Understanding the Success of Mass Civic Protest in Tunisia." *Middle East Journal*. 67 (4): 546–64.

Ashour, Omar. 2011. "Post-Jihadism: Libya and the Global Transformations of Armed Islamist Movements." *Terrorism and Political Violence*. 23 (3): 377–97.

Bayat, Asef. 2013. *The Arab Spring and Its Surprises*. 44 (3): 587–601. Oxford: International Institute of Social Studies.

Cavatorta, Francesco, and Fabio Merone. 2013. "Moderation through Exclusion: The Journey of the Tunisian Ennahda from Fundamentalist to Conservative Party." *Democratization*. 20 (5): 857–75.

Cavatorta, Francesco, and Fabio Merone. 2015. "Post-Islamism, Ideological Evolution and 'La Tunisianité' of the Tunisian Islamist Party al-Nahda." *Journal of Political Ideologies*. 20 (1): 27–42.

Chamkhi, Tarek. 2014. "Neo-Islamism in the Post-Arab Spring." *Contemporary Politics*. 20 (4): 453–68.

Clark, J. A., and E. Dalmasso. 2015. "State Actor-Social Movement Coalitions and Policy-Making under Authoritarianism: The Moroccan Party of Justice and Development in the Urban Municipality of Kenitra." *Middle East Law and Governance*. 7 (2): 185–211.

Donker, Teije Hidde. 2013. "Re-emerging Islamism in Tunisia: Repositioning Religion in Politics and Society." *Mediterranean Politics*. 18 (2): 207–24.

El Mellouki, Sanae. 2015. "The Infusion of Islam into Pluralistic Politics: The Need to Explore the Islamist Identity Beyond Ideological Boundaries: The Case of the Moroccan Party of Justice and Development." *Discourse and Society: an International*

Journal for the Study of Discourse and Communication in Their Social, Political and Cultural Contexts. 26 (6): 662–81.

El-Affendi, Abdelwahab. 2011. "Constituting Liberty, Healing the Nation: Revolutionary Identity Creation in the Arab World's Delayed 1989." *Third World Quarterly.* 32 (7): 1255–71.

Guazzone, Laura. 2013. "Ennahda Islamists and the Test of Government in Tunisia." *International Spectator.* 48 (4): 30–50.

Günes Murat Tezcür. 2010. "The Moderation Theory Revisited: The Case of Islamic Political Actors." *Party Politics.* 16 (1): 69–88.

Ismail, Salwa. 1998. "Confronting the Other: Identity, Culture, Politics, and Conservative Islamism in Egypt." *International Journal of Middle East Studies.* 30 (2) (May): 199–225.

Karakaya, Suveyda, and A. Kadir Yildirim. 2013. "Islamist Moderation in Perspective: Comparative Analysis of the Moderation of Islamist and Western Communist Parties." *Democratization.* 20 (7): 1322–49.

Kirdiş, Esen. 2015. "Between Movement and Party: Islamic Movements in Morocco and the Decision to Enter Party Politics." *Politics, Religion & Ideology.* 16 (1): 65–86.

Munson, Ziad. 2001. "ISLAMIC MOBILIZATION: Social Movement Theory and the Egyptian Muslim Brotherhood." *The Sociological Quarterly.* 42 (4): 487–510.

Roy, Olivier. 2013. "There Will Be No Islamist Revolution." *Journal of Democracy.* 24 (1): 14–19.

Schwedler, Jillian M. 2011. "Can Islamists Become Moderates? Rethinking the Inclusion-Moderation Hypothesis." *World Politics: A Quarterly Journal of International Relations.* 63 (2): 347–76.

Shehata, Samer, and Joshua Stacher. 2006. "SPECIAL REPORT - The Brotherhood Goes to Parliament." *Middle East Report.* (240): 32.

Voll, John, Peter Mandaville, Steven Kull, and Alexis Arieff. 2012. "Symposium- Political Islam in the Arab Awakening: Who Are the Major Players?" *Middle East Policy.* 19 (2): 10–35.

Volpi, Frédéric, and Ewan Stein. 2015. "Islamism and the State after the Arab Uprisings: Between People Power and State Power." *Democratization.* 22 (2): 276–93.

Willis, Michael. 2004. "Morocco's Islamists and the Legislative Elections of 2002: The Strange Case of the Party That Did Not Want to Win." *Mediterranean Politics.* 9 (1): 53–81.

CONTRIBUTORS

Mohammad Abu Rumman is a scholar on political Islam at the University of Jordan (Amman). His research interests include political Islam, political thought, and democratization in the Arab world. He has published several books including *Mysteries of the Sufi Path: The Sufi Community in Jordan and Its Zawiyas, Hadras and Orders* (2020), *Infatuated with Martyrdom: Female Jihadism from Al-Qaeda to the "Islamic State"* (2017), and *Political Reform in Islamic Thought: Approaches, Powers, Priorities, and Strategies* (2011).

Khalil al-Anani is Associate Professor of Politics and International Relations at the Doha Institute for Graduate Studies, Qatar, and a Senior Fellow at the Arab Center Washington. He has previously taught at the Paul H. Nitze School of Advanced International Studies at Johns Hopkins University (Washington, DC, USA), Georgetown University (Washington, DC, USA), George Washington University (Washington, DC, USA), and George Mason University (Fairfax, USA). His research interests include authoritarianism and democratization, state violence, religion and politics, political Islam, Egyptian politics, and Middle East politics. His latest books include *Inside the Muslim Brotherhood: Religion, Identity, and Politics* (2016) and *Elections and Democratization in the Middle East* (2014). He has also published several articles at leading research and academic journals such as *Politics and Religion, Democratization, The Middle East Journal, Sociology of Islam,* and the *Digest of Middle East Studies.*

Mubarak Aljeri is a doctoral candidate in the Department of Politics and International Relations at the University of Edinburgh (UK). His research interests include social movements in the Arabian Peninsula, political Islam, and tribal politics in the Middle East. His has published two books in Arabic on Islamism in Tunisia.

Hamzah Almustafa is a doctoral candidate in Middle Eastern Politics at the University of Exeter (UK). He holds a master's degree in Political Science and International Relations from the Doha Institute for Graduate Studies (Qatar) and has previously worked as a researcher at Al Sharq Forum (Istanbul, Turkey). His latest book is *The Virtual Public Sphere in the Syrian Revolution: Features, Orientations, and Mechanisms to Create Public Opinion* (2012, in Arabic).

Tarek Chamkhi is a doctoral candidate at the Crawford School of Public Policy at the Australian National University (Canberra). His research interests include

Islamism, geopolitics of the Middle East, and international relations. His latest publication is an article titled "Neo-Islamism in the post-Arab Spring" in the journal *Contemporary Politics* (2014).

Abdelwahab El-Affendi is Professor of Political Science and Provost, Acting President, Doha Institute for Graduate Studies, Qatar. Previously, he was the founder coordinator of the Democracy and Islam Program at the University of Westminster (London, UK, 1998–2015) and a visiting fellow and professor at the Christian Michelsen Institute (Bergen, Norway, 1995 and 2003), Northwestern University, (Evanston, USA, 2002), University of Oxford (UK, 1990), University of Cambridge (UK, 2010–12), and the International Institute of Islamic Thought and Civilization (Kuala Lumpur, Malaysia, 2008). He is the author of a number of books including *After the Arab Revolutions: Decentering Democratic Transition Theory* (2021), *About Muhammad: The Other Western Perspective on the Prophet of Islam* (2010), and *Turabi's Revolution: Islam and Power in Sudan* (1991).

Mohammed Masbah is Founder and President of the Moroccan Institute for Policy Analysis (MIPA) (Rabat, Morocco). He is also an associate fellow at Chatham House (London, UK) and an adjunct professor at Mohammed V University (Rabat, Morocco). He is a political sociologist whose work centers on public policy, democratization, and political Islam, with a focus on North Africa. His recent publications include "Rise and Endurance: Moderate Islamists and Electoral Politics in the Aftermath of the 'Moroccan Spring'" in *Islamists and the Politics of the Arab Uprisings: Governance, Pluralization and Contention* (2018), *Moroccan Jihadists: Local and Global Dimensions* (2021), and "Trust in Institutions Index 2020" (2020).

Taha Yaseen is a Yemeni scholar with an MSc degree in Conflict Management and Humanitarian Action studies from the Doha Institute for Graduate Studies (Qatar). His research interests cover civil conflicts, social movements, and dynamics of national and regional rivalry. His articles have been published in various journals including the *Journal of Peacebuilding and Development*.

INDEX

Page numbers with "n" refer to endnotes.

Abbas, Mohamed 13
Abbasi, Muhammad Eid 57
Aboud, Hassan 53, 63
Aboul Fotouh, Abdel Moniem 13
Abu al-Abbas's brigades 77
Abu Bakr, Jamil 85
Abu Jaber. *See* Sheikh, Hashim
AbuKhalil, As'ad 129
Abu Khalil, Hitham 13
Abu Yahya al-Hamwi. *See* al-Masri,
    Muhannad
accommodative strategy 12
adaptation strategies 34
El-Affendi, Abdelwahab 6
al-Ahmar, Sheikh Abdullah bin
    Hussein 70, 79
Ahmed, Mustafa 18
Ahrar al-Sham 53–7, 62–6. *See also*
    Jaysh al-Islam; Sham Legion
  competing currents 55–6
  internal divisions 56–7
  leadership 53–4, 56
    and constituents 63
  organizational transformation
      67–8
  post-Salafi Jihadism and 53–5
  transformation into politics 54
al-Akaily, Abdullah 85
Akhannouch, Aziz 42
al-Akour, Abdelrahim 85
AKP. *See* Party of Justice and Development
    (PJD)
al-Adl Wa al-Ihsane 37
al-Albani, ad-Din 57
Ali, Ben 19, 20, 24, 25, 27, 31
Aljeri, Mubarak 6
Alloush, Mohammed 67
Alloush, Sheikh Abdullah 57
Alloush, Zahran 57–9, 63
Almustafa, Hamzah 5, 6

al-Amoush, Bassam 85
Anan, Sami 12
al-Anani, Khalil 5, 20, 34
Angrist, Michele Penner 27
Ansar Allah. *See* Houthis
anti-Islamism 126
Arab culture 128, 129
Arabism 119
Arab Revolution. *See* Arab Spring
Arab Spring 1, 2, 5, 11–13, 16, 18–23,
      32, 33, 35, 52, 69–71, 73, 79, 81,
      82, 92, 98, 99, 101–2, 104–10,
      114, 122, 124, 125, 128
  Brotherhood after the 7–9
  Hadas' position on 104–8
  impact on Islamists 3–4
  repercussions of 89–90
"Arab" Sudanese identity 127
Arab uprising. *See* Arab Spring
Arab world 1, 33, 51, 76, 82, 119, 124,
      128, 129
al-Aradah, Sultan 78
Arnaout, Abdul Qader 57
al-Ash'ari, Abu al-Hasan 21
Ashour, Omar 5–6, 58
Al-Ashqar, Omar 84
Askar, Khalil 95
al-Assad, Bashar 4, 52
Al-Assaf, Nimer 86
al-Atoum, Ali 86
atrocities in Syria 129
al-Attar, Muhammad 86
autocracy 30
al Awwa, Muhammad Said 120
Ayoob, Mohammad 21
al-Azayida, Ahmad Qutaysh 85
Azayyida 150 n.9
al-Azm, Sadik 128–9
al-Azm, Sa'id 97
Azzam, Abdullah 83

Badran, Mudar   84, 99
Baha, Abdellah   39, 43
al-Banna, Hassan   2, 11, 82, 96, 107, 122
Bayat, Asef   21, 120
  post-Islamism   4
Belkoura, Abu Bakr   47
Benabdallah, Nabil   41
Benkirane, Abdelilah   33–6, 38–42, 45, 46, 48–50
Bennabi, Malek   119
Bourguiba, Ali   25
Brahmi, Mohamed, assassination of   25
Brown, Nathan J.   8, 105

Cavatorta, Francesco   26, 29, 30
centrist movement   85–7, 99
Chamkhi, Tarek   4, 5
"Charter of Revolutionary Honor"   55, 64
Chiki, Abdelrahim   43
Civil Protection Authority (CPA)   60–1, 66
civil war   78
Clinton, Hilary   126
CNT. See Central National Trend (CNT)
constitutional monarchy   88
Constitutional Monarchy Initiative in 2009–10   91–2, 100
coup of 2013   16–18, 45, 110
CPA. See Civil Protection Authority (CPA)
crass orientalism   129
cross-ideological alliances   46–7

Da'ud, Khaled   13
Da'wa. See religious preaching
Dayyah, Imad Abu   85, 86
decision-making process   13–14
deep state   111
democracy   30, 32, 87, 99, 104, 126
Democratic Constitutional Rally (RCD)   24, 31
Democratic Reform Initiative   37
"Democratic" Revolutionary Organization   60–1
demonization campaigns   78
Deshisat, Jamil   89, 94, 95
"Dignity of the Homeland" movement   102, 105, 106, 108
"Dignity of the Nation" movement   112

Directions of the Movement   43
disoriented adaptation   17–18
"Doves"   83–6, 94, 98–100, 106
al-Duwailah, Mubarak   105, 108

EAC. See Egyptian Association for Change (EAC)
Eddine, Abdelali Hami   50
Egyptian
  Islamist   122–3
  regime   126
  revolution   123–4
Egyptian Association for Change (EAC)   121
Egyptian Current   13
ElBaradei, Mohamed   121
Elbechri, Tarek   120
Ennahda Party   23–5, 31–3, 104, 107
  Brotherhood vs.   30
  democratic transition   24
  moderation through inclusion/ exclusion   25–7
Al-Erian   122
El-Erian, Essam   117
The Essays of the Islamists (al-Ash'ari)   21
extremist wing   86, 88
al-Ezz, Ibrahim Abu   95
Ezzat, Mahmoud   13

al-Falahat, Salem   85–91, 96, 97, 100
Fares, Mohammed Abu   83, 84
al-Faroukh, Alaa   93, 94
FJP. See Freedom and Justice Party (FJP)
Freedom and Justice Party (FJP)   9, 104, 122
Free Syrian Army (FSA)   53, 56, 60–2, 66, 67
"the Friday of Rage"   118, 121
functional entity   93, 152 n.32

GCC. See Gulf Cooperation Council (GCC)
GDP   23
generational divisions   60
gentleman's agreement   86
Ghafour, Abdulrahman Abdul   111
Ghannouchi, Rachid   21, 28–31, 83
Gharaibeh, Rahil   83, 86, 88, 89, 91–4, 98, 100

al-Ghazali, Sheikh Mohammed 119
GNA. *See* Government of National Accord
    (GNA)
GNC. *See* General National Congress
    (GNC)
gradualism 11, 20
    and flexibility 29, 47–9
Guidance Bureau 13, 89
Gulf Cooperation Council (GCC) 72
gun politics 75–7

Habib, Mohamed 13
Hadas. *See* Islamic Constitutional
    Movement
al-Haddad, Gehad 135 n.31
Hadi, Abd-Rabbu Mansour 74, 76
Hafez al-Assad 51
Hafter, Khalifa 3
al-Hajj, Abdul Rahman 60, 64
al-Hakim, Nazir 60, 63, 64
Hamas 85–9, 91, 99, 118, 123
Hamdawi, Mohamed 43, 44
Hamid, Shadi 22
al-Hammouri, Muhammad 97
al-haraka al-dusturiyya al-islamiyya.
        See Islamic Constitutional
        Movement
al-Harbash, Jamaan 106, 109, 113
hard-line movement 88, 98–9, 152 n.25
Hassad, Mohamed 41
Hassanein, Khaled 97
"Hawks" 83–6, 91, 98–100, 106
Heraks 77
Hezbollah 118
El Himma, Fouad Ali 41
Houthis 3, 69, 70, 74–80
Houthi-Saleh alliance 76
Howeidy, Fahmy 14
Hussein, Saddam 20

identity(ies) 45–6
    of insecurity 126–9
ideological conflicts 47
Ikhwan 118–23, 129
    leadership 121–2
inclusion-moderation hypothesis 5, 51
insecurity 126–9
intellectual dexterity 58
intellectual transformations 66–7

internal conflicts 63
Internal Reformist movement 99
intra-Jihadist conflicts and
        competition 65–6
Irsheid, Zaki Bani 86, 87
Islah Party 3, 69, 70
    challenge facing 79
    and democracy 73
    internal cohesion and external
        ties 77–9
    leadership 71, 72, 74
    during and post-Yemeni revolt 71–4
    and prerevolution politics 70–1
    regional powers 79–80
    religious discourse 72–3
    rise of power 75
    transition and war 74–5
    women's political rights and 73
Islam 125
    political 2, 21, 29, 32, 45, 90, 93, 94,
        98, 99, 101, 103, 105
    transformation of 45
Islamic Action Front 84–6, 90
Islamic Constitutional Movement
    and Arab Spring 104–8
    boycott of parliamentary
        elections 102, 106, 109–11
    emergence of 101–3
    political behavior 105
    political boycotts 109
    relationship with the Kuwaiti
        regime 108–10
    transformations of 110–12
    future challenges 113–14
Islamic identity 61–3, 66, 84, 97
Islamic Movement for Reform in
        2005 99
Islamic preaching (*da'wah*) vs.
        politics 42–5
Islamic revival 120, 124, 125
Islamic State in Syria (ISIS) 33–41, 54,
        55, 58, 59, 61, 65, 66, 129, 131
Islamic Tendency Movement (MTI) 26,
        29
Islamism 20–1, 119, 120, 124–7. *See also*
        neo-Islamism
    theorizing 4–5
Islamists 21
    identities of insecurity 126–9

impact of the Arab Spring on 3–4
moderation of 34, 35, 42
political movements 103–4, 115
revolutions 2–3, 121–4
transformation of (*see* transformation of Islamists)
in Yemeni politics 69–70
Islamist-secularist polarization 127
IS Organization. *See* Islamic State in Syria (ISIS)
"issue of Nationalism" 86–91, 96, 98, 99

Jaafar, Mustafa Ben 27
JaF. *See* Jaysh al-Fatah (JaF)
"Jailbreak", revisiting the 118–21
Jaysh al-Fatah (JaF) 61–3
Jaysh al-Islam 57–9, 63–6. *See also* Ahrar al-Sham
intellectual transformations 66–7
leadership and constituents 63
organizational transformation 67–8
JCP. *See* Justice and Construction Party (JCP)
Jebali, Hamadi 25
jihadis 12
jihadism 58
jihadist movements 53
Jomaa, Mehdi 27
Jordan, Brotherhood in 82–3
divisions 90–8
executive office 85, 87
extremist wing 86, 88, 99
Islamic Action Front party 84–6
"issue of Nationalism" 86–91, 96, 98, 99
moderate wing 86–90, 95, 99, 100
political reform and democracy 87
from religion to politics 83–4
repercussions of the Arab Spring 89–90
Shura Council 88, 89
Jordanian identity 93
Justice and Development Party (AKP). *See* Party of Justice and Development (PJD)
Justice and Development Youth 50

al-Kafawin, Ahmad 97
al-Kandari, Ali 107, 109

Karman, Tawakkol 73, 80
al-Katatni, Sa'ad 13
Kefaya movement 8
Ketchley, Neil 17
al-Khader, Talal 112
al-Khalfi, Mustafa 43
Khalifa, Abdul Rahman 85
"Khawarij" 58, 66
Kishk, Muhammad Jalal 120
al-Kofahi, Nabil 86, 88, 89, 91–4, 98, 100
Kuwait
democracy 104
economy 108
Hadas' position on Arab Spring 104–8
Islamic Constitutional Movement 101–3
Islamist political movements 103–4
Muslim Brotherhood (MB) 101
political power 108
political system in 103–4
Kuwaiti regime, Hadas' relationship with 108–10

Lahoud, Carine 103, 110
Larayedh, Ali 25, 27
Laufer, Rafael 60
Leader's charisma 62–3
Lewis, Bernard 120, 128
LIFG. *See* Libyan Islamic Fighting Group (LIFG)
LIMC. *See* Libyan Islamic Movement for Change (LIMC)
Lotfi, Islam 13
Lund, Aron 60
Lynch, Marc 14

Madi, Abu Ela 13
Mahfouz, Saud Abu 86
Mahmoud, Mustafa 119
Manji, Irshad 128
Marzouki, Moncef 27
Masbah, Mohammed 6
Mashhur, Mustafa 12
al-Masri, Muhannad 56
May 16 bombings 44, 49
Merone, Fabio 26, 29, 30
El-Messiri, Abdelwahab 120

Index

Military Operations Centre (MOC) 62, 65
Ministry of Family and Development, Morocco 46
Ministry of the Interior, Morocco 40–1, 48, 49
moderation 34
  Ennahda Party 25–7
modern Islamism 21
Mohammed VI 37, 44
monarchy 35, 38–42, 48, 49
Moroccan constitution 37
Morsi, Mohammed 10, 12–14, 16, 25, 30, 76, 89, 117, 118
Mourou, Abdelfattah 26
MTI. *See* Islamic Tendency Movement (MTI)
Mubarak, Hosni 7–11, 15, 20, 121
Mukhabarat 117, 119–21
"al-Muqata' Awjab" 109
Musallah, Nael Zaidan 89
Muslim Brotherhood (MB) 2, 33, 45, 59, 64, 75, 76, 79–81, 101, 107, 110, 118–19
  after the coup of 2013 16–18
  after the uprising of 2011 7–9
  ban of 95
  conservatism 11–12
  disoriented adaptation 17–18
  downfall of 10–16
  vs. Ennahda Party 30
  incompetence 15–16
  indoctrination 15
  Jordan (*see* Jordan, Brotherhood in)
  license for 94, 98, 152 n.34
  organizational adaptation 18
  organizational stagnation 12–15
  Palestinian 89
  political platform 9
  protests and demonstrations 17–18
  rise to power 9–10
  Sham Legion's relationship with 59–60
  socialization 15
  young members 18
Mu'tasim, Jama 47

al-Nafisi, Abdullah 110
Nahas, Ubaida 60

al-Nahhas, Labib 55, 56
Najdi identity 127
al-Najjar, Ghanim 107, 108
Nasir, Sheikh 57
Nasser, Gamal Abdel 21
Nasserism 119, 120
National Action Group 60
National Alliance to Support Legitimacy 17, 137 n.51
National Coalition to Support the Syrian Revolution 60
National Congress Party. *See* Zamzam Party
National Constituent Assembly (NCA) 25
National Democratic Party (NDP) 8
National Dialogue Conference 75, 78
"National Identity and Citizenship" 91
nationalism 98
nationalist identity 93
"National Reform Project" 96
National Salvation Front (NSF) 24
NCA. *See* National Constituent Assembly (NCA)
NDP. *See* National Democratic Party (NDP)
neo-Islamism 4, 20–2, 32
neo-Islamist parties 22–3
neo-Islamists 19–23, 31–2
  ruling failures 28–9
New Islamic Youth 59
New Muslim Brotherhood's Association 94–6
NFC. *See* National Forces Coalition (NFC)
Nidaa Tounes 24, 31
Nofal, Ahmed 83
non-confrontational strategy 12
NSF. *See* National Salvation Front (NSF)
NTC. *See* National Transitional Council (NTC)
Al-Nusra Front 56, 57, 61, 63, 66

Obama, Barack 126
al-Omar, Ali 56
O'Neil, Patrick H. 111
one-vote law 109
organizational crisis 92
organizational secrecy 96
organizational stagnation 12–15

168   *Index*

organizational transformation 67–8
Orientalism 128, 129
Othmani, Saadeddine 44–5, 48, 50
Oufkir, Mohamed 39, 41

Palestinian Brotherhood 89
pan-Arabism 120
"Parliamentary Break-In" 113, 114
Party of Justice and Development
     (PJD) 6, 15, 22, 27, 33–6,
     49–50, 67, 98, 105, 107, 111
  cross-ideological alliances 46–7
  electoral success 35
  governance 35
  from identity to administration 42–9
  maintenance of power 36
  and monarchy 35, 38–42
  political openness 37
  post-2011 victories 48
  rise to power 36–8, 48
Pashtun identity 127
"The People's Revolution" slogan 55
PJD. *See* Party of Justice and Development
    (PJD)
policy choice 46
political Islam 2, 21, 29, 32, 45, 90, 93,
    94, 98, 99, 101, 103, 105
"Political Reform Project" 107
Popular Front 24
post-Arab Spring 21, 22, 30, 34, 35, 125,
    127
post-coup regime 16, 18
post-Islamism 4, 22, 32, 124
post-Islamists 21–2. *See also* neo-
    Islamists
post-political Islam 90, 93, 94, 103
post-post-Islamism 125–6
post-Qaddafi Libya, transformation of
    Islamists in. *See* transformation
    of Islamists, in post-Qaddafi
    Libya
post-Salafi Jihadism 53–5
post-Yemeni revolt 71–4
"Project Nation" charter 54–5, 64, 66

al-Qaeda 66
Qahtan, Mohammed 74
al-Qahtani, Daham 109
El-Qassas, Mohamed 13

al-Qudah, Ghaith 97
Al-Qudah, Mohammed Abdul
    Hamid 86, 97
al-Qudah, Muhammad Sharaf 94, 95
Qutb, Sayyid 82, 83, 85

Rabaa massacre 16–17, 39
Rahim, Yasser Abdel 61
Rahma, Haitham 60, 63
Rajoub, Mohammed 97
Ramadan, Ahmad 60
Ramid, Mustafa 41, 47
Al-Rashad Union 77
al-Rashid, Imad al-Din 60
RCD. *See* Democratic Constitutional Rally
    (RCD)
reformist strategy 11
regional identities 127
*Religion and Politics: Distinction, not
    Separation* (Othmani) 44
religious discourse 72–3
religious-political relationship 42–5
religious preaching 2, 4, 22, 26, 31, 34,
    67, 82, 95, 105, 112
  vs. politics 42–5
Rescue and Partnership Party (RPP) 89,
    90, 93, 96–8
"The Return of Islam" (Lewis) 125
revolution
  Egyptian 123–4
  Islamist 2–3, 121–4
  Islamists in 121–2
  Syrian and Arab 128
revolutionary activism 17
"revolutionary" ideology 11
rhetorical populism 58
Roy, Olivier 3, 21, 124
RPP. *See* Rescue and Partnership Party
    (RPP)
Rumman, Mohammad Abu 6

al-Sabah, al-Mohammad Nasser 106,
    113
al-Sabah, Nasser Mohammed 102
Sadat, Anwar 120, 121
al-Sadiq, Abu Muhammad 56
al-Sadr, Muhammad Baqir 119
Saeed, Hammam 83, 86, 88
Salafi Jihadis 21

Index

Salafi jihadism. *See* post-Salafi Jihadism
Salafi jihadist identity 56
Salafis 8, 12, 123, 127
Salafism 58
Salafists 53, 69, 70, 75, 77
  clergy 58
  influence 24
Salah, Abu 56
Saleh, Ali Abdullah 3, 6, 72, 74–7, 79
al-Sanad, Ali 105, 112
Saudi Arabia 16, 72, 73, 76, 79, 80, 119
Saudi-Islahi relations 79
Saudi-Qatari divide 79
al-Sawa, Ali 84
al-Sawag, Falah 106, 109
SCAF. *See* Supreme Council of Armed Forces (SCAF)
El-Sebsi, Beji Caid 24
sectarianism 127–9
Self-Criticism After the Defeat (Al Azm) 128
Sha'araoui, Sheikh Muhammad Mutawlli 119
shadow organization 86, 87
al-Shaheen, Osama 112
El-Shaikh, Kafr 13
Sham Legion 59, 63–6
  democratic revolutionary organization 60–2
  Islamic approach 61
  Islamic identity 61–2
  military leadership 61
  relationship with the Brotherhood 59–60
Sharia 4, 20–2, 30, 90
shariatization 20, 22
al-Shater, Khairat 13–14
al-Shayb, Raed 95
Shehatah, Ahmed 14
Sheikh, Hashim 55–6
Shia 127
Shura Council 13, 14, 88, 89, 95
SIF. *See* Syrian Islamic Front (SIF)
El-Sisi, Abdel Fattah 7, 16, 18, 45
Six-Day War of 1976 82
Soufan, Hassan 63
specialization policy 43
strategic moderation 45–6

student protest movement 120
"Students Against the Coup" 17
Sudanese Islamists 127
Sultan, Essam 13
Sunni 103, 127, 128
Supreme Council of Armed Forces (SCAF) 10, 14
Syria, transformation of Islamists in. *See* transformation of Islamists, in Syria
Syrian
  crisis 52, 59, 61, 65
  Islamist faction 51–4, 58–60, 64, 65
  revolution 52, 60, 63, 128
  sectarianism 129
Syrian Islamic Front (SIF) 54
Syrian Islamic Liberation Front (SILF) 53

al-Tabatabaie, Waleed 113
Tahan, Abu Saleh 56
tamarod 25
al-Ta'mneh, Fathi 95
Tantawi, Mohamed Hussein 12
Thesis of the Democratic Struggle 45
Thunibat, Abdul Majid 85, 86, 89, 90, 94–5
Thunibat, Hassan 97
totalitarianism 31
traditional Islamic ideology 99
transformation of Islam 45
transformation of Islamists 5
  in Syria
    Ahrar al-Sham (*see* Ahrar al-Sham)
    behavioral 67
    generational divisions 63–4
    intellectual 66–7
    internal conflicts and balances 63
    international pressure on 65
    intra-Jihadist conflicts and competition 65–6
    Jaysh al-Islam (*see* Jaysh al-Islam)
    leader's charisma 62–3
    local pressure on 64
    organizational 67–8
    regional pressure on 64–5
    Sham Legion (*see* Sham Legion)
transformations of Islamic Constitutional Movement 110–12
"trans-Islamic" 124

Tunisian General Labour Union (UGTT) 24, 25
al-Turabi, Hassan 21, 83
2011 constitutional amendment, Morocco 37, 48–9

UAE. *See* United Arab Emirates (UAE)
al-Udini, Abdullah 78
UGTT. *See* Tunisian General Labour Union (UGTT)
underground organization 96
Unification and Reform Movement 42–4, 49
United Arab Emirates (UAE) 16, 73, 76, 78–80

Voll, John 30

al-Wadi'i, Muqbil 70
Wedeen, Lisa 51
Wickham, Carrie 8
Wright, Robin 21

al-Yamani lil-Islah. *See* Islah party
Yaseen, Taha 6
Yatim, Mohamed 39, 43
Yemeni Congregation for Reform. *See* Islah Party

El-Za'farani, Ibrahim 13
al-Zamie, Ali 106, 107
Zamzam Party 90–8, 100
al-Zarqan, Ahmad 86
al-Zindani, Abdul Majeed 71, 78, 79

CPSIA information can be obtained
at www.ICGtesting.com
Printed in the USA
LVHW022229280423
745601LV00004B/267

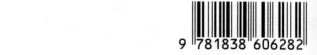